All You That Labor

RELIGION AND SOCIAL TRANSFORMATION
General Editors: Anthony B. Pinn and Stacey M. Floyd-Thomas

Prophetic Activism:
Progressive Religious Justice Movements in Contemporary America
Helene Slessarev-Jamir

All You That Labor:
Religion and Ethics in the Living Wage Movement
C. Melissa Snarr

All You That Labor

Religion and Ethics in
the Living Wage Movement

C. Melissa Snarr

NEW YORK UNIVERSITY PRESS
New York and London

NEW YORK UNIVERSITY PRESS
New York and London
www.nyupress.org

References to Internet websites (URLs) were accurate at the time of writing.
Neither the author nor New York University Press is responsible for URLs
that may have expired or changed since the manuscript was prepared.

Library of Congress Cataloging-in-Publication Data
Snarr, C. Melissa.
All you that labor : religion and ethics in the living wage movement /
C. Melissa Snarr.
p. cm. — (Religion and social transformation)
Includes bibliographical references (p.   ) and index.
ISBN 978–0–8147–4112–2 (cl : alk. paper) —
ISBN 978–0–8147–8389–4 (e-book : alk. paper)
1. Minimum wage—Moral and ethical aspects—United States.
2. Living wage movement—United States. I. Title.
HD4918.S55   2011
261.8'5—dc23   2011021035

New York University Press books are printed on acid-free paper,
and their binding materials are chosen for strength and durability.
We strive to use environmentally responsible suppliers and materials
to the greatest extent possible in publishing our books.

Manufactured in the United States of America
10 9 8 7 6 5 4 3 2 1

Come to me, all ye that labour and are heavy laden,
and I will give you rest.

Matthew 11:28 (KJV)

Contents

Acknowledgments

A book requiring fieldwork and dialogue across disciplines greatly expands the number of people to whom I am indebted. Insights that contributed to a word, a sentence, or an entire section of the book sometimes came from a conversation in the hallway, a late night beverage, or a quick email. In other words, many thanks to all those who were interested enough in my work as a scholar and in the working poor as persons that you shared the journey with me—even for a brief moment. Many organizations openly accepted an academic in their midst who wove together participation and observation on an almost daily basis. I am particularly grateful to Interfaith Worker Justice and several of their affiliates for extending me their trust. Kim Bobo and Megan Macaraeg in particular were great sources of inspiration for the book.

My research also benefited materially and intellectually from two research groups at Vanderbilt University. The Robert Penn Warren Center hosted a research group that placed me in conversation with feminist social movement theorists as my project commenced. Combined with my ongoing collegium of the past four years, the Global Feminisms Collaborative, I have been able to pursue interdisciplinary conversations that were vital to this text. Thanks especially to Lyndi Hewitt, Katy Attanasi, Sarah VanHooser, Brandi Brimmer, Anastasia Curwood, Susan Saegert, Marilyn Robinson, Darcy Freedman, Andrea Tucker, Kate Lassiter, Stacey Clifton, and Sonanali Supra. In both of those groups and in my life, Brooke Ackerly has been my continual champion and intrepid conversation partner. I am also grateful to Vanderbilt Divinity colleagues who have supported this work: Victor Anderson, Stacey Floyd-Thomas, Ted Smith, Graham Reside, Barbara McClure, Trudy Stringer, Ellen Armour, Viki Matson, and Alice Hunt. Friends and colleagues across time and space such as Monya Stubbs, Khette Cox, Lyndsey Godwin, Heather Caudill, Barbara Andolsen, Christine Hinze, Toddie Peters, Pamela Brubaker, Laura Stivers, and Harlan Beckley also enriched this project in many ways. My students also continually press me to connect theory and practice, and they teach me through the varied activisms of their lives. They give me confidence that "even ministers" think social movement theory can be helpful. Thank you as well to my NYU editor Jennifer Hammer and her willingness to take a chance on this kind of book, and her continual encouragement to make it better. The fine editing work of Jane Katz also sharpened my prose along the way. Finally, thank you to Bart Dredge and Jeff Rogers who taught me in two undergraduate courses whose simultaneity would set me on a life path: "Social Movements" and "Old Testament Prophets." Your pedagogy and passion continue to inspire me.

Biblical quotations are drawn from the King James Version, the New Revised Standard Version, the New American Standard Bible, and the TaNaK (Jewish Publication Society).

Parts of some chapters in this book have been previously published in journals. The articles are "Working Women and Complex Coalitions: Feminist and Religious Activists in the Living Wage Movement," *Journal of Feminist Studies in Religion*, Spring 2011 (forthcoming); "Waging Religious Ethics: Living Wages and Framing Public Religious Ethics," *Journal of the Society of Christian Ethics* 29, no. 1 (Spring/Summer 2009): 69–86; "Religion, Race, and Bridge Building in Economic Justice Coalitions," *Working USA: The Journal of Labor and Society* 12, no. 1 (March 2009): 73–95; "Oh, Mary Don't You Weep: Progressive Religion in the Living Wage Movement," *Political Theology* 8, no. 3 (July 2007): 269–79.

Abbreviations

ACORN	Association of Communities Organized for Reform Now
AFL-CIO	American Federation of Labor-Congress of Industrial Organizations
AFSCME	American Federation of State, County, and Municipal Employees
BUILD	Baltimoreans United for Leadership Development
CA CLUE	California Clergy and Laity United for Economic Justice
CLUE LA	Clergy and Laity United for Economic Justice, Los Angeles
DART	Direct Action Research and Training
EPI	Economic Policy Institute
FBCO	Faith-based Community Organizing
IAF	Industrial Areas Foundation
ICWJ	Interfaith Committee on Worker Justice
IWJ	Interfaith Worker Justice (the national organization and many locals dropped "Committee" in the late 1990s)
IWPR	Institute for Women's Policy Research
KJV	King James Version
Mid TN JwJ	Middle Tennessee Jobs with Justice
NASB	New American Standard Bible
NCC	National Council of Churches
NRSV	New Revised Standard Version
PERI	Political Economy Research Institute
PICO	Pacific Institute for Community Organizing

SCLC   Southern Christian Leadership Council
SEIU   Service Employees International Union
TANF   Temporary Assistance for Needy Families
WIN   Worker's Interfaith Network
UU   Unitarian Universalist

Introduction

At a southern university rally for living wages in 2005, a middle-aged African American woman rose to introduce herself and speak to the crowd. Standing there in her uniform, she stated her name and job title (custodian), then paused before saying slowly and deliberately, "Everyone keeps telling me not to speak today. They say I'll lose my job or not get my raises. But I'm telling you today that I'm not afraid. There's nothing they can do to me, with God on my side." In front of a hundred students, faculty, and other staff, she relayed her story of working two jobs, one of them full time, to feed her daughter and take care of an aging mother. She expressed her frustration at not having enough time with her family, with her seemingly ceaseless work. With strength and clarity in her voice, she ended by stating her hope for "a fair day's wage for a fair day's work."

Later that year, the local African American ministerial fellowship and an influential Unitarian Universalist church, joined by many university faculty and staff members, wrote to the university's chancellor, strongly pressing the wealthy institution to understand living wages as a moral issue with significant related concerns for racial justice. As the campaign grew, faith leaders led rallies, supported workers who risked speaking publicly, and provided organizing space for meetings. By the end of the union contract negotiations, the workers had secured a guaranteed starting rate of $10 an hour by 2009.

While religious persons and organizations were not the whole story in this campaign, every major actor in the coalition acknowledged religious activists' role in its success. In fact, to ignore religious activists' multiple contributions to the campaign would be to miss a major dimension of the campaign and its later influence on the rise of a faith-labor coalition for living wages, for city workers, those contracted through the metropolitan government, and other low-wage workers who sought their help.

Religious Foundations of the U.S. Living Wage Movement

Whether the campaigns are at a university, business, city, or state level, persons of faith and religious organizations regularly play important, but generally under-analyzed, roles in the living wage movement in the United States. The contemporary living wage movement emerged in the early 1990s from the grassroots coalition of churches in Baltimore, Maryland. These churches, which provided social services to the poor in Baltimore during this time, noticed a disturbing trend. In spite of national rhetoric about growing prosperity and a booming stock market, more people were showing up at church soup kitchens, clothes closets, and rental assistance programs. And more of them had full-time jobs. Over spaghetti dinners in church basements, people talked about trying to survive and provide for their families on inadequate full-time wages. As stories accumulated and patterns emerged, a coalition of forty-six Baltimore churches decided they had seen enough. As members of Baltimoreans United in Leadership Development (BUILD), a congregation-based community organizing network affiliated with the Industrial Areas Foundation (IAF), the churches activated their organizing model to address the pressing issue in their community of working poverty.[1] Having identified the problem through one-on-one conversations and congregational leadership teams, they created a group to research the possible causes of "working poverty" in their city and to plan for action. What they found both confirmed their instincts and alarmed them: the city of Baltimore and its downtown redevelopment strategies were themselves responsible for the new low-wage jobs.[2]

Like many cities in the United States, Baltimore in the late 1980s and early 1990s sought to revitalize its downtown through a series of financial incentives and public subsidies to private firms in order to encourage investment in new office, hotel, and residential projects, which would remake the downtown district. In 1981, the newly elected President Reagan had cut seven billion dollars in aid to municipalities; as a result many cities were forced to cut budgets, and they turned to federally funded "urban renewal" programs, which offered interest-free grants for private redevelopment in targeted urban areas. When most of that federal funding ended in 1987, cities turned to alternate strategies in the form of tax incentives and subsidies for downtown redevelopment.[3] Proponents argued that local government assistance would, in the long term, result in additional tourist dollars, a larger tax base, and a more stable local economy.[4] Yet despite two billion dollars in subsidies for the downtown Baltimore hospitality industry during the 1980s, the percentage of working Baltimoreans living in poverty continued to increase.[5]

The BUILD network identified three primary problems through their research on the city's working poverty. First, private companies involved in government urban renewal projects were paying low wages in order to win low-bid government contracts. The government's own system of contracting rewarded poverty-level job creation in order to "save" the government money. Second, tax abatements and other subsidies given by the city went to private firms that paid workers at or barely above minimum wage. No criteria in government subsidies compelled contractors to meet a certain wage- or job-quality creation standard. Third, and simultaneously, the city was privatizing (that is, outsourcing) government jobs such as janitorial and food service. As a result, low-wage, private-sector contractors were replacing higher wage government jobs, which had often been unionized.[6] Although Baltimore was indeed creating new jobs, they were primarily low-wage jobs with few benefits, which offered little hope of breaking the cycle of poverty.

In the 1980s, BUILD's (and IAF's) strategy had been to fight for housing and education subsidies for the urban poor.[7] But as Arnie Graf, the East Coast director of the IAF, recalls, "We came to realize that we could not subsidize our way out of the crisis. And why did we need so much subsidy? Why do people who are working everyday need this subsidy in order to send their kids to school or buy a home? We had to get to the root of it. We had to deal with people's work and wages."[8] Joining forces, BUILD and American Federation of State, County, and Municipal Employees (AFSCME) identified the city itself as the major contributor to working poverty and called for an accounting of the "municipal subsidization of poverty."[9] The contrasts between the newly thriving urban corporate/hospitality sector and its surrounding impoverished neighborhoods thus became a moral rallying call for faith-based and union organizing in Baltimore.

Working with AFSCME, BUILD's first legislative action was to encourage the mayor to pass a "right to organize" ordinance, which protected workers by voiding municipal contracts of those companies that fired workers for union organizing. This law opened the door for a strong labor organizing drive among privatized building-service workers, which built a power base for a new low-wage worker organization: the Solidarity Sponsoring Committee, or simply Solidarity.[10] While this legislative effort strengthened the union politically, religious activists' involvement and framing were central from the beginning. In fact, at the launch of Solidarity, one of the local affiliated pastors, Rev. Vernon Dobson, proclaimed BUILD's support for the new organization with the passion of a shepherd protecting his flock: "The church is going to protect these workers. I have a message for employers—people who are upset because they don't want to pay workers more money . . . who don't want workers to organize. You keep your hands off these people because they are children of God."[11] Such was the public beginning of a primarily worker-run organization described as "a little bit of church, a little bit of union, a little bit of social service, and a whole lot of politics!"[12]

The coalition of BUILD, AFSCME, and Solidarity created an even larger campaign in 1993 during a $165 million bond drive to renovate the Baltimore convention center. Together, these organizations launched the "Social Compact" campaign to demand that hotels and businesses funded by the new government bond offer higher wages and training. Because the development was made possible through public subsidies, BUILD argued that downtown businesses were obligated to create jobs that "would enable families to support themselves without having to rely on public subsidy."[13] Soon after, the coalition expanded its campaign to require all businesses that had contracts with the city to pay their workers at least a "living wage."

Defining the *living wage* as a wage sufficient to lift a family of four above the federal poverty line ($14,350), religious activists and union organizers sought to create a different sort of campaign for a very different kind of ordinance. Rather than the usual rallying with the usual suspects, union leaders were invited into pulpits and religious leaders into union halls to emphasize the importance of this new kind of low-wage worker organizing and advocacy.[14] Union and religious solidarity across economic class became a central theme for the campaign. Identifying businesses that received government subsidies but paid poverty wages, the coalition organized municipal subsidy tours in which they displayed huge price tags on buildings around the city, listing the amount of government subsidy each received and how little their workers were paid.[15]

Priests and ministers, often in clerical collars, accompanied the tours and marched through major hotels denouncing those immense subsidies, occasionally going floor by floor to speak with custodial staff.[16] The coalition also convinced some major convention clients to offer area hotels a dollar more per room if that dollar would go *directly* into the salaries of workers.[17] With strategies such as these, coalition activists worked with numerous laypersons, clergy, workers, and allies to make visible the seemingly invisible hands that were shaping the city's economy. In so doing, they built the *moral agency* necessary to introduce a form of economic democracy and accountability into the dynamics of municipal politics. By "moral agency" I mean, most simply, the moral knowledge, judgment, and motivation to take actions related to the right and the good.

In December 1994, the Baltimore coalition of faith, labor, and community organizations managed to pass their municipal living wage ordinance. With a cost increase to city contracts of less than the rate of inflation, the ordinance set the minimum starting wage of all workers on city service contracts at $7.70 by 1998. While not a panacea for working poverty in Baltimore, the ordinance benefited approximately four thousand workers and established a political power base for those previously marginalized in the local economy.[18]

The economist Deborah Figart and the political scientist Janice Fine, conducting separate studies of the Baltimore living wage campaign, concluded that faith-based activism was essential to the campaign's success and emergent power base. When a local newspaper reporter aggressively questioned an activist about Baltimore's new labor and religion alliance, the Christian activist, tired of being called a union puppet, quipped, "It is the church's traditional role, its prophetic calling [and] if anyone has any problems with it, let them take it up with our chief organizer, Jesus Christ."[19] Local newspapers later described the clergy involved in the campaign as the "city's collective soul fighting a holy war."[20] Empowered by its mission, BUILD lobbied gubernatorial candidates in 1998 to implement their "Joseph Plan" (referencing the Hebrew biblical character) that called for 20% of the state surplus be used for job creation and training whenever the state had three consecutive months of economic downturn.[21] When Baltimore's Democratic governor won reelection, in part because of BUILD's get-out-the-vote drive, he established the plan and appointed BUILD's lead organizer to chair it.[22] This organization continued its work, winning the governor's support for including college training in welfare-to-work requirements, constructing more than seven hundred affordable housing units, and seeking to establish a hundred-million-dollar affordable housing fund for low-wage workers.[23] Solidarity, with the support of BUILD and AFSCME, also won an ordinance, which gave workers the right to stay on the job when contracts changed hands, and an executive order that forbade full-time workers from being replaced by $1.50-an-hour workfare recipients. Solidarity eventually even established its own healthcare program and worker-run temp agency.[24]

Perhaps the greatest legacy of the Baltimore campaign was its inspiration for a wave of living wage organizing across the nation for nearly two decades. Even before the Baltimore campaign was concluded, word spread about the success of this new organizing form and strategy, and activists in other cities began establishing their own coalitions for municipal living wages. Two other cities passed ordinances in 1995, three in 1996, and forty-four between 1997 and 2000.[25] Since 1994, more than 144 municipalities and counties have enacted varied forms of living wage ordinances and at least thirty-four more campaigns are active at this time (not including university, state, and business sectors).[26] Even opponents of living wage ordinances have acknowledged the movement's powerful reach. In 2002, the former congressman Newt Gingrich invited corporate leaders to an "anti–living wage" conference, bemoaning that "In 2001 alone, advocates of a free market have lost one living wage battle every fourteen days on average."[27] Political power was shifting, and many conservative politicians, chambers of commerce, and corporations that relied on low-wage labor felt its tremors.

Baltimore's model coalition of religious, labor, and low-wage worker organizations has been repeated in cities across the nation since 1994. Yet much of the academic analysis of the living wage movement has largely ignored the role of religious activists and their resources in the movement's success. Often subsumed under the larger heading of "community coalitions," religious activism is a neglected category of analysis in this seemingly secular movement. In fact, it largely disappears in the analytical gap between sociologists of social movements, who undertheorize the roles of religious activists, organizations, and ideology in social change, and religious ethicists, who focus on the abstract issue of living wages but not on the ethical practices of the movement itself. Here, we look at key practices of religious persons and organizations in the U.S. living wage movement, arguing that these practices build the *moral agency*—a person's commitment and capacity to discern and work for the needs, rights, responsibilities and flourishing of oneself and others—of low-wage workers and their allies, and help mitigate the sociodemographic barriers that keep the working poor outside of public policy making. Enhancing moral agency is never easy work. But through practices such as moral framing, racial bridge-building, gendered leadership development, and ritual enactment, religious activists help to build the moral agency necessary to imagine alternative policies for the working poor.

By analyzing religious activists in the living wage movement, we gain three major insights. First, we better understand the roles of religious activists and their ethical underpinnings even in a seemingly secular movement. In addition to the obvious invocations of religious rhetoric and ritual, we identify the more subtle and complex enactments of religion in social movement activism. We see, for example, the roles of religious leaders in reconciliation work among advocacy organizations that harbor deep divisions based on race and ethnicity. We also begin to notice the key leadership roles that women of faith play in the movement and their relationship to feminist organizations.

Second, we better understand the actual, rather than imagined or projected, challenges of ethics and agency that the movement faces, which can aid in its scope and effectiveness. Where must we draw on neoliberal economic models to make arguments for living wages, and where is it dangerous to do so? How might we address the deep "Brown/Black" divides among low-wage workers? In what ways might we address the staffing of the movement by underpaid women? How do we guard against religious ritual becoming manipulative political performance? Answering these questions can provide a perspective from which allies can contribute to the movement in valuable, integral ways.

Third, we begin to understand the movement's goals more broadly, which helps us contextualize the movement in larger efforts toward the expansion of democracy in the United States, both politically and economically. In their work, religious activists are not merely mobilizing for a specific policy measure, however important it may be. They are also seeking and enacting an expanded vision of democratic polity founded on greater economic equity and representation. As these progressive people of faith embody it, religious activism seeks to cross barriers of public/private, race, class, and gender, and allows them to practice the polity they preach. While living wage campaigns often focus on one specific public policy measure, they also embody a larger goal of renewing democracy by cultivating broad-based moral agency focused on the political economy. Widening our analytical lens allows us to see the living wage movement as part of a larger vision of recent progressive religious activism (some term this the "religious left"), which seeks to reincorporate economic democracy into the dynamics of political representation in the United States. By paying attention to religious rhetoric and practice in this seemingly secular movement, we are able to better understand the ethical and agential challenges involved in building a more inclusive democratic polity in this country and how religious sources might develop some of the moral agency necessary to navigate these challenges.

Listening to the Movement

This book arises out of several years of regular participant observation in living wage campaigns in Atlanta, Georgia, and Nashville, Tennessee, as well as periodic participant observation and primary document reviews of campaigns in Memphis, Tennessee, and San Diego, California.[28] I chose Atlanta, Nashville, and Memphis because I have lived in (or nearby) these cities and became active in their campaigns. I complemented these sites geographically with San Diego because it sheds light on the dynamics of the Southwest with its enormous immigrant influx and diminished union density, without the "Bible belt" context of southern cities. San Diego was also the last major city in California to pass a living wage ordinance, which in fact points to the challenges that campaigns face in a more conservative but less "religious" political region.

Because the Atlanta, Nashville, and Memphis campaigns led to thicker description from a southern regional perspective, I offer some balance to this through extensive literature review, e.g. Orin Levin-Waldman, Stephanie Luce, or Jared Bernstein's studies. However, this southern regional focus is an advantage in studying the living wage movement. The sociologist Isaac Martin, reporting on the diffusion of living wage ordinances, concludes that the southern regional location is one of the strongest factors deterring the passage of these ordinances.[29] Before the Atlanta campaign, there had not been a living wage campaign in a major city in the South (unless one considers Miami). When the Atlanta coalition called Jen Kern, the director of the Living Wage resource center at the Association of Communities Organizing for Reform Now (ACORN) to ask her to lead a training session, she replied, "Atlanta, this is the phone call we've been waiting for." Thus, the challenges and successes of southern campaigns offer particular insights into grassroots economic political activism in hostile environments.

My two years of participant observation in Atlanta (2001–3; ordinances passed in 2003 and 2005) included multiple campaign meetings, public rallies, city council sessions, campaign intern supervision, and a subsequent seminar session with two movement leaders through my academic research group at Vanderbilt University. My ongoing involvement in the Nashville campaign is the most extensive, beginning in 2004 (resolution passed in 2010) and included numerous meetings, trainings, public rallies, supervisions of interns and personal consultations, the development of needs-based living wage estimates for community organizers, and the formation of an Interfaith Worker Justice affiliated committee. In my work on the Memphis campaign (2006–8; ordinances passed in 2006, 2007, 2008), I reviewed primary documents, attended two public rallies, and participated in strategic consultations with the executive director during the inception of the Nashville campaign. In the San Diego campaign (ordinance passed in 2005), I reviewed primary documents and, in 2007, consulted with campaign leaders on the development of the Nashville campaign.

At the national level (2004–8), I conducted primary document reviews and participated in two national annual conferences and seven smaller affiliate tele-meetings of two national faith-based economic justice networks, Interfaith Worker Justice and the National Council of Churches' Let Justice Roll living wage campaign, which coordinate their work closely.[30] Supplementing this participant observation, I conducted an extensive review of the academic, nonprofit, and advocacy literatures on the U.S. living wage movement.

Centering Ethical Practices

There is no attempt here to recount the complex technical dimensions of passing and implementing living wage ordinances or their financial impact.[31] Instead, the focus is on how religious organizing builds economic political agency among those supporting the campaigns. There is also no attempt to outline, in a more abstract manner, all the ethical and political arguments for and against living wages. Our focus is instead on analyzing, evaluating, and learning from the organizing *practices* that religious activists use to build moral agency, in ways rarely discussed in the scholarly literature.[32]

Maintaining the focus on religious practices is not meant to imply that by themselves, people of faith or religious organizations have caused, or been the tipping point for, the movement's successes. Social movement theory is too complex to sustain the first claim, and the second would require quantitative research beyond the scope of this project. However, the current academic literature has largely ignored the presence and practices of religious activists in the movement. This book seeks to address this gap, and centers on the argument that important lessons are available about the ways religious ideology and practices contribute to moral agency—again, a person's commitment and capacity to discern and work for the needs, rights, responsibilities, and flourishing of oneself and others. Rev. Alexia Salvatierra, the director of California Clergy United for Economic Justice (CA CLUE), explains, "What do we hope for? Not just that a job is a better job. That's not enough." She describes a scene from the movie *Bread and Roses* in which the cleaning women reflect on how they do their jobs, disappearing into hallways and elevators, occasionally getting stepped over, and they comment wryly, "We have magic powers—to become invisible." Salvatierra continues, almost as a benediction, on the purpose of low-wage worker organizing: "We want to say it is possible . . . we have the power to stop making people invisible."³³ Living wage campaigns, and the religious organizations that support them, seek to build the moral agency of workers and their allies to make low-wage workers visible and powerful in the U.S. political economy.

Sustaining Moral Agency

In 2006, an article in the *New York Times* and a segment on a PBS national television series featured several of the custodians who had risked their jobs during the 2005 university campaign mentioned earlier. They glowed with pride in the television segment as they told their stories of struggle and activism. They became mini-celebrities among allied staff, students, and faculty at the institution. But many of them later told stories of having their shifts changed, their sick days closely monitored, and continual disruptions to their work life after the union contract was signed. The female organizer for the union and her female divinity school intern reported being escorted off campus by police the following summer as they attempted to speak with workers at clock-ins. Union density dropped precipitously over the next two years.

Religious activists' role in building the moral agency of many of the workers, their allies, and the coalition as a whole was significant in this campaign. But maintaining and developing that agency among those most marginalized is, at best, tenuous in our current political economy. Enhancing moral agency is hard work. In the United States, religious organizational involvement continues to be one of the few resources that can mitigate political alienation based on race, education, and economic status. Understanding how religious involvement does this work for and with low-wage workers, the challenges religious activists face, and how we might better nurture the building of moral agency in relation to the political economy is at the heart of this book.

Particularity and Religious Pluralism

While multiple faith traditions in the living wage movement are discussed here, a core Christian focus runs through the text in two primary ways. First, Christian clergy and practitioners dominate the movement's public self-presentation and staffing. Certainly rabbis (including the director of San Diego Interfaith Committee on Worker Justice [ICWJ]), imams, and laity from many faiths are present in the living wage movement and were active in my participant observations. Jewish foundations such as Jewish Funds for Justice and other local organizations also contribute financial and technical resources and skills to the movement. But as is true in much of American religious life, Christian practitioners and resources heavily influence the movement and tend to frame its public and private work; for example, even if the hymns that the movement uses remove specifically Christian language, the hymn as a worship form is still decidedly Christian.

Second, because my primary training and religious commitments are broadly Christian, I focus on the subtlety of Christian discourse more clearly and am more capable in offering constructive sources for its enhancement, thus clarifying possible Christian contributions to a pluralistic discourse on worker justice. The people of faith within the movement are primarily Christians, and they can enhance the depth of their contributions to multifaith dialogical conversations and moral agency by attending to the richness of their traditions and inviting others to do the same.

Social Ethics and Accountability to Social Activism

This book is aimed directly at a wide range of readers including sociologists of religion, social movement theorists, progressive religious activists and their allies, grassroots political strategists, those who study the intersections of race, gender, religion, and politics more generally, and Christian social ethics. It is of particular resonance for this latter field.

From its beginning as an academic discipline, Christian social ethics relied heavily on the social sciences, and on sociology in particular, to develop accounts and strategies for combating contemporary suffering and injustice. As the historian and ethicist Gary Dorrien explains, Christian social ethics began "as a successor to required courses in moral philosophy [and] approached ethics inductively as the study of social movements addressing social problems."[34] In fact, early twentieth-century academic social ethicists such as John Ryan, Henry Ward, and Walter Rauschenbusch collaborated with the incipient living wage movement to analyze its social concerns and enhance its theological arguments and movement practices. These ethicists were deeply concerned with enhancing the capacity of persons to discern and advocate for peoples' needs, rights, and flourishing in the midst of often devastating work conditions. In drawing on sociology to understand the importance of moral agency and how it can best be cultivated by the living wage movement, we follow a long line of Christian ethicists who have partnered with social movements in order to understand and contribute to religious ethical practice.

While strict attention to social science and political intervention has become controversial in the larger discipline of Christian ethics, social ethicists continue to be "political, activist, and pragmatic" in their engagement of social issues.[35] The goal of Christian social ethicists has been not just to advance the guild but also to transform social structures.

Religious ethicists offer attentive eyes and analytical categories for understanding how religious resources help persons and communities construct their commitments and capacities for action. They are adept at framing moral arguments and can draw on intellectual traditions that give these arguments greater resonance in public debate. But, curiously, they often lack an understanding of how social and political change actually happens. While many ethicists see social change as their goal, few analyze the processes for social change that would enact our goals. Religious activists invite academics to learn from the grassroots ethical work of their movements and to evaluate their moral arguments and theories of moral agency against the hard realities of people's lives and incremental work for social and political change. Sustaining relationships with religious activists can help academic ethicists better judge whether their work is resonant, or at least not at odds, with building that agency. By listening to religious activists more carefully, we all deepen our understanding of practices for social change and the concrete cultivation of moral agency.

Exploring, Evaluating, and Enhancing Economic Political Agency

Religious activists offer significant resources for building the economic political agency of the working poor and their allies. But this work also requires the continual evaluation of the use of those resources so that activists can sustain the critical edge needed to expand the agency necessary to pursue economic democracy. If a democratic polity based on economic justice is a primary goal of progressive religious activists, they need to focus their attention on how religious worldviews and practices can, and do, cultivate moral action in relation to the political economy. This evaluative process helps to provide clarity on how to continue to cultivate, renew, and expand religious resources dedicated to the moral agency of low-wage workers and their allies.

A complex constellation of activities is needed to enhance the power of those who are normally excluded from policy making. Good arguments, however important, are never enough for social change. Robust economic political agency for the working poor entails parallel work in reconciliation, leadership development, and ritual renewal in order to sustain involvement. Thus, moral agency becomes a multidimensional concept dependent on greater institutional work and continual cultural nurturance.

The living wage movement is a story about the intertwined issues of economic poverty and political poverty, issues the movement must address together. In the midst of economic and political deprivations, religious persons are building a movement not just to pass a single economic triage policy but also to reinvigorate a moral worldview that requires greater economic political power of, with, and for the poor. In many ways, their efforts parallel and illuminate the reemergence of progressive theology more generally in the last decade and its focus on putting poverty back on the national and global political agenda.

The following chapters focus on specific areas of the movement in order to enhance our understanding of the contributions and challenges that religious worldviews and practices offer for building moral action focused on the political economy. Each chapter explores a primary practice of the movement, analyzes religious contributions to this practice and its cultivation of moral agency, identifies an ethical issue around agency arising from this work, and offers a way forward from religious sources for the ongoing agential work of the movement.

Chapter 1 contextualizes the emergence of the contemporary living wage movement in the United States. By conscious political choice, U.S. politicians have opted to undermine the original intent of the minimum wage by refusing to raise it adequately over the last half-century. Despite increased worker productivity, the minimum wage is far below what is necessary for a small family to pay for their basic needs in this country. The increase in working poverty thus signals both the economic and political poverty of low-wage workers. Religious organizations join coalitions for a living wage precisely to counter these intertwined poverties. Faith-based community organizing is second in size only to the labor movement in advocacy and mobilization for social justice among low-wage workers in the United States. Moreover, the reemergence of progressive religious activism and the rebirth of religion-labor-community coalitions for living wages have been mutually reinforcing. Religious activists seek to enhance the economic political agency of low-wage workers and their allies and put poverty back on the national agenda.

Chapter 2 analyzes the ways that the moral framing of the movement and its religiously resonant arguments on the moral nature of government and wages facilitate an alternative vision of the political economy. Religious activists not only define what is unjust about working poverty but also identify culpable actors (businesses and especially government), offer an action plan (living wage ordinances), and provide the motivation to move people to action. While drawing implicitly and explicitly on long-standing religious traditions for their arguments, religious activists also carefully include pragmatic economic appeals. The social equity strand of neoclassical economics encourages governments to focus their economic corrections on lower and middle classes for greater economic growth. While this framing has great resonance with U.S. voters, activists must be careful not to embrace the neoliberal ideal of independence from government. Religious activists can better support the working poor by emphasizing the theological goods of interdependence as a foundation for a moral economy.

Chapter 3 explores the role of religious organizations in multiracial and ethnic living wage organizing, and chapter 4 analyzes the gendered nature of living wage organizing. Religious activists in the living wage movement ground much of their moral motivation and argumentation in what is perceived as God's special concern for the poor. Economic class is certainly the focus of much religious organizing.[36] In the United States, however, economic class can rarely be separated from race and gender.

Within this intersection, progressive religious organizations offer particular strengths and challenges for building movements in raced and gendered political economies. Chapter 3 explains that religious activists take on two major racialized functions within the living wage movement: bridge building and political activation. Bridge building involves the work of ideology translation, relational repair, and inclusion monitoring in coalitions. Political activation involves cultivating the resources (public speaking, personal connections, and the like) necessary to enhance political participation. Through these activities, activists augment the moral agency of low-wage workers and their allies by offering pathways for building a collective identity across difference and by providing opportunities for more marginalized persons to cultivate key civic skills. While religious organizations and activists offer these resources, they can also be the source of significant resistance to cross-race and cross-class political engagement. Even some forms of well-intentioned "grass-tops" religious organizing can ultimately undermine the economic political agency of low-wage workers. Continued meditation on the multiple dimensions of theological solidarity—preferential accountability (or responsibility to the poor), structural conscientization (developing critical analyses of social reality), complex identity recognition (or realizing we are not defined by merely one identity), and expansive moral agency (building and embracing further capacity to act for the good)—can help religious allies continually evaluate their work.

Chapter 4 also traces the contributions of feminist organizations to living wage activism and discusses their connections to religious activists. Motivated in part by the feminization of poverty, certain feminist foundations, organizations, and researchers provide important resources for the living wage movement. Moreover, women represent half of all the organizers and board members in religious organizing. This is particularly important because women are generally underrepresented in political engagement, and these women often provide crucial role models. Yet this "feminization of organizing" can be a problem when women professional religious organizers also lack the structural support (childcare, healthcare, retirement) necessary to sustain their positions. In addition, religious organizations that are close allies with feminist organizations sometimes encounter resistance from other religious entities over reproductive rights issues. In response to these challenges, this chapter reflects on the "sacrificial" demands of low-wage worker organizing and the needed supports for women organizers as well as on the call of Christians to reach across even grave difference to "remember the poor" (Gal. 2:10).

How activists utilize religious ritual to strengthen moral commitment and moral agency within the movement is featured in chapter 5. Religious ritual gives activists a vital way to cultivate collective identity, offer low-risk participation, challenge the boundaries of sacred and profane, and display embodied testimony. Through ritual practice, activists ultimately "re-member" the sacred, or expand the places and persons included in its scope. Yet the use of religious ritual is also vulnerable to becoming a form of theater for political expediency, losing its larger meaning and legitimacy. In order for religious ritual to maintain its integrity, its power, and its meaning, religious activists must build and maintain connections with other more continuous worshipping communities (congregations, intentional communities, etc.). These connections help keep religious rituals lithe and authentic, renew the whole context of faith that makes sense of political work, and provide a longer-term vision of the liturgical nature of activism itself.

The final chapter reflects on the next stages of the living wage movement. While there are fewer municipal living wage campaigns active in 2010 than in 2005, the living wage movement is best seen as an important gateway to other worker justice struggles such as raising state and federal minimum wages, developing and enforcing anti-wage theft laws, fair treatment of undocumented workers, and negotiating community-benefit agreements. As with previous campaigns, religious activists not only seek to enact concrete policies but also build the moral agency of low-wage workers and their allies in order to alter the landscape of the political economy. Participatory justice is their ultimate goal, not just policy development. As the movement enters these new stages, we briefly reiterate the lessons and challenges the movement's complex work has presented so far. Robust economic political agency for the working poor and their religious allies entails not only making good moral arguments (or framing), but also parallel work in bridge building, alternative political development, gendered leadership, and ritual renewal. Through these organizing practices, religious activists ask us to think and to act more thoroughly about the moral and theological meanings of wages, work, government, political engagement, and the political economy.

1

U.S. Poverties and Religious Resources

Movement Context

Oh Mary, don't you weep, don't you mourn
Oh Mary, don't you weep, don't you mourn
Pharaoh's army got drowned
Oh Mary, don't you weep.

Oh Worker, don't you weep, don't you mourn
Oh Worker, don't you weep, don't you mourn
Pharaoh's army got drowned
Oh Worker, don't you weep.

Oh Pharaoh, don't you know what you do
Oh Pharaoh, don't you know what you do
Pharaoh's army got drowned.
Oh Mary, don't you weep.

Woe to the powerful, justice will prevail
Woe to the powerful, justice will prevail
Pharaoh's army got drowned.
Oh Mary, don't you weep.

Oh Council, won't you pay a living wage
Oh Council, won't you pay a living wage
Pharaoh's army got drowned
Oh Mary, don't you weep.

When I get to Heaven goin' to put on my shoes
Run about glory and tell all the news
Pharaoh's army got drowned
Oh Mary, don't you weep.[1]

Through an African rhythm, an oppressor's folly, and justice's triumph, a new version of a familiar spiritual declares the presence of a growing social movement. This recent adaptation of "Oh Mary, Don't You Weep," while echoing old labor hymns, has several novel features that reflect the living wage movement.[2]

First, the activists singing these songs are on the lines of a burgeoning frontier in the labor struggle—municipal living wage ordinances. They are not just singing to factory bosses but to city councils and county commissioners, who, in an era of privatization, are contributing to lower wage work in America. Second, this song is found in Interfaith Worker Justice's *Rally Song Book*, circa 2005, not the *Little Red Song Book* of the International Workers of the World (or the "Wobblies") of 1904. Interfaith Worker Justice, founded in 1996, serves as an innovative movement halfway house for the support, coordination, and integration of religion and labor activism in the United States.[3] Third, this song appears in a rally book that includes numerous African spirituals, Appalachian hymns, and Spanish folk songs. The compilation represents the diversity of contemporary work in the United States and labor and religious organization's efforts to deal with these changes. Finally, a religious laywoman, Kim Bobo, the founder of Interfaith Worker Justice, composed the hymn's new verses. She is just one of the hundreds of women of faith who play a primary role in leading this movement, a movement whose primary beneficiaries are most often women living in poverty.

Religious activism has been absent from much of social movement theorists' analyses of the living wage movement. However, progressive religious coalitions are fundamental to the new labor activism rising in the United States. As the political scientist Richard Wood recognized in his analysis of faith-based community organizing, religious community organizing is "second in size only to the labor movement among drives for social justice among low-income Americans today."[4] At a time when the media and academia still focus regularly on the strength of the "religious right" at the federal level, the success of the living wage movement demonstrates the underrecognized power of progressive religious activists in cities around the nation.

The 1994 coalition of Baltimore churches provided the impetus for that city's living wage ordinance. While often cited as the first living wage ordinance in the nation, Baltimore's ordinance was not really the first. In 1988, the city of Des Moines, Iowa, set a minimum compensation package for its economic development projects, and Gary, Indiana, implemented a similar measure in 1991. But Baltimore's ordinance was the first to be prompted by a grassroots campaign.[5] Moreover, Baltimore activists articulated the failures of the minimum wage program and reintroduced the term "living wage" while developing a new successful model for building local economic political power.[6] In Andy Merrifield's assessment, these new living wage campaigns offered "progressives everywhere a new big idea at a time when we're not supposed to need big ideas anymore: the working class is getting back on the offensive, reorganizing in the workplace, [and] seeking allies."[7] These campaigns breathed new life into the economic political agency of workers and their allies. As a result, they became stepping stones for other struggles as coalitions extended their power base to statewide minimum wage victories (Arizona), increases in the Earned Income Tax Credit (Boston), the election of third-party candidates to city councils and mayoral seats (Santa Monica), and to the increase in the federal minimum wage in 2007.[8]

While the specifics of living wage ordinances vary according to local contexts, the logic and strategy of municipal campaigns have not varied dramatically from the Baltimore model of developing religion, community, and labor coalitions to establish higher wage floors. Municipal living wage ordinances typically propose that those who work full time for a local government (and often those who work for businesses that have contracts with or receive subsidies/tax abatements from local government) should receive an hourly wage that lifts them out of poverty. Proponents generally calculate the appropriate wage level either by dividing the federal poverty threshold for a family of three or four by one or two full-time, full-year, wage earners or by using a more precise local needs assessment that enables families to provide for their basic needs from earned wages. The logic offered is straightforward: full-time work should ensure basic economic needs. Workers paid by the government (or supported by their contracts and/or subsidies) should not have to return to the government for basic economic assistance (such as food stamps); taxpayer money should not be used to create poverty-level jobs.

Strategically, numerous organizations have played important roles in developing the living wage movement nationally. ACORN and the New Party provided centralized information centers and trained personnel for numerous campaigns.[9] Their websites and experienced personnel, such as Jen Kern and David Reynolds, have been a repository of organizing guides, sample ordinances, and campaign updates, all essential resources for establishing a consistent framework and strategy in the movement.

Inspired by the Baltimore victory, ACORN's Kern laboriously poured over state constitutions and documents from around the country in 1995 to determine other places where citizens could legally develop campaigns to raise the minimum wage above the federal level.[10] In other words, were there any state regulations or court decisions that could block the development of ordinances or a ballot initiative to raise wages? With this list in hand, ACORN began by working for statewide minimum wage increases in Missouri (a successful campaign, but quite expensive), and citywide minimum wage increases in Houston and Denver (which were defeated). Eventually, ACORN returned to more limited, city government-focused ordinances, and local ACORN affiliates served as a direct partner in fourteen successful ordinance campaigns.[11] Nationally, ACORN held three living wage conferences for those interested in running successful local campaigns. The IWJ founder and director Kim Bobo notes, "[ACORN] had provided much of the leadership for the living wage movement (thanks especially to Jen Kern [the director of the ACORN's living wage resource center for ten years])."[12] While the national ACORN office provided important early training for the Atlanta coalition and shorter consultations with several other campaigns, local ACORN affiliates were not integral to the cities in my research, as many did not even have local affiliates in the area.[13] Yet ACORN's training expertise and national activity as an information clearinghouse assisted almost every campaign in the United States.

Independent and university economic think tanks also contributed to the success of the movement. In San Diego, the local Center for Policy Initiatives researched the economic feasibility of the living wage ordinance and testified regularly before the city council. In Atlanta and Nashville (as well as numerous other cities), the Political Economy Research Institute (PERI), based at the University of Massachusetts–Amherst and directed by the economist Robert Pollin, provided analyses and reports on the economic impact of specific municipal ordinances. These documents were often submitted directly to city councils to counter opposition arguments. In a more general manner, the Economic Policy Institute in Washington also provides crucial studies of the effects of ordinance implementation around the nation. The Brennan Center for Justice at New York University Law School, particularly Paul Sonn of the National Employment Project there, supplied key legal advice for the movement and helped write several wage ordinances and ballot measures.[14] The Strategic Press Information Network (SPIN) and the Communications

Consortium Media Center's Fairness Initiative on Low Wage Work also provided consultations and organizing guides on movement messaging.[15] Although part of the national infrastructure of the movement, none of these organizations directly organizes local living wage campaigns.

In contrast, the locals and central labor councils of various unions provided important infrastructure, funding, and organizing for numerous local campaigns.[16] Although labor is not particularly powerful in Atlanta, Memphis, Nashville, or San Diego, each of these coalitions still received some funding (direct and in-kind contributions) from union networks, drew on union connections with key government officials, relied on union organizers to identify low-wage workers, and benefited from unions mobilizing turnout. When many of these coalitions formed, among their first phone calls were those to allies in the local labor movement for endorsement and advice. As an organizer in Nashville explained, "No one knows the political landscape better than [the head of the local AFL-CIO (American Federation of Labor-Congress of Industrial Organizations)] and [their lobbyist]. Their insight was vital." Calls from these union leaders also arranged the first metro council-member sponsor of Nashville's municipal living wage campaign.

Despite the fact that religious organizations are often less obvious in other campaigns than in Baltimore, they continue to shape the "new" living wage movement. Religious activists help influence the movement through their participation in local coalitions and national networks such as Interfaith Worker Justice (with their forty local affiliates and worker centers), the National Council of Churches' Let Justice Roll campaign, various denominational social justice offices, and the four major interreligious faith-based community organizing networks (IAF, Pacific Institute for Community Organizing [PICO], Direct Action Research and Training [DART], and Gamaliel).[17] As the political scientists Margaret Levi, David Olson, and Erich Steinman conclude, "Besides lending legitimacy and authority to living wage campaigns, church involvement provides significant contributions to organization building for campaigns."[18] Rabbi Lori Coskey, the executive director of San Diego's ICWJ, states this clearly: "We were the face of the living wage here in San Diego. We turned out over half of the participants at every rally and testified for months before the council." The 5–4 metro council vote could not have happened without them.

Municipal living wage ordinances are the backbone of the new living wage movement. Yet the movement encompasses a range of worker justice campaigns including various public policies, business practices, and organizing strategies. In addition to municipal living wage ordinances, these include cost-of-living increases, health care co-payments, paid vacation time, and workplace equity. For example, among the stated principles providing the "basis of [San Diego's ICWJ's] formation" is this:

> People have a basic right to productive lives, including compensated employment. Part of compensated employment is the right to just and living wages and other benefits to sustain a life with dignity. Included in the benefits are adequate health care, security for old age or disability, unemployment compensation, healthful and safe working conditions, weekly and daily rest, family leave, periodic holidays for recreation and leisure, and reasonable security against abuse, harassment, and arbitrary dismissal.[19]

This principle correlates with the goal of the organization "to educate the community on the rights of workers to obtain just and living wages and other benefits that allow for a life with dignity."[20] As in San Diego, other cities' lead organizations saw municipal living wage ordinances as only one dimension of their campaigns. They participated regularly in "living wage" organizing for universities and local businesses.

During Atlanta's municipal living wage campaign, successful campaigns occurred concurrently at Agnes Scott College and Emory University. Campaigns at Belmont and Vanderbilt Universities in Nashville (where a wide-ranging ordinance had been withdrawn in 2000) nurtured a new municipal campaign with new organizers. In Memphis and San Diego, the success of the municipal campaign led to support for new university campaigns. Religious activists and organizations also participated in wage-related campaigns focused on local business concurrently with their municipal campaigns. In Nashville, this included aiding the mostly immigrant Metro taxi drivers to document their low pay (around $2.10 an hour) and organize for new contracts.

Moreover, living wage organizing is not just about wages; it also focuses on health care coverage, retirement benefits, vacation days, and various "right to organize" protections. San Diego's living wage ordinance included $2 per hour in required benefits for workers, as well as three ordinances that focused on worker retention, worker anti-retaliation, and responsible contractor policies.[21] Each of these components was seen as part of insuring the stability of a living wage "package of benefits."

The breadth of the movement enables numerous actors to identify themselves with the living wage movement. What they share is a call to address working poverty not only in their cities but also in the nation as a whole. To do this, they must respond to both the economic and political poverty of low-wage workers wherever it exists. The larger dimensions of these poverties is thus important for understanding the context in which these religious activists are building the movement and moral agency in the current political economy.

Intersecting Poverties

Discussions of poverty usually focus on the economic deprivation people experience when resources are limited or unevenly distributed. But poverty is a multifaceted reality, which appears in multiple dimensions of people's lives. Deprivation can arise in spiritual (e.g., alienation from God), bodily (disease), social (isolation), and political (disenfranchisement) realms as well as economic.[22] Most people in poverty experience the intersection of multiple poverties simultaneously. For example, economic deprivation may interact with declines in bodily health as health care is harder to obtain and preventative practices become too costly. For growing numbers of the working poor who lack a livable wage, economic poverty pairs with political poverty as the voices, votes, and concerns of the working poor are marginalized in policy making and in political campaigns. "Working poverty" is now a common feature of the United States' economic landscape; because of inadequate pay millions of people who work full-time jobs still live in poverty, and many more teeter on the edge. Despite increases in worker productivity over the last forty years, the purchasing power of the federal minimum wage has been in absolute decline for decades: the inflation-adjusted wage of 2009 was 17% lower than it was in 1968 (the federal minimum wage's peak purchasing power). Through a conscious practice of erosion-by-neglect, politicians have made the federal minimum wage a poverty wage that no longer pretends to track inflation or increases in worker productivity. How the federal minimum wage has declined is thus the story both of economic and political poverty of low-wage workers in the United States and the wider context in which the "living wage" movement operates.

Poverty Wages, Political Poverty

An early article in the *Washington Post* stated, "If you hold the line on the minimum wage and inflation continues, it has the net effect of a rollback."[23]

In 2007 the U.S. Congress voted to raise the federal minimum wage incrementally to $7.25 by July 2009. This legislation marked the first minimum wage increase since Congress had reset it at $5.15 in 1997. Those ten years were the longest period *without* an increase since the minimum was created in 1938.[24] Because of the 2007 legislation, almost 4.5 million people, or 4% of the U.S. workforce, received a wage increase.[25] Women (63% of all minimum wage workers) benefited the most from the raise, as did a disproportionate share of minorities (African Americans are 11% of the total workforce but 18% of workers affected by the increase; Hispanics are 14% of the total workforce and 19% of the beneficiaries).[26] While celebrating the raise, activists also recognized that the increase only returned the minimum wage to its 1972 value.[27] As one Let Justice Roll leader explained, "Yes, the ten-year wait is over. It's a victory. This raise will certainly help some people. But it's in no way enough. We are already organizing for $10 by 2010." After controlling for inflation, even the $7.25 wage floor represented only about a 4% increase over the $5.15 wage of 1997.[28] And while the rate of inflation between 1997 and 2009 was about 3% per year, the buying power of the minimum wage fell by almost 40% since 1997.[29] Thus, the final 2009 incremental wage increase covered, at most, one year in real wage loss for low-wage workers in the last decade.

Despite the myth that wages track worker productivity, the minimum wage declined in real value while worker productivity grew during the same period. Worker productivity increased by nearly 30% during the last decade while the minimum wage decreased by almost 40%.[30] This meant that business owners and their shareholders benefited from the increase in worker productivity at the expense of those same workers, both by not sharing the economic benefits of worker productivity with their employees (to the tune of a 30% increase) and by effectively cutting their employees' wages during the same period (by nearly 40%). As the economist Robert Pollin asserts, "The fact that the minimum wage has been falling in inflation-adjusted dollars while productivity has been rising means that profit opportunities have soared while low-wage workers have gotten nothing from the country's productivity bounty."[31] This drop in real income also meant that workers entered the 2008 recession with little cushion to ride out the business cycle. In fact, unlike previous business cycles where workers' median income saw at least some increase (i.e., from 1979 to 1989), the last business cycle (2000–7) saw almost no median wage growth. This at a time when average CEO pay rose 167%, or sixteen times the average worker's pay.[32] Activists argue that this dynamic made workers even more vulnerable in one of the harshest recessions since the Great Depression: they, the workers, had nothing in reserve.

The recession of 2008, and, more specifically, the loss of 4.6 million full-time, full-year jobs contributed both to an increase in poverty rates overall (from 12.5% to 13.2%, or 2.6 million more people) and to the greatest single-year drop in median income on record (3.9%).[33] Even among those who were able to keep full-time, full-year jobs, more workers fell into poverty (a rise from 2.5 to 2.6% in 2008).[34] While income growth slowed for all income levels during the recession, the story is starker at lower income levels, or the working poor. Income for those in the bottom 40% of income earners (or bottom two quintiles) dropped 2.7% in 2008 while the top 40% of income earners still saw an increase of at least 1% in earned income.[35] Although the gap in average earnings between the highest 20% and lowest 20% of income earners did not grow significantly during 2008, more people fell into poverty than in the previous three years.[36]

While these numbers speak to the growing economic poverty of low-wage workers, a political poverty is growing as well. The current disconnect between worker productivity and minimum wages is central to understanding this new political poverty. Between 1947 and 1973 worker productivity rose at a rate of 104% while the minimum wage rose at 101%, adjusting for inflation. But between 1973 and 2004, worker productivity rose 78% while the inflation-adjusted minimum wage fell 24%.[37] Pollin explains, "This means if the real value of the national minimum wage had risen exactly in step with average productivity growth—and no more than that—the minimum wage of 2008 would be more than $19.80."[38] In the last several decades, workers and their allies have been unable to compel politicians to maintain a fair relationship among inflation, worker productivity, profit distributions, and minimum wages.

The inadequate purchasing power of the current federal minimum wage signals a gap between the original goals of minimum wage legislation and its economic and political reality in the last half-century. Minimum wage laws originated in Australia, Britain, and France in response to the "sweating of labor" or "work at wages so low that [workers] could not, and did not, support a socially acceptable level of wholesome family life."[39] Efforts to secure wages that would sustain persons and families at "a socially acceptable level of well-being" became known as the "living wage" at the turn of the twentieth century.[40] In the United States, state laws in Massachusetts and Oregon laid the groundwork for combating "sweating," and in 1938 the federal government finally enacted the national Fair Labors Standard Act (FLSA), which established the federal minimum wage, as well as limits on work hours and child labor.[41]

Proposals for, and debate around, a federal minimum wage began in the midst of rampant unemployment and skewed distribution of wealth during the Great Depression. As the historian Willis Nordlund explains, the primary goal of federal minimum wage legislation was to insure that "economic depression did not depress wages even farther. The federal minimum wage program was designed to be a floor under wages in addition to an income enhancement and poverty reduction mechanism."[42] From the beginning, such legislation was both a pragmatic and moral intervention. Pragmatically, Franklin D. Roosevelt declared in 1933 that the slow decline of wages was "a serious form of unfair competition against other employers [that] reduces the purchasing power of workers" and threatens the stability of industry."[43] Striking a more moral tone while encouraging the passage of the FLSA in 1937, President Roosevelt asserted that a "self-supporting and self-respecting democracy can plead no justification for the existence of child labor, no economic reason for chiseling workers' wages or stretching worker's hours."[44] With the economy unstable and labor unions weak, federal politicians debated the FLSA and the federal minimum wage vigorously but eventually approved them overwhelmingly.[45]

Defining Poverty

Certainly, the minimum wage never provided for luxurious living. In 1968, though, a minimum-wage earner lived 20% above the poverty line (set for a family of three); today she and her family would live 30% below this same line.[46] And, as an adequate measure of poverty in the United States, even this line is highly controversial and generally discredited. Kathleen Short, the former chief of Poverty and Health Statistics as the U.S. Census Bureau, states, "We haven't changed the way we determine the poverty level since the 1960s. That is a political issue, not because we think it's the best way to measure poverty."[47]

The federal government's poverty threshold, developed by Mollie Orshansky of the Social Security Administration in the early 1960s, was based on U.S. Department of Agriculture (USDA) estimates of the "economy food plan" (now called the "thrifty food plan") multiplied by three. The multiplier was derived from the findings of a 1955 survey showing that families of three or more spent one-third of their after-tax income on food.[48] From the beginning, the poverty threshold was set extremely low. The "economy food plan" was the least costly food plan, included no meals eaten outside the home, and was intended by the USDA for "temporary or emergency use when funds are low"; it was not "a reasonable measure of basic money needs for a diet."[49] The Office of the Budget overruled subsequent efforts to revise the food plan and increase the multiplier. Now, the poverty threshold is updated only by the yearly consumer price index universal, or the government's calculation of the differences in prices paid by consumers for a "representative basket of goods and services" over time.[50]

Thus, the official federal poverty threshold began artificially low and has not reflected the economic changes since 1960s that should have altered both its baseline and its multiplier. For example, food currently accounts for only one-sixth of the after-income spending of families in the lowest 20% of income earners while housing, childcare, and medical costs have increased much more rapidly and consume more of family budgets.[51] On the other hand, the official poverty threshold also uses pre-tax income and does not include subsidies such as the Earned Income Tax Credit (EITC) or food stamps in an accounting of family income. In fact, a 1995 report commissioned by the Joint Economic Committee of Congress from the National Research Council of the National Academy of Sciences argued for developing new, federal poverty thresholds that "represent a budget for food, clothing, shelter (including utilities), and an additional amount to allow for other needs (e.g., household supplies, personal care, non-work-related transportation)" that would be calculated from "actual expenditure data" for families.[52] We can understand the need for this shift when we hear testimonials of minimum wage workers such as this Atlanta resident:

My name is Santina Story. I am a thirty-three-year-old mother of three and the only wage earner in my house. I have two years of experience in housekeeping and until recently, was making $6.75 an hour for my work at the Crowne Plaza Hotel in Atlanta. I worked forty hours a week, but due to the fact that I had to take MARTA [public transportation], my days ended up being longer and more tiring. Because of the hours I was never able to see my children. My baby would spend all day at PeachCare and by the time I would get home from work, I was too busy preparing dinner and getting the kids ready for bed so they can be ready for school the next day. I couldn't help them with homework or catch up with them on their day. . . .

I choose to do this type of work because I like to clean and I like the people I get to interact with. I no longer have to depend on welfare just to survive. But due to the low wage, I still have to depend on food stamps, PeachCare child care, and sometimes I have to use MARTA passes which I get at the Atlanta Day Shelter. I had to quit because I didn't qualify for medical leave or sick days and I needed time off to take my youngest child to the doctor for health problems. . . . Earning $6.75 an hour I was basically living paycheck to paycheck. I still have to live with things like no heat in my one-bedroom apartment. My kids never have anything new.[53]

If one sits in on an organizing meeting with low-wage workers, these stories are all too common.

I want to work and have to work but daycare takes so much of what I make. And if there's Section 8 housing, it's nowhere near work. The daycare charges you extra if you're late. And if you're late more than five times, they won't let you come back. Work writes me up if I'm late there too. It doesn't matter that I'm relying on the bus to get everywhere.

When my husband left, my kids and me had to go to the shelter. People are like—you got a full-time job and you have to live there? But I'm proud of how I work. I want my daughters to see my work ethic. But it's gotta pay off, you know. That's why I'm at this meeting.

Simply averaging the eight alternative poverty measures presented in the report, the new poverty threshold would be 42% above the official poverty line.[54] With this in mind, many advocate for a poverty threshold between 150% and 200% of the official poverty line, in order to address families' minimum needs, not just emergency budgeting.[55] Most means-tested government programs in the United States already use multipliers of the poverty threshold to determine eligibility: food stamps eligibility

TABLE 1

	Percentage of Population in Poverty in U.S., 2008
Total Persons below 100% of Poverty Threshold	13.2%
Total Children	19%
Total 65 or over	9.7%
Women	14.5%
Men	11.7%
Whites (non-Hispanic/Latino)	9.2%
Blacks	25%
Latinos	21.2%
Total Persons below 200% of Poverty Threshold	31.9%

extends to 130% of the poverty line; nutrition programs such as school lunches and Women, Infant, and Children (WIC) extends to 185%; and most State Children's Health Insurance Programs (SCHIP) cover children up to 200% of the poverty line.

Working Poverty

According to government poverty statistics, 13.2% of the U.S. population, or 39.8 million people, lived in poverty in 2008, including 19% of all children and 9.7% of all those sixty-five and older (see table 1).[56] Although whites dominate poverty statistics in sheer numbers, women, blacks, and Latinos are over-represented in absolute numbers as percentages of the population. Almost one quarter of all blacks, 21.2% of Latinos (compared to 9.2% of non-Latino whites), and 14.5% of all women (compared to 11.7% of men) fall below the official federal poverty threshold in the United States.[57] Over 96 million people (or 31.9% of the total population) qualify as working poor, that is, living below 200% of the poverty line.[58]

In 2009, 3% of all hourly waged workers in the United States worked at or below the minimum wage.[59] Expanding the category to include all workers earning less than ten dollars an hour, we find that 30% of all hourly waged workers, including 35% of all waged women (compared to 24% of men), 35% of blacks and 36.5% of Latino workers (and 45.7% of Latinas) also fall into this category and, consequently, come under official poverty guidelines.[60]

Despite claims that most persons working low-wage jobs are teenagers earning spending money after school and in the summers, 81% of low-wage earners are over the age of nineteen.[61] For example, in Atlanta in 2003, 21% of all workers, with an average age of thirty-five and an average job tenure of seventeen years, earned less than a living wage. Of these low-wage earners, 56% were female and 43% were non-white. Only about 7% of these workers were teenagers.[62] Most of the teens earning minimum wage were no longer in school but were working full-time to provide for their families. The typical low-wage worker, however, is an adult woman with children. Fifty-nine percent of those benefiting from the 2009 minimum wage increase (either by the mandatory increase or ripple effects) were women; again, while minorities are disproportionately represented in the low-wage worker pool, 61% of minimum-wage workers receiving wage increases were white.[63]

Elizabeth Rosita, from San Diego, is one of those minimum-wage women struggling to care for her family. Ms. Rosita works thirty-seven-and-a-half hours a week as a public restroom attendant, including regular night shifts, as well as twenty-five hours a week at McDonalds. Both jobs pay minimum wage with no benefits. Her family struggles to pay rent for their small, one-bedroom apartment. Her son works as a public restroom attendant and at Albertson's grocery store; his wife takes care of their young son. Ms. Rosita sleeps on the living room couch while her son's family sleeps in the bedroom. Everyone is on California's MediCal, and they are on a waiting list for Section 8 housing. At the time, she hoped the living wage ordinance (subsequently passed) would give her more time with her grandson.[64]

Considering that a full-time, year-round worker earning $7.25 an hour still falls 13% below the federal poverty threshold of $17,346 for a family of three, the minimum wage increase is significant for family incomes and children's poverty. Wages and salaries account for approximately three-fourths of total family income in the United States (and more in the lowest 20% of income earners). The Economic Policy Institute therefore argues that wage trends are "the driving force behind income growth and income inequality trends."[65] Conversely, neglecting the minimum wage affects families and children significantly. The son of Santina Story, from Atlanta, speaks to the impact low-wage work has on his life.

> Hello, my name is Dontavious Story and I am in fifth grade. I'm going to tell you about my life. My life is about school and family. I start my day off when I wake up at 3:30 in the morning. I help my mom get

my baby brother ready for day care. . . . I go back to sleep until I go to school with my sister and friends. When school is over, my sister and I go to the after-school program. Then we come home and wait for my mom to come home from work. When mom comes home she needs help with dinner and the baby, so I help. . . . I feel bad because I get a bed and my mom sleeps on the floor.

I don't get to spend any time with my mom. She is always tired and stressed from work and us. I feel bad because I miss out on things because my mom says we can't afford them. I can't play football at school because we can't afford a uniform and my sister almost missed a fieldtrip because it cost too much. . . . It makes me feel really sad because my mom spends all her money on us. She hasn't bought anything for herself in two years.[66]

The United Nations Children's Fund reports that the United States has both the highest percentage of low-wage workers and the highest child poverty rate among the fourteen industrial nations.[67]

Political Poverty and Erosion-by-Neglect

The efficacy of the minimum wage has always been debated, both on the macro level as policy and on the micro level as a specific hourly rate. As Rev. Trina Zelle of Arizona Interfaith Alliance for Worker Justice explains it, "In any debate where the business guys are complaining about a specific wage rate, I simply ask—'do you believe in a minimum wage?' That usually sends them scrambling. Because the reality is most Americans do; most Chambers of Commerce don't."[68] The Reagan presidency and Senate Republicans in the 1980s advanced an erosion-by-neglect strategy concerning the minimum wage.[69] Murray Weidenbaum, the chairman of Reagan's Council of Economic Advisers noted in 2001, "If we . . . had had our druthers, we would have eliminated the minimum wage." This, in fact, would have been a "painful political process" so the administration was instead content to let inflation turn the minimum wage into an "effective dead letter."[70] Or, in the words of a lobbyist for the National Chamber of Commerce in 1981, "If you hold the line on the minimum wage and inflation continues, it has the net effect of a rollback."[71] This intentional neglect serves as a backdrop for understanding the 1997–2007 gap between minimum wage increases and the continuing erosion of the wage's purchasing power.

That gap signals a loss of political power for those who see wage floors as vital to low-wage workers' economic well-being. Low-wage workers in particular rely on government wage policies because they have little bargaining power in the marketplace, both for jobs and for raises. Clinton's welfare reform, which required recipients to work in order to receive Temporary Assistance for Needy Families (TANF), only deepened workers' powerlessness.[72] "Welfare reform" increased the pool of workers in the low-wage labor market and depressed their prevailing wages and their power even more.[73] Minimum wage increases thus become the primary way that low-wage workers receive cost-of-living adjustments in the current political economy.[74]

The virulent effects of the erosion-by-neglect strategy in the 1980s and 1990s became the oppositional field into which the contemporary living wage movement arose in the mid 1990s: "Even those workers who were playing by the rules were getting crushed."[75] With growing poverty, absolute declines in wages for the bottom income earners, and expanding gaps between the rich and poor, a new political mobilization emerged from the collaborations of labor, community, and religious groups. For the living wage movement at the turn of the twenty-first century, the economic and political decline of the federal minimum wage foregrounded deep structural issues both in waged work and the political power of waged workers in the United States.

In this economically and politically impoverished context, religious activists draw on the resources (or multidimensional "wealth") of theology and religious organizations to counteract deprivation. Religious activists are intentional in their framing, coalition building, leadership development, and ritual practice not merely to pass legislation but to build a political power base for moving the concerns of low-wage workers into the center of the political process. Through this work, they are also intentional in building the moral agency of low-wage workers and their allies toward collective action in the current political economy. Their poverty focus and alliance building speaks both from and back to the larger efforts for progressive social reform by progressive religious activists in the United States at this point.

Reviving the Religious Left? Building Progressive Religious Activism

Although progressive religious organizations have been a powerful force in activist organizing, including the black civil rights movement, the war on poverty, the antiwar/nuclear weapons movement and the Central

American peace and sanctuary movements, most academic and popular press writing in the last several decades have focused on the rise and dominance of the "religious right." Alliances among the Christian Coalition, Moral Majority, Family Research Council, Focus on the Family, and the Republican Party have spawned waves of scholarly research on the religious right. Yet in the past two decades many religious organizers also have sought to counter these more conservative religious activists with a new kind of organizing meant to bolster progressive religious organizations' presence in local, national, and international politics, particularly around poverty issues.[76]

In 2006 a front-page *Washington Post* article announced, "The Religious Left is Back."[77] But even the term "religious left" is not a moniker embraced by most progressive religious activists, as ethicist and religious researcher Robert Jones reports.[78] Emerging as a broad countermovement to the Christian Right in the 1980s and '90s, a constellation of progressive religious activists made the case that "God is not a Republican . . . or a Democrat."[79] While these activists sought, in part, to counter the alignment of the Christian conservatives with the Republican Party, they did not want to build a "mirror image" countermovement to align with the Democratic Party to become merely the polarized religious left.[80] Rather, they wished to transcend the culture war dichotomies of right versus left and focus instead on what brought them together, "broad commitments to social justice, democratic pluralism, and equality of all people."[81]

There has been little academic research on this revitalization of progressive religious activism, in part because it is not a unified political movement that can be studied easily. The progressive religious activist movement is perhaps best understood as a broad sector of religious groups that organize political action around values of peace, justice, and support for marginalized persons. More specifically, the new progressive religious coalition brings together local Protestant (progressive black, white mainline, and historic peace churches), Catholic, Unitarian Universalist, and Jewish (Reformed, Reconstructionist, and Conservative) congregations; social justice agencies associated with those religious denominations (such as the Catholic Campaign for Human Development); and the National Council of Churches, as well as numerous independent religious organizations (such as the Children's Defense Fund, Sojourners, Tikkun, Bread for the World, Evangelicals for Social Action, Interfaith Worker Justice, Interfaith Alliance, Faith in Public Life, Faith Voices for the Common Good, the Network for Spiritual Progressives); and various faith-based community organizing networks (such as the IAF, the Gamaliel Foundation, PICO, and DART).[82]

For most progressive religious activists, eliminating poverty is the unifying mission. Not all progressive religious groups, such as Religious Leaders for Reproductive Choice, subscribe to this as their primary mission. Yet the explicit coalition building that emerged around "poverty activism" in the 2004 and 2008 presidential campaigns has consistently garnered the attention of the popular press, creating the perception that progressive religious organizations were back on the political scene.[83] When then-candidate Barack Obama delivered a speech on faith and politics at the Call to Renewal conference in 2006, Jim Wallis of Sojourners called it "a landmark speech for the religious left."[84] The political commentator E. J. Dionne argued that the midterm elections of 2006 marked the end of the religious right's dominance and the emergence of a new religio-political landscape.[85] Political analysts subsequently argued that Obama's election in 2008 (including his religious organizing emphasis) signaled the return of progressive religious networks and ideology, and the closing of the "God gap" in partisan voting.[86]

In their 2009 survey of religious activists, Robert Jones and the political scientist John Greene observe that progressive and religious right activists are surprisingly similar demographically. Most hold a college degree (with progressives having more graduate degrees), most consider religion as extremely important in their lives (conservatives having a slight edge), and most attend worship at least once a week.[87] Ideologically and theologically, however, these two groups of activists differ more significantly. While 92% of conservatives see moral decay as "the main cause of America's problems," 49% of progressives explicitly disagree with this statement, and 47% think "poverty and discrimination" are the main sources of social problems. Seventy-four percent of progressive religious activists see poverty as their top priority; by contrast, conservative activists identify abortion and same-sex marriage as their top priorities (at 83% and 65%, respectively).[88]

Activists differ in how they interpret the roots of social problems. Progressive activists emphasize structural understandings of social problems while conservatives emphasize the failure of individual responsibility (or as the sociologist Charles Hall concludes in an earlier study, "system-blaming" versus "individual blaming").[89] Theologically, 88% of religious right activists identify as traditionalists as compared with 28% of progressive religious activists. With evangelical organizations such as Sojourners and Bread for the World playing major roles in antipoverty work, the role of theological liberalism in progressive religious activism is not hegemonic. In the living wage movement, ministers such as Bishop George McKinney (of St. Stephen's Church of God in Christ Cathedral in San Diego), a self-proclaimed social conservative and diehard opponent of teaching evolution, advocated for living wages because, "As a pastor actively involved in the [Bush] administration's faith-based initiative, we have provided services to people who work hard but still cannot make ends meet."[90] Still, most economically progressive religious activists build on Roman Catholic social teaching, liberation theology, and/or Protestant social gospel theology (which thrived in the Progressive era) to focus on "the least of these," especially in terms of poverty.[91] In the end, compared to conservatives, progressive religious activists do not subscribe completely to a particular theological viewpoint (that is, traditional versus liberal), but they do overwhelmingly embrace a social and political outlook that systematically seeks to build greater economic and political democracy and eliminate poverty.[92]

Religious activists in the living wage movement fit squarely within this broad story of the revival of progressive religious activism in the United States. Moreover, in addressing the structures of working poverty, religious living wage activists help to define progressive religious organizing in the United States. The relationship is reciprocal: lessons learned within the living wage movement speak from and back to this larger community of activism as it gains strength for addressing the myriad economic justice issues that concern persons of faith. The fissures, strengths, and strategies of the living wage movement provide a barometer for much of progressive religious organizing around economic justice in the United States more generally.

Pharaohs and Unexpected Agency

While new progressive religious activism carries forward the legacy of progressive and Black civil rights organizing, in many ways "God is also doing a new thing."[93] With shrinking union density, growing municipal privatization, and increased diversification of the low-wage workforce, new targets, new power arrangements, and new leaders have emerged at the turn of the twenty-first century. In this mix, new religious leaders and organizations come forward with a decidedly multicultural and multifaith approach to their work.

The rephrasing of an old black Christian spiritual as one of the movement songs also speaks to continuity: mourning is not the only option, pharaoh is sometimes defeated. And persons of faith have a particular gift for cultivating the moral agency to make that happen.

2

Living Wages

Religious Ideology and

Framing for Moral Agency

In a small classroom on the campus of North Park Seminary in Chicago, three leaders from the National Council of Churches' (NCC) Let Justice Roll campaign gathered with a student activist from the University of Notre Dame and a local Chicago alderman to train other activists on building successful living wage campaigns. While handouts and handbooks were circulating, Rev. Paul Sherry, the retiring director of the NCC's national campaign, mused, "One of the most important parts of the campaign was to find a phrase that really captured the imagination. I think we did it with 'A job should keep you out of poverty, not in it.'"[1] Conversation moved to the importance of infusing and maintaining a moral tone in any discussion of living wages.

This national workshop was just one among the many in which lead organizers emphasized a key strategy to their living wage victories: sticking to the "moral high ground" rather than arguing numbers (such as how the living wage was calculated, the probable costs, and so on). Attention to numbers was certainly critical, and many living wage campaigns hired economists to track economic impacts. But numbers-crunching did not draw the most "conversions," or new allies, and it certainly is not what motivated persons to join the fight. In fact, when asked what major lessons they wanted other activists to take from their campaigns, lead organizers echoed each other: "Don't get caught in debating numbers" but emphasize the values of fairness, hard work, and just wages. In other words, "framing" the living wage required keeping the moral dimension of this issue front and center in the movement's message.

Religious living wage activists navigate deep cultural assumptions about the "nature" of the economy and its nonrelationship to morality. To do this well, they must be creative enough to enter the dominant political/economic discussions convincingly while simultaneously challenging them by offering alternatives to reverse the tidal wave of damaging policies. They also seek to cultivate the engagement of persons and communities that are largely tangential to the insider conversations of most government economic policies. In other words, they want the working poor and their allies to be legitimate policy contributors in American democratic capitalism, not just objects. To do this, religious activists intertwine ethical arguments about the moral nature of the economy with pragmatic claims about proper economic interventions in the market. They document and, importantly, teach others to document the sociological reality and theological good of people's social, economic, and political interdependencies. They identify and explain our collective responsibility for the creation and continuation of working poverty. By developing and practicing new combinations of religious political speech, religious activists cultivate analytical capacity and moral commitment—or moral agency—for challenging the current political economy.

The effectiveness of framing in the living wage movement is built on amplifying core economic ideals of the "American dream" and its surrounding civil religion.[2] Many religious activists are well versed in the moral arguments on political economies from theologians such as Walter Rauschenbusch, John Ryan, and Martin Luther King Jr. Their political success depends, in part, on using religious values and tropes that resonate with dominant U.S. culture and its neoclassical economic ideals. This framing strategy introduces, at minimum, an effective triage mechanism for falling wages and, optimally, a pathway for ongoing moral education that enables persons to criticize and concretely re-envision the current political economy.

But as with all ethical and rhetorical work, some of the movement's current framing for "living wages" has implications that may be damaging in the long run. Promoting such neoclassical ideals as independence from government, for example, could be seen as stigmatizing any necessary and good government "dependence." These potentially undermining implications must be addressed in order to support other poverty-fighting measures and recognize everyone's "dependencies" on government for their well-being (or welfare). By remembering the sociological and theological importance of our interdependencies, religious activists can hold these neoclassical ideals in check and better support long-term economic political change.

Moral Agency and Framing

As ethical and social movement theories inform us, moral agency is analytically cultivated, in part, by helping people dissect and deconstruct the "givenness" of social structures and discern the impact those structures have on their lives. The capacity to act for social change deepens as people come to understand reality, not as "naturally" occurring but as the product of human choices guided by certain values, which can be countered by other choices guided by different values. Connecting a person's isolated sense of suffering or injustice with others and constructing groups with shared interpretations help people demystify social structures (and the ideologies that keep them in place) and open them to reconfiguration. When activists work on the collective moral meanings of a movement, therefore, they are cultivating their own and others' moral agency through reexamining "what is" and imagining "what ought to be."

The importance of crafting the moral meanings and messages of a movement may seem evident to ethicists who make their living crafting moral arguments. In recent years, however, sociologists who study social movements ("social movement theorists") have analyzed the importance of framing for the emergence and success of movements. "Resource mobilization theory"—the idea that resources were key to movement success—that dominated U.S. social movement theory in the 1980s and 1990s, largely ignored mobilizing beliefs (e.g., moral arguments), seeing them, much like social stress or grievances, as constants in society that did not by themselves determine the emergence or success of a movement. More vital and volatile structural resources, such as money or organizational leadership, enabled aggrieved populations to act on their concerns. For example, racism has always existed, but it took a synergy of growing black wealth, strong autonomous social institutions, and coordinated leadership to start the black civil rights movement; message crafting was secondary.[3]

In the last decade, though, sociologists working with the concept of "framing" recognized how interpreting grievances can mobilize individuals to join movements.[4] They argued that ideology and galvanizing beliefs emerge as social productions through an interactive process[5] and emphasized "meaning work . . . [or] struggle over the production of ideas of meanings" as a central task and goal of movements.[6] Theorists began to see framing as essential, conscious work that built the agency of others to see and act in the world differently. The sociologist James Jasper describes this form of agency as "artfulness" and contends:

> Individuals are not mere bearers of structures or dupes of culture. They act, albeit within certain limits. They monitor their actions and the outcomes, make adjustments, imagine new goals and possibilities, respond to others. . . . Art pulls these dimensions together succinctly for it consists of experiential efforts to transmute existing conditions into new creations by problematizing elements that have been taken for granted. . . . Protesters, just as clearly, rethink existing traditions in order to criticize portions and experiment with alternatives for the future, in both large and small ways. They offer ways of getting from here to there.[7]

Activists then do not merely act out predetermined scripts or apply traditions to contemporary problems. Instead, they artfully and consciously reconstitute multiple moral traditions and encourage others to do the same.

Religious activists bring great gifts to this intentional framing for social change. Religious practitioners are immersed in the art of moral argument. The narratives, symbols, principles, and rituals of faith communities regularly encourage ethical reflection in the daily lives of these practitioners. While the practices and resources look different in different faith communities, consistent themes and approaches to moral persuasion regularly emerge as believers practice the public, political nature of their faith. In the living wage movement, religious activists draw on long legacies of arguments for the moral nature of wages, the moral responsibilities of government, and accountability to the poor to compel and motivate commitment to the movement. They both display and extend the moral agency of movement participants by accessing strong alternative (or nondominant) traditions on the "nature" and purpose of the political economy. In this manner, they expand the palette and materials for the artfulness of politics.

Framing the Moral Economy

There is nothing but a lack of social vision to prevent us from paying an adequate wage to every [American] whether he be a hospital worker, laundry worker, maid, or day laborer. There is nothing except shortsightedness to prevent us from guaranteeing an annual minimum—and livable—income for every American family.[8]

While activists in the early twentieth century used the term "living wage," the term was reborn as an activist and public policy frame in the late 1990s. Why was this phrase such an effective frame for altering policy for low-wage workers? To understand both the power of the living wage concept and religious activists' role in its resonance and diffusion, we must first understand the dynamics of framing.

According to social movement theorists, effective frames perform two vital functions: (1) *Punctuating*—underscoring, embellishing, or redefining what is just or unjust; and (2) *Attributing*—identifying culpable agents, prescribing a general line of action, and motivating people to carry out the action.[9] The first function interprets a situation as morally wrong, and the second identifies the human action involved in creating the problem and the alternative human action that can and must change the outcome. The most effective frames define what is unjust by providing a diagnosis of the situation, a prescription of what should and can be done, and the motivation to do it. Each dimension of effective framing focuses on the role of human agency in history and seeks to redirect participants to a different historical end.

At the heart of the living wage movement is the moral claim, based on fairness, human dignity, and fundamental justice, that full-time work should lift a person and her or his children out of poverty. The NCC's slogan is, "A job should lift you out of poverty, not keep you in it." A full-time wage should provide a "living" not just subsistence. The living wage justice frame signals the flourishing that should come with fulfilling the duty of work as opposed to the injustice of working full-time and remaining in poverty. In this frame, proponents articulate the diagnostic element by focusing on people who "play by the rules" but are not able to move beyond basic survival, and present these working poor families as the epitome of what is unjust in the current U.S. political economy. In the words of one clergy activist,

> The face of hunger is changing. An increasing number of working people are not able to provide for their basic needs. About twenty of these hard-working Americans visit the Trinity Episcopal Soup Kitchen in Bethlehem [Pennsylvania] each day . . . they play by the rules. They contribute to the economy. And yet, they do not have enough to eat.[10]

Or as the NCC's general secretary declared, "Our concept of justice holds that no person who works should be impoverished."[11] Here is the basic moral assertion: hard work in the United States should provide a measure of security and even prosperity. The working-poor frame points to a fundamental injustice by naming the incongruity of working full-time and still finding yourself unable to pay for adequate housing, health care, transportation, and food for yourself and your family..

In offering this frame, activists draw on the experience of the working poor to call people to recognize a recurring record of suffering: this is not about individuals occasionally falling "down on their luck" but points to a larger structural problem. When homeless workers at soup kitchens share their stories of low-paid, full-time work, patterns of suffering emerge that beg for explanation. Through this intentional storytelling a sense of collective suffering and systemic failure replace individual failure.

Yet underscoring the problem is not enough to foster the agency for social change. Working poverty could be seen as resulting from economic downturns, globalization, or other "natural" market shifts. The frame requires an explanation and attribution to an accountable party. Here, activists target corporate greed and CEO salaries: the benefits of increased worker productivity and profits have accrued only to corporate elites, not to workers themselves. As the NCC states in its widely circulated guide on raising the minimum wages:

In 1980, CEOs of major U.S. corporations made on average 45 times the pay of average full-time production and nonsupervisory workers. By 1991, CEOs made 140 times as much as workers . . . the gap has doubled since then. CEOs made more than 300 times as much as average workers in 2004.[12]

In this way, activists connect statistics about the nature of working poverty to a larger diagnosis of what has gone wrong in the U.S. economy in the last forty years: a greedy fixing of the economies to benefit those already in power. The NCC guide again states:

Workers have not been getting their fair share of the benefits of rising worker productivity. For decades after WWII, the benefits of rising productivity were widely shared. Between 1947 and 1973, worker productivity rose 104 percent while the minimum wage rose 101 percent, adjusting for inflation. Income and wealth inequality decreased. Since then, productivity has gone up, but worker pay has not . . . between 1973 and 2004, worker productivity rose 78 percent, but the real minimum wage fell 24 percent. For average workers (production and nonsupervisory workers, about 80 percent of the employed private workforce), hourly wages fell 11 percent, adjusting for inflation.[13]

The rich are indeed getting richer off the sweat of the workers they employ. These statistics are repeated around the country in living wage educational forums, submitted as testimony before city councils, and included in newspaper op-eds. Familiar graphs from the Economic Policy Institute and United for a Fair Economy show up in PowerPoints in multiple cities. Activists hope that tracking the human choices that create this pattern of suffering increases people's capacity to see the culpable fingerprints on the economic political system. By supplying a clear account and defining a target, they seek to empower low-wage workers and their allies to alter that problematic system.

While elite corporate greed is the ultimate diagnosis of working poverty, activists also see the government as a collaborator or at least an absent gatekeeper in the current "race to the bottom."[14] The government has resisted increasing the minimum wage to maintain its buying power, thus expanding the ranks of working poor. Simultaneously, as the Baltimore story demonstrates, municipal governments' low-bid contracts and subsidies to corporations regularly encourage lower wage floors as cost-cutting mechanisms for governments and corporations. The disturbing irony, activists contend, is that the government regularly spends additional taxpayer funds on these same companies' employees since workers often require government subsidies for basic survival (Section 8 housing, food stamps, health care safety nets, etc.), and because of their low income, they contribute little to the tax base via property, income, and sales taxes.

Jamie Gates, an ordained Nazarene minister, sociology professor, and ICWJ board member, stated in his testimony before the San Diego City Council, "Let me say two things about why NOT having a living wage will cost the city far more than what it pays for a living wage."[15] He detailed how two minimum-wage earners raising two children in San Diego would qualify for $23,471 a year in public assistance: "The City of San Diego is currently *among* the local employers that force their employees onto tax payer funded public assistance programs." He argued that contractors who do not provide health care also shift the costs of basic medical care onto the other businesses: "The cost of uncompensated medical care for San Diego hospitals in 2002 was $325 million. These costs . . . are shifted onto the rest of us who *have* health insurance. Employers who *do* provide health care for their employees pay for it in the form of increased premiums."[16] In essence, activists like Mr. Gates argue that low-wage government jobs create a double tax-burden on taxpayers and punish more than just businesses. In other words, activists frame local governments not only as actively contributing to the growth of working poverty, but also placing an even greater burden on taxpayers and more ethical businesses. The NCC summarizes:

> Low-wage employers rely on taxpayers and charitable groups to subsidize them by providing a safety net, however inadequate and full of holes, for workers who don't earn enough to support themselves and their families. Low-wage employers shift health insurance costs to other businesses that provide family health plans.[17]

Wal-Mart is the most cited example of profitable corporations benefiting from tax subsidies and yet having employees in need of government assistance:

> A state survey in Georgia, where Wal-Mart is the largest employer, looked at enrollment in PeachCare, which provides health insurance to children in low-income families. It found that Wal-Mart had one child in PeachCare for every four families. The ratio for the next ranked company, Publix, was one child in PeachCare for every 22 employees. In Florida, Wal-Mart which is getting millions of dollars in state incentives to create jobs . . . has more employees and family members enrolled in Medicaid than any company in the state.[18]

In this way, Wal-Mart has become an exemplar of the "working poor" frame. By dissecting the causal activity of the government and corporations in relation to working poverty, activists seek to create a counterbalance of agency among low-wage workers and their allies and a target on which to focus this agency.

Because of the greater feasibility of lobbying local governments, activists turn their way for intervening into working poverty. Municipal living wage ordinances require city contractors, and often those subsidized by government tax-breaks, to pay their workers a living wage. In the Atlanta living wage campaign, activists outlined the logic simply:

The living wage movement is based on two principles:

⊕ People who work full time should be able to support their families above the poverty line.
⊕ Employers who receive public dollars should pay their employees a living wage.[19]

In part because county and municipal governments cannot leave—and businesses must stay to serve them—municipal living wage ordinances are a focused and politically viable intervention for improving wage standards. In the local context, the living wage gains its full import as a wage that eliminates the double taxpayer burden: full-time government (and government subsidized) workers need not rely on government assistance for their "living."

Rounding out this public frame, activists intertwine the diagnosis (working poverty) and prescription (government living wage ordinances) with the motivational claims that supporting the living wage is both "ethically and economically right." The first motivational claim often relies heavily on religious moral arguments. At the public announcement of the Atlanta living wage campaign, Rev. Joseph Lowery, the civil rights hero and former president of Southern Christian Leadership Council, roused the gathered crowd with the refrain, "What would Jesus pay?" At a Memphis interfaith service to extend the coverage of their living wage ordinance, Rev. Rebekah Jordan, a Methodist clergyperson and executive director of Workers Interfaith Network (WIN), stood before the faithful and declared to a chorus of "amens" and applause, "The wages of sin are death . . . but deadly wages are a sin." Echoing this religious ethical motivation at the national level, NCC's Let Justice Roll campaign sums up their position stating that "All our faith traditions call us to show compassion to the poor and do justly toward our neighbors"[20] and that "Among the key principles shared by all faiths are the importance of paying workers fairly for their labor and the right of workers to perform their responsibilities with dignity."[21] Because of theological arguments for special attention to and compassion for the poor, people of faith are required to act with justice in all their economic dealings. Rev. Jordan argued in a 2004 op-ed in the Memphis *Commercial Appeal*:

It is immoral to ask people to work full time but pay them so little that they remain mired in poverty. As a person of faith, I believe

that God asks us to respond to poverty not just by generous charitable giving, but also by ensuring the jobs in our local economy pay
enough to meet a family's basic needs.[22]

Thus, it is justice, not just charity, that God desires.

Activists consistently interweave these assertions about morality, fairness, and dignity with claims about justice grounded in scripture. In San
Diego, bright yellow postcards encouraging officials to enforce the living
wage ordinance featured a quote from Deuteronomy 24:14–15: "You shall
not take advantage of hired workers. . . . You must pay them their due on
the same day before the sun sets; they are in need and urgently depend on
it." The Union of American Hebrew Congregations also concludes their
statement in support of living wages with scriptural references.

> The Torah instructs us to treat workers with justice . . . Jewish tradi-
> tion recognizes the importance of wages to a worker's sustenance. We
> are taught that "one who withholds an employee's wages is as thought
> he deprived him of his life" (Talmud Baba Metzia 112a). Based on
> these teachings, the [Union of American Hebrew Congregations] has
> long advocated measures that would insure every worker willing and
> able to work "a wage which makes possible a decent standard of liv-
> ing." (*The Eradication and Amelioration of Poverty, 1968*)[23]

The NCC continues this approach, interspersing their arguments with
passages such as:

> Woe to him who builds his house by unrighteousness, and his upper
> rooms by injustice; who makes his neighbors work for nothing, and
> does not give them their wages; who says, "I will build myself a spa-
> cious house with large upper rooms," and who cuts out windows for
> it, paneling it with cedar, and painting it with vermillion. Are you
> a king because you compete in cedar? Did not your father eat and
> drink and do justice and righteousness? Then it was well with him.
> He judged the cause of the poor and needy; then it was well. Is not
> this to know me? says the Lord. (Jer. 22:13–16)[24]

In this manner, religious activists link traditions of religious argument
with founding scriptural documents and authoritative interpreters. They
also extend their protest community temporally by connecting with his-

torical legacies of moral interpretation and political action. Past generations stand with contemporary activists to enlarge the sense of collective
power and emphasize both the capacity and necessity of religious action
for change.

Because of their desire for an expansive understanding of collective
obligation and agency, religious activists do not use scripture as an argument sufficient in and of itself but rather to highlight the basic economic
equation of a "fair day's pay for a fair day's work." One of the lead organizers from Let Justice Roll noted that "Sacred texts are very powerful, as
long as they are pithy and trigger long understandings of the faith. But
long tracts don't work, scripture needs to immediately relate to an inherent sense of fairness; that cuts across ideological difference."[25] Deeply
committed to the necessity and good of building interdependent networks across/within difference, religious activists quickly connect exclusive scriptural traditions to universal norms. The head of the San Diego
living wage campaign observed that their diverse coalition united on the
conviction that all their traditions proclaimed the basic dignity of workers because they, the workers, were "created in God's image." Thus, scripture is never the last word or an uninterpreted public claim by movement
activists; activists work carefully to connect scriptural claims to more
widespread moral norms.

Religious activists are also careful not to use scriptures that have a
more ambiguous legacy with coalition members. For example, fellow academics have asked whether the movement has considered using the par-
able of the laborers in the vineyard (Matt. 20:1–16) to justify living wages.
Their interpretation of the passage runs along this line: the owners' equal
payment of workers who arrived at the beginning and end of the day
reminds readers that all workers should be paid a wage that will sustain
them. In practice, religious organizers rarely cite this scripture because
union allies dislike it immensely. What they hear in it is an owner who,
for no apparent reason, favored one set of workers over another and who
sought to disrupt the ill-favored workers' efforts to organize for a more
just wage structure. Knowing their efforts are not best spent redeeming
a certain reading of scripture for a movement, religious activists choose
more unifying scriptures while linking them to universal norms.

Although activists lead with ethical and religious arguments, the economic claim that living wages are good for businesses almost always
quickly follows, even for religious activists. They argue consistently that
living wages lower turnover and training costs, increase productivity,

expand the local tax base and consumer spending, and even improve shareholder value. Here the contrast between Costco and Wal-Mart becomes one of the markers of "high road vs. low road" business practices. Activists note that "Comparing the two, *Business Week* reported, 'Costco's high-wage approach [averaging $17 an hour] actually beats Wal-Mart at its own game on many measures . . . [and] found that by compensating employees generously to motivate and retain good workers, one-fifth of whom are unionized, Costco gets lower turnover and higher productivity.'"[26] They continue by citing studies from compensation experts who argue that "overpaying CEOs and underpaying workers is bad business as well as bad ethics. . . . Corporations with significantly higher than average shares of employee stock options going to the CEO and the next four top executives had *lower* average shareholder returns for the decade."[27] Ken Cramer, a founding partner of Costco, cited this high road approach when he testified in favor of the municipal living wage ordinance in San Diego.

> Our wage structure is exemplary, and it works. A living wage makes social sense. It reduces stress on welfare agencies and it reduces crime. . . . We've found ways to build ballparks, convention centers and libraries. Being decent to our low-income citizens is surely more important than concrete monuments. The city should not only pass the living wage ordinance but also guarantee in your current labor negotiations that no city employee be paid below a contract employee. A city worker is worth their keep.[28]

With support from key business allies, religious activists lead with ethical claims but interweave pragmatic business claims for persuasive effect. This dual motivation for living wages is perhaps best captured in the closing line of NCC's literature and public speeches: "Living wages are good for workers, business and our nation's future."[29]

Producing "Effective" Public Religious Ethics

Jesus was a low-wage worker.[30]

According to sociologists, frames move people to action when they cohere with people's personal experiences, connect with their emotions, and resonate with a community's cultural values.[31] While living wage activists' public rhetoric is explicit in its attention to experiential credibility and emotional impact, its use of certain ethical and economic traditions in framing its message is less definitive. But as in all movements, activists simply will not be successful in public policy change without a dynamic interplay between contemporary framing and the cultural heritage of the country and its major institutions.[32] For the living wage movement, cultural salience comes, in part, from its capacity to draw on enduring religious and economic values that challenge the current practices of the economy without radically disrupting fundamental neoclassical assumptions concerning the political economy. Activists themselves rarely discuss these traditions explicitly in their day-to-day organizing work. Nonetheless, the influence of these traditions is apparent in the principles and values that activists now deem familiar or logical.

Relationship to Religious Traditions

As important as Rauschenbusch is to social thought, I daresay that few religious leaders are engaged in just wage issues either because of what he said or didn't say. People of faith are engaged in challenging economic injustice because all our faith traditions' sacred texts condemn greed and advocate just treatment of workers. The teachings, combined with their own faith journeys of seeing poverty in their congregations, propel their actions.[33]

The historical writings of theologians and ethicists are rarely enlisted (and sometimes even resisted) in movement arguments, despite the rich theological tradition of writing on just wages. Even the words of Martin Luther King Jr. break through this barrier only occasionally.[34] San Diego's living wage sign-on letterhead included King's summons to

[B]e dissatisfied until those that live on the outskirts of hope are brought into the metropolis of daily security. Let us be dissatisfied until slums are cast into the junk heaps of history and every family is living in a decent sanitary house . . . and people will recognize that out of one blood, God has made all people to dwell upon the face of the Earth.[35]

Direct quotes from historical theological figures rarely drive the framing of the movement, yet theological arguments still feed the movement by providing the moral reservoir from which frames emerge. Religious, and particularly Christian, arguments for *the moral nature of wages, the moral responsibilities of government*, and *the priority of the poor* inform basic assumptions and motivations of many religious activists in the contemporary living wage movement. The themes in these religious traditions provide activists with a varied collective values repertoire (a "values tool-kit,") with which they can counter arguments to more dominant ideologies.[36] Without the variety and depth of these moral traditions, contemporary actors would be hampered in their efforts to reimagine the world and express their agency.

Of the major theological arguments implicit in the living wage movement, perhaps the most influential is the early twentieth-century consensus on the *moral nature of wages*. This argument comes from thinkers such as Fr. John Ryan, who helped establish the first state minimum-wage laws in the nation, working with the National Consumer's League.[37] This tradition draws on Catholic anti-individualism and natural rights traditions (seen in the papal encyclical *Rerum Novarum*) in arguing for society's, and particularly government's, responsibility to workers.[38] Writing in 1906, Ryan is credited with the first major theological treatise on the living wage, which he grounded in three fundamental principles. Beginning with a strong doctrine of creation, Ryan argued that "God created the earth for sustenance of *all* His children; therefore . . . all persons are equal in their inherent claims on the bounty of nature."[39] As children of God, then, everyone has the right to sustenance. As he told the National Consumers' League in 1910, "The most insignificant child, the most degraded and exploited worker, is equal in moral importance and in the eyes of God to the greatest statesmen or the most efficient captain of industry . . . [and each has an] indestructible right, either against his employer or against society, to the minimum conditions of a decent livelihood."[40] But like the current living wage movement, Ryan added an important caveat to this universal right. Drawing on John Locke's claim that labor was the basis of claims to property, Ryan asserted that "The inherent right of access to the earth is conditioned upon, and becomes actually valid through, the expenditure of useful labor."[41] Alluding to scripture, he continued, "The general condition is that men must work in order to live. 'If a man will not work neither shall he eat.' For those who refuse to comply with this condition the inherent right of access to the earth remains suspended."[42]

On these principles, Ryan established the obligation of capital owners who as "possessors must so administer the common bounty of nature that non-owners will not find it unreasonably difficult to get a livelihood."[43] Ownership of capital was a privilege derived from God that entailed responsibilities to the rights of those who work diligently. Private property and industrial capital were valuable and necessary, but only when they served the end of developing human personality; thus, the "private right of any and every individual must be interpreted consistently with the rights of all."[44] The interdependence of the common good trumped the radical individualism of unfettered industrial capitalism.

Perhaps most important for the early twentieth-century movement and its late twentieth-century sister was Ryan's distinction between a living wage and the survival wages on which so many workers subsisted. Again referring to the created dignity of human beings, Ryan claimed that "the intrinsic worth and sacredness of personality imply something more than security of life and limb and the material means of bare existence . . . the opportunity of pursuing self-perfection through harmonious development of all his faculties."[45] For Ryan this included "reasonable" opportunities for recreation and education as well as security against future sickness. His influence on this point can be heard when FDR's secretary of labor Frances Perkins stated that the Fair Labor Standards Act "had anticipated that we would regard the minimum wage as being a living wage—that is, we would make it above the subsistence and regard the definition of 'living wage' to be about what Father John Ryan called it in his book."[46] In the end, Ryan helped set a tone for later living wage activists when he summarily stated, "Not the economic but the ethical value of the service rendered, is the proper determinant of justice in the matter of wages; and this ethical value is always the equivalent of at least a decent livelihood for the laborer and his family."[47] Wages were an ethical and theological issue.

Almost a century later, the NCC would argue that "wages are a bedrock moral issue."[48] Or as San Diego religious activists stated in their support of living wages, "All economic life should be shaped by moral principles. Economic choices and institutions must be judged by how they protect or undermine the life and dignity of the human person, the family, and the environment in service of the common good."[49] Summarizing this point, Jamie Gates began his address to the San Diego City Council this way: "Budgets are moral documents, they reveal who we are as people and what we value."[50] From John Ryan to contemporary religious activists, advocates stressed the moral nature of wages and the sacred obligation to pay living wages.

Ultimate responsibility for the economy and ethical wages leads to the second major theological tradition implicit in the contemporary movement, and a subject of perennial debate in Christianity: *the moral responsibilities of government*. Denominational statements tip their hand to this legacy more regularly:

> The United Methodist Church recognizes the responsibility of governments to develop and implement sound fiscal and monetary policies that provide for the economic life of individuals. Every person has the right to a job at a living wage.[51]

The living wage movement resonates deeply with Catholic social teachings and Protestant social gospel on the role of government in promoting the common good. While some movement leaders may choose not to reference a heritage such as Rauschenbusch's quotation earlier in this section states, the movement's interpretation of scripture relies heavily on these theological traditions.

Within the vast literature on Christian understandings of government, we highlight Ryan, Rauschenbusch, and King's writings as examples of a Christian consensus on government intervention in the economy for the common good. For Ryan, the Catholic tradition clearly prescribed the state's role in safeguarding natural rights: "As protector of natural rights, the State is obliged to enact laws which will enable a laborer to obtain a living wage."[52] Drawing on past encyclicals, Ryan emphasized the moral education of and rights of owners but also conceived of the state as the guarantor of economic rights for all. Speaking from that legacy, Janet Mansfield, a member of Christ the King Parish in San Diego, declared moments after that city's successful council vote, "As a Catholic, I think San Diego is starting to live up to the Catholic social teachings of treating the working poor with dignity and respect."[53] Government as an employer has ethical wage responsibilities and also as a public guarantor of rights in the economic sector as a whole.

Rauschenbusch argued that God's intention for all social institutions was to act humanely and to nurture liberty, equality, and brotherhood. Christians were meant to regenerate social institutions so that they would serve God's desire for human flourishing; this was the path of sanctification (or, participation in the life of God). But government had a special role in the struggle for humanization when economic greed was infecting other social institutions. "The State" Rauschenbusch argued, "is like a breakwater, pounded by hungry seas."[54] He understood the necessary cooperation (but not conflation) of church and state in this effort and argued:

> Church and State both minister to something greater and larger than either, and they find their true relation in this unity of aim and service. . . . When the Church implants religious impulses towards righteousness and trains moral convictions of people, it cooperates with the State by creating the most delicate and valuable elements of social welfare and progress. . . . Together they serve what is greater than either: humanity.[55]

For Rauschenbusch, Christians were morally required to be involved in politics, to insure that politics sought liberty, equality, and brotherhood in all aspects of society, and, particularly, to reform the economy's materialist greed that was literally dehumanizing people on a daily basis.

King also emphasized government's expansive moral responsibilities. He argued that his vision of the beloved community required a robust social democracy where government helped empower its citizens to reach their full potential through education, employment, and housing.[56] Government served God's love and purposes by establishing justice in society, and because of its ultimate accountability to God, government was required to be a steward of its resources and to ensure that the basic necessities of all citizens were met.[57] "Christians must encourage, yea demand, that their governments act as though the financial and technical resources entrusted to them belong to God, and that these resources are used to the Glory of God for the care of God's children wherever they may be in need."[58] Government was not to be just a "night watchman" protecting liberty from the incursions of others; government was responsible for taking action to meet people's basic needs. Anything else was deeply sinful and a rejection of government's moral purposes.

The responsibility for meeting the basic needs of all people is anchored by the third major theological tradition in the living wage movement: *the priority of, or preferential option for, the poor*. Kim Bobo, the executive director of Interfaith Worker Justice, noted that one of the three most formative experiences in her college education was a course with Latin American Catholic liberation theologian Gustavo Gutierrez, who argued that a preferential option for the poor was the beginning of Christian theology.[59] Bobo, like so many others in the movement, takes from this credo the ethical nature of wages and moral responsibilities of government. The preferential option for the poor emphasizes humanity's radical interdependence and particular responsibility to the "least of these."

Grounded in the teachings of the New Testament's Sermon on the Mount, Hebraic Jubilee practices, and the Hebrew prophets' call for justice and care for the widow, orphan, and stranger, "preferential option for the poor" describes God's relationship to the poor and the call of discipleship for those who would follow God's teaching. In this theology, God is understood as especially attuned to the cries of the poor; those in covenant with God must provide care.[60] Or as Walter Brueggemann contends, "The Exodus narrative, Mosaic legislation, and the prophetic poetry are all agreed. The rich are not autonomous, but under divine mandate to act in solidarity with the poor."[61] In an article reflecting on the necessity of living wages, he argues that although "popular religion" focuses on the parting of the Red Sea as the focus on the Exodus story, "This defining memory is not about water; it is about rescue from unbearable poverty and abuse in debt slavery."[62] Deuteronomic codes sought to halt the ongoing creation of poverty; the psalmists and prophets continually reminded God's followers never to forget the dignity and concrete needs of the poor.

While theologians across the centuries and denominations have interpreted biblical texts as testaments to God's special concern for the poor, the specific phrase "preferential option for the poor" emerged only recently, developed by Latin American Catholic bishops in the late 1960s and 1970s. Liberation theologians (as they came to be known) radicalized a stream in Vatican II's *Gaudium et Spes* (Joy and Hope), which stated that "The joys and the hopes, the grief and anguish of the people of our time, especially those who are poor and afflicted, are the joys and hopes, the grief and anguish of the followers of Christ." In response to this claim, the Latin American bishops began developing the concept of the church for the poor during their meeting at Medellin in 1968; at their meeting in Pueblo in 1979, they declared "a clear and prophetic option expressing preference for, and solidarity with, the poor."[63] Eventually, the preferential option for the poor came to be seen throughout Catholic social teachings as a summons to analyze unjust distributions and reorder society to serve the most oppressed. Poverty and oppression became moral and epistemological starting points for theology; those who were last in society needed to be first in the Kingdom of God and its work. Whether in liberation theology, Catholic encyclicals, or Protestant adaptations, a preferential option for the poor shifts the focus of poverty onto the social structures that produce oppression and call followers to provide justice, not just charity.

Although seldom named explicitly, these arguments for the moral nature of wages, the moral responsibilities of government, and the priority of the poor feed the cultural/theological reservoir from which the more explicit framing of religious activists emerges. In light of these traditions on God's provision of resources and the purpose of life itself, government is enlisted in a special task: to serve God's purpose by helping to produce and distribute common goods in a way that prioritizes the poor and interdependence. In this framework, wages become a moral issue that may not be sacrificed to radically individualistic views of unfettered capitalism.

Relationship to Economic Traditions

While this vision of the moral economy, bolstered by these religious legacies, helps to give the living wage movement its moral thrust, the public policy approach of the movement is also effective because it does not fundamentally diverge from the economic cultural inheritances of the United States. Rev. Paul Sherry, former director of Let Justice Roll, explained it this way: "We had to make the ethical and economic argument. We couldn't just be decent, well-meaning people who are naïve."[64] More specifically, the fact that the movement's economic frame coheres with the "social equity" strand of neoclassical economics strengthens its potential resonance. The "laissez-faire" and "social-equity" strands of neoclassical economics share the assumptions that production and consumption are the source of wealth and that increasing labor productivity is the key to economic growth.[65] But while the laissez-faire side of neoclassical economics emphasizes privatization, deregulation, and trade liberalization for healthy economies, the social-equity side (exemplified by John Keynes) argues for government stabilization of markets, basic economic security, and social development for economic health. By embracing social-equity liberalism, the living wage movement challenges current market inequities while maintaining Americans' deep cultural affinity for neoclassical economics.

Laissez-faire liberalism, or neoliberalism, contends that government intervention in capitalist markets increases inefficiency and hampers the innovation necessary for economic growth. Government therefore should be limited to those functions the market cannot provide: "maintenance of law and order . . . the enforcement of contracts; the defining of property rights and arbitration of discrepancies related to property disputed; and finally, the provision and maintenance of a monetary system."[66] Within this theory, the best approach for reducing poverty is "investment in the business sectors of economies (i.e., owners of capital) [that] would eventually 'trickle down' to the rest of the population through increased job opportunities and better social services provided by a stronger economy."[67] Limiting government intervention through deregulation or tax breaks theoretically helps supply-side economies even out great inequities in the market.

By contrast, social-equity liberalism takes a more active view of government's role in the political economy. Undergirding social-equity liberalism is the recognition that governments have a responsibility to care for society's most vulnerable. Moreover, the government can and should take on the role of stimulating the economy and "providing a social safety net for the failures of the market."[68] While the capitalist market is still the mechanism for promoting prosperity and wealth, government must also occasionally stimulate the economy to insure its health and help those at the lower rungs of society. The Keynesian economic logic behind this model is highly pragmatic, not just moral. Keynesians argue that when economies slow, the best spark for new growth comes from economic relief to the lower and middle classes. Because those classes spend higher percentages of their income on necessities, relief targeted their way increases consumer demand that then sparks production.

In arguing for the positive effects of wage increases, the living wage movement draws its economic arguments from Keynesian logic. Here the NCC articulates an argument seen in local editorials and rallies in multiple cities:

Higher wages increase consumer purchasing power, which increases sales. Low-income workers by necessity spend more of their increased wages than those with higher incomes and spend largely at businesses in their communities. Increased demand for goods and services results in increased employment in a multiplier effect that generates additional purchasing power and business revenues.[69]

By exposing the incongruity between increased productivity and slowed wage growth, activists also counter the laissez-faire myth that "diligence and efficiency in the marketplace are rewarded with wages and the potential for upward mobility."[70] At a 2005 workshop session at the IWJ national conference, two "framing" specialists argued explicitly that activists needed to emphasize that the "economic rewards system is broken." Drawing implicitly on social equity liberalism, these experts and religious activists argued that when the market fails, government has an obligation to act for market stability. Because activists' reform proposals still embrace part of the larger neoclassical vision, they can persuade potential adherents to adopt social equity liberalism. While the movement does not embrace the absolutist individual freedom of neoliberalism, it still relies heavily on the assumptions and positive appraisal of the independent capitalist market of neoclassical economic theory and its goal of independent economic freedom. In fact, the framing experts above argued that because polling data showed "low-wage workers are generally respected . . . [but] they are mostly seen as former welfare recipients. We need to emphasize independence and hard work." While this could be seen as part of cynical spin for political efficacy, we see these values embedded in denominational statements supporting living wages. The living wage statement in the "social principles" of the United Methodist *Book of Discipline* asserts: "Since low wages are often a cause of poverty, employers should pay their employees a wage that does not require them to depend upon government subsidies such as food stamps or welfare for their livelihood."[71] Even when informed by religious convictions, neoclassical economic goals are still present. It is still a job that should lift you out of poverty, still economic independence that is the goal of a living wage.

Enhancing Moral Agency: The Theological Goods of Interdependence

Because the movement's goals are not just implementing policy but also enhancing the economic political agency of the working poor, evaluating the movement's longer-term effects on moral agency is important. While the religious and economic legacies described earlier make it possible to construct an alternative vision for wage setting, they (particularly neoclassical economics) also entail constraints and risks. The social equity approach is effective as an economic triage mechanism for the U.S. capitalist economy (that is, keeping workers out of radical poverty). But religious activists should thoroughly examine their use of an economic model that idealizes economic freedom from the state and sees welfare provision as interference into capitalist markets.[72] Prizing independence from the state and stigmatizing means-tested government assistance only serves to undermine the agency of the working poor. A leader from Let Justice Roll, in contrast to some of her peers on a previous panel, said, "I don't like the language of self-sufficiency. Everyone should get benefits and no one should be ashamed of it."[73] A return to interdependence as the foundation of divine economy (or, God's work in the world) may continue to strengthen religious recognition and support for welfare provision (that is, the myriad government provisions for well-being) in the United States. By deepening the movement's theological commitment to inter-dependence through meditations on the social nature of the self and the sociality of God, activists can help shore up their resistance to neoclassi-cal biases and provide a stronger foundation for long-term, anti-poverty action. Without this tradition of interdependence, religious activists lose a significant repertoire for resisting dominant patterns in the current political economy.

Pragmatic Interdependency and Well-Being

Relying on the neoclassical ideal of economic independence from govern-ment reinscribes the stigma of receiving certain forms of welfare from the state. Neoclassical ideals tend to shame poorer recipients of government benefits (such as TANF) while obscuring the myriad government welfare all of us receive. Everyone, at every level of society, depends on govern-ment for welfare provision, through elaborate interdependent systems of giving and receiving. Whether it be public roads, mortgage tax breaks, air and water quality, traffic regulation, and the like, every member of soci-ety relies on government-sponsored and -regulated activity for maintain-ing and developing their welfare, or well-being.[74] Rather than idealizing largely nonexistent "independence," we should be moving closer toward, rather than farther away from, cultivating the quality of our necessary interdependencies on both pragmatic and theological grounds.[75]

Martin Luther King Jr. reflected pragmatically on our interdependence in his 1967 meditation on the way of peace.

It really boils down to this: that all life is interrelated. We are all caught in an inescapable network of mutuality, tied into a single garment of destiny. Whatever affects one directly, affects all indirectly. We are made to live together because of the interrelated structure of reality. Did you ever stop to think that you can't leave for your job in the morning without being dependent on most of the world? You get up in the morning and go to the bathroom and reach over for the sponge, and that's handed to you by a Pacific Islander. You reach for a bar of soap, and that's given to you at the hands of a Frenchman. And then you go into the kitchen to drink your coffee for the morning, and that's poured into your cup by a South American. And maybe you want tea: that's poured into your cup by a Chinese. Or maybe you're desirous of having cocoa for breakfast, and that's poured into your cup by a West African. And then you reach over for your toast, and that's given to you at the hands of an English-speaking farmer, not to mention the baker. And before you finish eating breakfast in the morning, you've depended on more than half the world. This is the way our universe is structured; this is its interrelated quality. We aren't going to have peace on Earth until we recognize this basic fact of the interrelated structure of all reality.[76]

Even persons who seek to live "off the grid" and foster a more narrow interdependency are bound by intersecting social conditions, such as the emissions of neighboring communities and far-off nations that eventually affect their air quality and climate conditions. Relationally, humans are talked into talking, and loved into loving; our interdependence only becomes more complex as we age. To be a self then is to be "a being which not only knows itself in relation to other selves but exists only in that relation."[77] We are reliant on and formed by our ongoing interactions with others for identity, possibility, and purpose.

Theological Interdependence and Welfare

In his address to the 2007 IWJ national conference, Bishop Zavala of Los Angeles gave a detailed and compelling plenary reflection to over the four hundred gathered activists. Reminding some and introducing others to the themes of Catholic Social Teachings, he launched into a strong defense of the right of workers to organize. He stated four foundations for this right in Catholic teachings. "First, human beings are created in God's image. . . . Second, they are called to living in communion and so called to the common good. . . . Third, they are called to the least of these. . . . Fourth, they are called to preach and bring about the Kingdom of God." The bishop's remarks underscored two points that are particularly relevant to our discussion of interdependence.

In Christian theology, our interdependence is informed theologically by (1) our creation by God as social beings; and (2) God's own nature, in Trinitarian formulation, which attests to the good of this sociality and interdependence. Recognizing the social origins and development of human persons, Christian ethicists emphasize the theological necessity of relationships for human flourishing. God's call of love, service, and care for others can be accomplished only through relationships of mutual giving and accountability.[78] Sanctifying the human person (or, being incorporated ever more fully into the life of God) comes through communions and imagined institutions with metaphorical names such as the "kingdom of God" or the "beloved community." Our human institutions (such as work, education, family, and so on) enable or limit this sanctification through the everyday practices in which persons are habituated and constructed. There is a banality to good, as there is to evil, which comes in how our institutions are structured to cultivate the dignity and worth of persons and the quality of relations among them. Thus to speak about the self, moral formation, sanctification, and even salvation (that is, reconciled wholeness with God and creation) is to talk about the necessity and the good of our interdependencies and how institutions support the interrelated complexity of our well-being.

A vision for human society grounded in the theological goods of interdependence includes relationships of justice and mutual accountability. As one Catholic activist reflected:

> I guess my worldview is that ultimately we're all connected, and that biologically and spiritually and environmentally we're all connected to each other. And even though some people are able to remove themselves from that connection based on wealth and privilege, ultimately we are all connected. . . . It's not spiritually healthy to be one of those people that removes yourself too much from all that. . . . Ultimately we need to be accountable to the people that work for us and with us.[79]

Catholic writings on solidarity with the poor are quite clear on this point. John Paul II argues for seeing interdependence as a "moral category." This framework gives rise to the virtue of solidarity that is not "a feeling of vague compassion or shallow distress at the misfortunes of so many people" but rather "*a firm and preserving determination* to commit oneself to the *common good*; that is to say to the good of all and of each individual, because we are *all* really responsible *for all.*"[80] God creates us as social beings who require communions of interdependence, not only pragmatically but also theologically.

For Christians, the life of God symbolized in the Trinity also models a form of interdependence that God desires to see in the world. The Trinity points toward the nature of God as a society of persons who infinitely give to and receive from one another in infinite mutuality and reciprocity in order to embody a holistic practice of love.[81] The early Cappadocian doctrine of the Trinity understood the persons of the Trinity as each having their own work and character yet mutually constituted by their relationship with the others. They are because of each other and yet each has its own place and distinctive worth in the whole.[82]

While controversy persists over the nature of the Trinity and how it applies to human relations, the theologian Joyce McDougall's assessment that the "social Trinitarian analogy of fellowship" functions as a "divine archetype . . . [or] elastic rule of faith for right relationships" is helpful.[83] Ultimately, this vision of the Trinity reminds us that the primary nature of God is "not the will-to-power but the will-to-fellowship."[84] Being with and for others in love marks out the parameters of relationship that God models and offers the world. In fact, living into our nature as the Image of God (or *Imago Dei*) might be better understood as living into the Image of the Trinity or *Imago Trinitatis*.[85] This relational metaphor marks the beginning, end, and center of Christian salvation history as the desire of God for creating interdependent relationships of loving justice. As people of God, we are invited to receive this gift of Trinitarian becoming and thus to free others to love and nurture their welfare. We are certainly not the same as the divine; the challenges of sin and finitude alter the landscapes of our relationships profoundly. But for Christians, a turn to Trinitarian imagery can encourage continued meditation on God's interdependent becoming and God's vision for interdependent human relationships.

This interdependent nature and welfare is necessarily supported by institutions that coordinate and honor the exchanges of resources, goods, values, and relations necessary for the full development of persons. *Polis* (or, a body politic) is necessary for *oikus* (household). A political ordering is necessary for the proper coordination of the vast goods of the household of God, or creation. Political or social orderings, often found in government, extend transient moments of individual obligations of social responsibility to "fixed principles of mutual support" and systematize the creative, life-giving purposes of human sociality.[86] When institutions undermine or ignore our interdependent coordination of well-being, they literally de-humanize persons as they move them farther away from understanding and living through their connectivity.

A theological vision of interdependence can open our eyes, not only to the lived reality that we all do and should receive numerous forms of welfare (provisions for well-being) that arise from our interdependent relationships, but also to the practices of solidarity that are necessary in light of this vision. Acknowledging that everyone receives numerous kinds of welfare through our interdependencies can refute the stigma of government welfare that is so prominent in the United States. Ultimately, a vision of God's interdependent economy should invite us to understand welfare provision as cultivating all our capacities to live life abundantly, whether it be through more equitable education, health care, housing, child care, environmental regulations, and the like. Removing the stigma of welfare provision for basic well-being can alter both economic and political poverty. Understanding the breadth of our interdependencies can provide a ground for economically poor persons to further claim their agency in the political process rather than alienating them from it as "mere" dependents of the state. Interdependent capacity building should entail participating in the political mechanisms of government rather than constructing poor persons primarily as objects of surveillance until their dependency is overcome. Both theologically and pragmatically, assuming that a wage should and will move us away from institutional interdependencies is dangerous at a time when need is growing while government services are rescinded.

Frame Bridging

In exploring some of the constraints of the current living wage frames, we should not underestimate the very hard work of organizing and changing public policy, nor should we write off some of the benefits of this neoclassical economic frame for the movement. Social movement theory reminds us that framing is a dynamic, ongoing process of struggle within a movement, among movements, and with targets. Movements always emerge in response to multiple cultural dynamics and ideologies. Movement leaders must craft messages that are salient enough to mobilize adherents, neutralize opponents, and persuade policy makers.

And so it is with the living wage movement. It emerged through a dialogue on dominant values in municipal politics and it grew because of its ability simultaneously to draw in community allies, counter chambers of commerce, and appeal to shared values with local politicians. In utilizing the social equity message, the movement goes a long way toward challenging the neoliberalism that has driven wage policies in the last fifty years while simultaneously presenting a salient persuasive argument. In social movement terms, this "frame bridging" is essential to growing movements: it combines elements of shared interpretation with new ideas that might differ from dominant thinking.[87] Bridging the pragmatic benefits of government intervention and demand-side economics with the moral obligations of government to care for the poor re-inscribes a vision of the moral economy in U.S. political-economic discourse.

But if frames are to survive, they must also adapt and change over time as the struggle continues. If the living wage movement is to develop as a larger economic justice movement that addresses issues such as wealth inequality and economic democracy, movement leaders will need to continue frame-bridging toward other religious, moral, economic, and political values. Eventually, they will need to move away from the neoliberal assumptions about individual economic freedom and toward a nuanced position on interdependence as a moral and theological good.

Activists already work diligently to reveal the structural interrelationships of the political and economic, both in the United States and globally. They carefully track the political history of wages, inflation, productivity, and wealth distribution. They identify how decreases in family income reduce local tax bases and lead to declines in education, public safety, and health care. From a sociological perspective, they cultivate economic political agency, in part, by tracking the history of politicians' choices that have trapped persons in working poverty, and they argue that there is another way possible. From a theological perspective, they have drawn on religious traditions that champion the good of government, in part because the gifts of creations are to be tended by the whole, for the whole, in light of God's desires for the world. By amplifying additional theological approaches to interdependence, we are building on their core work while challenging one potentially insidious strand in the movement's framing. Seeing the living wage merely as a way to eliminate government dependence ignores the sociological interdependence of current political economies (which mostly benefit the wealthy) and interdependence itself as a key principle of the divine economy. Elevating independence as the goal of the political economy disregards both the reality of everyday interdependence in the global economy as well as the theological good of interdependence for well-being. Pope Benedict XVI recently stated that "The risk for our time is that the *de facto* interdependence of people and nations is not matched by ethical interaction of consciences and minds that would give rise to truly human development."[88] The living wage movement has the potential to wed these two interdependencies together.

Theological concepts such as the Christian Trinity will certainly never be the movement's public frame in a pluralistic context. Yet theological reflection on the interdependent nature of persons and even God can be an important part of background conversations for activists. As the political scientist Amy Caiazza's report on women activists in religiously based community organizing notes, interdependence is one of the core values that inspires women to do organizing work. In the words of one of her Jewish interviewees, "God is the space between human beings, and all these ethical commandments and ritual commandments are all bound up together, and any relationship you have with God, any relationship with human beings are tied together."[89] In the end, ongoing theological and ethical reflection on interdependence can help people of faith resist the dominance of neoclassical assumptions about independence and motivate alternative frames.

Pragmatically, this may entail describing the living wage as the wage that allows one to pay for costs of living through full-time work, not as independence from government assistance. No one in the U.S. political economy ever achieves independence from government assistance, nor should it be reified as a goal. From most Christian perspectives, government is not a necessary evil but an institution permitted by God for the good of humanity. Healthy interdependence for flourishing should define our relation to government, rather than avoidance or, worse, shame. Building larger efforts for poverty reduction depend upon this interdependent vision.

Building Economic Political Agency

With these criticisms noted, we must celebrate the important work the movement has already accomplished. When activists around the nation teach communities about living wages, they start by telling the story of municipal subsidies of low-wage jobs. Through these accounts they invite citizens to understand the ways in which government is already "intervening" or, more precisely, intertwined with the economy. Drawing both on economic and moral frames (with their theological underpinnings), the living wage movement enables citizens to have a voice and claim their analytic and political agency in the economy beyond possessive consumerism. Enhancing people's sense of their economic moral agency lays the foundation for further action for worker justice. In the process, activists teach other political actors, ethicists included, about the delicate work of framing public religious ethics and invite us to join the framing struggles with greater care and efficacy.

3

"I Was a Stranger and You Welcomed Me"

Bridge Building and Political

Engagement in Racialized Economies

Leaders of the Mississippi Poultry Workers for Equality and Respect knew they had to overcome significant racial and ethnic barriers if they were to challenge the power of the poultry plant owners.[1] Yet the plant owners had to be challenged. Conditions in the plants were atrocious—sweltering temperatures, a toxic environment—and the work was certainly low paying. But black and Latino workers viewed each other uneasily, fearfully, and sometimes disdainfully. In the midst of this tension, management could pit workers against each other for jobs, promotions, raises, and shifts. In an effort to cultivate "Black-Brown solidarity," Poultry Workers leaders brought plant workers together in a series of workshops. They seated black and Latino workers alternately and asked them to introduce each other to the group by answering specific questions. Latino colleagues asked black co-workers, for instance, "What difference did the civil rights movement make in your life?" Black workers asked their immigrant Latino colleagues, "Why did you come to the United States to work?" Through these introductions, a dialogue developed: Latino immigrants were desperate for jobs to feed their families as work in Central America disappeared, while African Americans feared that their civil rights gains were eroding and that another immigrant group might be used against them. From this starting point, workers began to talk from and across their differences. What they shared helped them to work for greater justice in their workplaces and to resist the divide-and-conquer strategy of their bosses.

66

Raising the wages of the working poor is, according to activists, a "decidedly raced issue." Organizations ranging from the National Association for the Advancement of Colored People (NAACP) to Tennessee Immigrant and Refugee Rights Coalition endorse living wages as part of their efforts at racial and ethnic justice. They understand that stagnant wages disproportionately affect African American and Latino workers since full-time work no longer guarantees economic security for low-wage workers. Therefore, they see the political economy as a major battleground for dismantling institutionalized racism in the United States.

In the midst of this racialized landscape, religious organizations are also major players in connecting economic and racial justice issues within the living wage movement. While Sunday morning (or Friday Prayer and Saturday Shabbat, for that matter) is still the most segregated time in America, Tuesday night council meetings present a different picture. The living wage movement is, overall, one of the more racially and ethnically diverse movements in recent social movement history, and religious organizations regularly take the lead in cultivating this diversity. Religious activists, their organizations, and their theological mandates provide a psychic and physical space for confronting and mediating racial and ethnic divisions that could conceivably divide this economic justice movement.

Drawing on theologies grounded in a "preferential option for the poor," "being reconcilers of humanity," and "welcoming the stranger," religious activists make racial economic justice one of their central organizing goals. To accomplish this goal, religious coalition organizations take on two major racialized functions within the living wage movement: *bridge-building* and *political development*.[2] Through both these activities, religious activists build the moral agency of low-wage workers and their allies by offering pathways for creating a collective identity across difference and by providing opportunities for more marginalized persons to cultivate key civic skills.

Within living wage coalitions themselves, religious organizations regularly serve as "bridging organizations," mediating the economic justice concerns of labor, immigrant, and black civil rights groups.[3] Their mediation takes the form of *ideology translation, relational repair*, and *inclusion monitoring*. *Ideology translation* involves interpreting the frameworks, values, and strategies of one movement to another in order to foster better collaboration and respect for differences. *Relational repair* focuses on building trust and negotiating conflicts among organizations within the coalition. *Inclusion monitoring* entails advocating for inclusion within the coalition by asking regularly "Who is not at the table?" All of this work is central to forming and maintaining a coalition, and building agency for a sense of collective will and capacity.

Many religious organizations also identify and cultivate the involvement of those who are regularly excluded from the key pathways of political engagement. As the political scientists Sidney Verba, Kay Schlozman, and Henry Brady document in their book *Voice and Equality*, religious organizations are among the few in American civil society, especially with the waning of labor unions, that mitigate political alienation based in the intersection of race, lack of income, and limited formal education.[4] While U.S. workers who belong to unions do have a slightly higher level of political involvement than those involved in religious institutions, religious organizations have an edge in mobilizing the disadvantaged. By emphasizing *indigenous leadership,* religious organizations cultivate levels of political participation among poor people and people of darker colors that often outstrip their economic and educational demographics.[5]

Cultivating bridge building and political participation among minorities can place religious organizations at the forefront of anti-racist political work in the United States. While there are certainly examples of institutionalized racism within them, many religious organizations in the living wage movement are proactive in building the agency necessary for multiracial networks. By analyzing this work, we can see how religious activists practice theological solidarity. For it is through this solidarity that we can construct the collective agency needed for challenging the structures of working poverty.

The Racial and Ethnic Economy

Poverty in the United States is painted disproportionately in hues of brown and black. "Poor" and "black" are certainly not synonymous, although they are too often assumed to be so. But even a cursory reading of government statistics on poverty and income distribution reveals how income disparities are racialized in the United States. While Whites are certainly affected by income inequality (9.2% falling below the poverty threshold in 2008) and dominate the face of poverty by sheer numbers, African Americans and Latinos are overrepresented in low-wage labor sectors and poverty statistics. While these minorities (soon to be a collective majority) represented only 12.8% and 15.4% of the overall population respectively in 2008, 24.7% of blacks and 21.2% of Latinos fell below the federal poverty line in that same year.[6] The numbers are no better when we look at the working poor. While 16.4% of whites had an income below 130% of the poverty threshold (and thus qualified for food stamps), 32.7% of blacks and 32.8% of Latinos fell below the line.[7] When the upper limit of the "working poor" is set at 200% of the federal poverty line (where persons are considered able to pay for their own food, housing, transportation, child care, health insurance, taxes, etc.),[8] 29.4% of whites, and a startling 48.4% of blacks and 52.1% of Latinos fall below the line.[9]

These racialized patterns extend to recent immigrants to the United States. Generally speaking, immigrant workers earn about 17% less per year than native-born U.S. workers. But foreign-born (which is not to be equated with undocumented) workers from Mexico and Central America earn 44% percent less per year than their U.S.–born counterparts.[10] In San Diego, Einstein Novarro shares his struggles as one of those workers. In 2004, he was a forty-year-old Navy veteran who was a security guard at a public building in downtown San Diego. He earned $9.00 an hour but could not afford the health benefits offered by his government-contracted employer. Einstein had previously lived with his family in San Diego, but in 2001 he had to make the hard decision to move his family across the border to the more affordable Tijuana. He currently works three jobs to make ends meet. He testified for the living wage ordinance "because it can change my life . . . I can move back to San Diego and get health care for my family and save a little money for my retirement."[11] Immigrants—from all regions—comprise only 14% of all U.S. workers, but they comprise 20% of low-wage workers.[12] Undocumented immigrants (who come disproportionately from Mexico and Central America) represent only about 5.4% of the U.S. work force but are a much larger presence in lowest wage sectors: 24% of farm laborers, 17% of building cleaners and maintenance workers, 14% of construction workers, and 12% of food preparation workers.[13] While the median yearly income of U.S.–born Latinos has risen slightly, the median yearly income among noncitizen Latinos has actually declined steadily since 2000 and decreased dramatically during the recession.[14]

In the stagnant low-wage economy, much tension arises around whether immigrants (particularly Latinos) are "taking" jobs from native-born workers. However, recent analyses show that there is little, if any, correlation between "growth in foreign-born population and the employment outcomes of native-born workers."[15] In fact, between 2000 and 2004, twenty-seven states reported a positive correlation between increases in immigrant population and a rise in employment of native-born workers (these states account for 67% of all native-born workers).[16] Moreover, the Economic Policy Institute's analysis of government data from 1994 to 2007 shows that immigration had a positive effect of a .4% increase (or $3.68 a week) on U.S.–born workers take-home earnings. Even among the lowest wage workers, recent immigrants tend to have a negative effect only on the wages of earlier immigrants, not native-born workers.[17] Recent waves of immigration did not cause the low-wage economy in the United States.

While blacks and U.S.–born Latinos have seen some gains in median yearly income, the income gap between those with darker skins and whites has held steady over the last twenty-five years. Moreover, Latinos still have the lowest median income of all racial and ethnic groups. As the Pew Hispanic Center reports, Latinos' average median yearly income in 2008 was $21,488 (with U.S.–born Latinos earning 17% more than foreign-born Latinos) compared to $24,951 for blacks and $31,570 and $35,542 for whites and Asians respectively.[18] Income inequality based on race and ethnicity is built into the U.S. political economy.

A Bridge-Building Vocation

Religious organizations enter this racial and ethnic landscape with a unique social position and skill-set for bridge building. This bridge building is necessary because the collective agency of the working poor is often untapped and uncoordinated, sometimes even divided. This situation echoes the larger struggle of organized labor in the last twenty years. With the 1980s' assault on labor from the "corporate right," and the resulting declines in union membership and negotiating power, labor has had to develop new strategies to survive. Much of the subsequent work of "new labor" is coming from grassroots initiatives that build "bridges" among social movements and various community constituencies for effective local campaigns. In these more decentralized campaigns, bridge builders are crucial: they make "deliberate efforts to educate different groups about each other, to reduce fear and hostility based on ignorance by bringing individuals together, and to encourage the valuing of cultural diversity."[19] Fluidity in coalitions, the flattening of decision-making hierarchies, and attention to overlapping interests pushes toward a new model of social movement unionism.[20] In this model, "coalitions . . . represent not the competition among constituencies for their 'piece of the pie,' but rather their alignment with other movements and with broad social interests."[21] Rather than dictating the terms of local campaigns, labor becomes a partner in a larger movement for economic justice.

Sociologists such as Margaret Levi stress that these coalitions are "no small feat, given the immense animosity that has characterized these relationships in the past decades" over issues of racism, sexism, xenophobia, and classism (i.e., among "skilled" and "unskilled" workers).[22] In these tension-ridden contexts, religious coalition organizations regularly draw on their ideological commitments and structural location to emerge as bridge builders.

The Complexity of Religious Coalitional Organizations

Activists form religious coalitions out of a complex mix of organizations, demographics, and ideologies. Congregations are often the first organizational type that many think of when analyzing "religious practice." However, the most influential and powerful organizational forms in religious living wage organizing are national and regional interfaith networks. For example, Interfaith Worker Justice has grown to an affiliate network of fifty-two local interfaith worker justice organizations. These local affiliates draw clergy and laity from various congregations, as well as unaffiliated believers. Similarly, congregation-based community organizing networks such as the IAF, PICO, Gamaliel, and DART draw on neo-Alinsky models of congregational engagement to form coalitions of faith leaders across a geographic area.[23] By 2001, there were more than 130 congregation-based community organizing networks across the United States, which included over four thousand religious institutions.[24] While each geographic network differs in its demographics, these networks coordinate much of the organizing across race, class, and gender that happens in the living wage movement. Congregation-based community organizing groups tend to have a higher percentage of both female and African American participants than random samples of regular churchgoers.[25] Given the homogeneity of most U.S. congregations, this is a significant accomplishment.

Within these networks, different congregations, clergy, and laity have varied motives for participating. Poorer congregations, which are often predominantly made up of minorities and immigrants, join these networks and living wage activism for the direct benefits of their members. Wealthier congregations, which tend to be more European American, join these networks from a sense of service to a struggle and, generally, a progressive orientation to the political economy. Clergy who join these networks are often motivated by a desire for wide-ranging community relationships.[26] Sitting in a private meeting with Nashville mayor Karl Dean, clergy members took pains to explain to him why they were part of this interfaith coalition for living wages. As an African American pastor from North Nashville explained, "My people are struggling. They get one step ahead financially and then their benefits are pulled. Even as we move forward we have to give folks enough that they don't lose, say Section 8 housing, and then don't have enough to pay for an apartment." At the same meeting, a Jewish rabbi spoke of his congregation's call to stand with the most needy and insure that fair wages were paid and a Unitarian pastor explained how she "knows that we are all struggling financially right now, with many in her congregation losing jobs and hours, but the low-wage workers she encountered [through the organizing network] were always struggling and in a permanent recession." Cohering for varied reasons, interfaith economic justice networks are the nexus for a tremendous amount of race and class-conscious organizing. Even multiracial and multiclass congregations rarely drive this organizing. Rather, relationships and institutional power are built at the network level of interfaith organizing; it is in those meetings and workshops that the bridge-building practices and political engagement are most apparent. These interfaith networks also facilitate relationships with labor and other community economic justice organizations. Interestingly, the most significant resistance to this bridge building often occurs at the congregational level from wealthier moderate and conservative congregations.

"In Our Own Languages We Hear Them": Ideology Translation[27]

Any one group may encompass multiple ideologies. When the beliefs are different but relatively complementary, bridge builders help people understand each other to strengthen their collaboration. The sociologists Rhys Williams and N. J. Demerath explain it this way: "Ideologies are belief systems—articulated sets of beliefs . . . primarily articulated by a specific class/group, that function primarily in the interests of that class or group, and yet are presented as being in the 'common good' or as generally accepted."[28] Ideologies are those committed beliefs that motivate and justify the challenge to existing power structures. When social movement subcultures in a coalition differ in their meaning making and activist strategies, *ideology translation* crosses those gaps. For example, while coalition members might share the goal of worker dignity, issues can arise when one organization speaks of "workers united will never be defeated" and another focuses on the individual dignity of each "as a child of God," leading to disagreements over patterns of decision-making and consensus-building vs. obedience to leadership. Bridge builders can help coalition partners understand how differing organizational patterns can be tied to varied group cultures and belief systems (e.g., "priesthood of all believers" informs consensus building vs. a strong apprentice system that emphasizes obedience).

Religious coalition leaders are well prepared for ideology translation because their formal education and vocational practice provide them with the hermeneutic and homiletic training for translating ideas across cultures (e.g., between ancient sacred texts and contemporary cultures). Their preparation actually encourages them to seek out opportunities to translate across social movement ideologies. The sociologist Fred Rose elaborates on this in his analysis on cross-class coalitions: "Bridge builders are able to translate or interpret the concerns of another movement into the language and frameworks of their peers. . . . This is particularly critical at the beginning stages of a coalition, before trust is developed among participants and a clear agenda established."[29] Religious bridge builders regularly reframe and translate key terms, approaches, and worldviews among coalition constituents.

Rev. C. J. Hawking, from the Chicago Interfaith Committee on Worker Issues, who has facilitated the growth of several local interfaith worker justice organizations, provides movement leaders in a workshop with a one-page sheet divided into two columns; one is labeled "Faith Movement," the other "Labor Movement." In each column are organizational and ideological terms in parallel: congregants vs. rank and file; lay leaders vs. stewards; ministerial association vs. central labor council; new church start vs. organizing drive; tithing vs. dues; "when one suffers we all suffer" vs. "an injury to one is an injury to all;" and so on.[30] The final lines of the sheet are blank for additional comparisons. As participants discuss this sheet, they begin to work through some of their apprehension at negotiating their different movement cultures. The goal is not simply vocabulary but an avenue for better understanding the other's work and respecting differences. And, as a union leader in the audience shares at the end of the session, "It's like a light bulb went off; of course—organized labor and organized religion—we're both about economic justice!" In a meeting later in the conference, a labor organizer talks about "activating the rank and file" and then turns to a religious colleague and asks, "Now, what's your term again?" "Laity" she answers, and they go on to discuss their respective leadership development programs.

Rabbi Lori Coskey, director of the San Diego ICWJ, sees this as a central purpose of her organization.

> The religious community and labor community often share common values and goals, but speak in different languages. While a Catholic, for example, might speak of "building the kingdom of God" or a Jew of "tikkun olam," labor organizers and worker activists speak of "card-check neutrality," "NLRB elections," and "mandatory bargaining subjects." Members of both communities often fail to see their common interests because of these different vocabularies. The ICWJ, however, is in a unique position of being able to translate between the two communities, and in doing so, to bring them together in partnership.[31]

Through this translation work, independent religious organizations are able to cultivate an important and powerful political coalition and moral synthesis for social change.

A similar model appeared at a Nashville vigil for a living wage. The head of the Tennessee AFL-CIO and the minister from a local Unitarian Universalist congregation took turns leading the liturgy adapted from IWJ for the assembled as described in Table 2 on the following page. Labor leaders commented afterwards that never before had their voices been included in worship in the South; they later wrote the event organizers to ask how they could best support the new interfaith committee.

Labor-pulpit exchanges in various U.S. cities extend this translation work even further. In Los Angeles, Clergy United for Economic Justice (CLUE LA) countered the "rent-a-collar"[32] model of labor's relationship to clergy by creating a program in which labor leaders and clergy visit each other's workplaces for a day. Through this exchange, the contexts of coalition partners become more mutually transparent, building trust among

TABLE 2

Labor Community	Religious Community
The Labor Community chants: No Justice! No Peace!	*Isaiah 32:17 says:* The work of justice will be peace.
The Labor Community chants: What do we want? Justice! When do we want it? Now!	*The Holy Quran says:* You who believe, stand firm for justice, as witness to Allah.
The Labor Community chants: We're overworked and underpaid!	*Baba Metzia 111a says: (Jewish)* He who withholds an employee's wages is as though he deprived him of his life.
The Labor Community chants: An injury to one, an injury to all!	*1 Corinthians 12:26 says:* If one member suffers, all suffer together with it.

the coalition organizations. One organizer attested that it also helped mediate differences in protest cultures between union and religious activists: "Union activists are often about 'attack, attack, attack.' But religious activists want to offer prayers and seek the good in the other." By visiting with each and going on smaller protests together, clergy and union leaders began to understand each other's approach more deeply. "We took both sets of leaders to deliver a letter to a nursing home that had consistent labor violations. The management started yelling at us, but the clergy were up front, so they were yelling at the clergy. The clergy were shocked. They helped calm everyone down, but they also gained insight into the abuse workers and their union stewards often face."[33] This network organizer affirmed that this type of bridge building helped the coalition move from a list of endorsees to partners in concerted and ongoing strategic collaboration.

While religious organizations have expended much energy in bridging the faith-labor divide, they also have effected crucial ideology translation while building multiracial/ethnic coalitions. At an organizing committee meeting in a southern city, labor leaders, clergy, and immigrant rights advocates gathered to discuss extending their work to develop a "worker rights center" to parallel their living wage campaign. As the meeting closed, a labor organizer approached the faith leaders and suggested that rather than framing their discussion primarily in terms of "immigrant rights," an appeal to "racial justice" would make the union base (and their leadership) less anxious. During the next wave of organizing, the faith leaders reframed the discussion (even changing the briefing paper they were distributing) without changing the composition of the coalition or the organizing agenda for low-wage immigrant communities. This translation helped labor to endorse the workers' center eventually and to become a permanent presence in coalition meetings.

Ideology translators do not seek to merge group identities or cultures but to provide pathways for communication and strategic resonance. Differences are not removed or dismissed but are put into intentional conversation in order to identify obstacles and possibilities for collaboration. Through this process, groups that are seemingly divided begin to see their connections more deeply and thus construct a collective agency that extends the capacity and strength of their coalition.

"Be Reconcilers": Relational Repair[34]

While ideology translation helps facilitate greater understanding and trust in relatively stable coalitions, *relational repair* is needed when there have been more significant ruptures in working relationships. Relational repair involves identifying the historical and contemporary conflicts affecting the coalition (or, potential coalition) and working to remedy fissures so that coalition work is possible. As the sociologist Silke Roth explains, "Bridging work is a form of social movement interaction that focuses explicitly on efforts to overcome and negotiate conflicts that result from different collective identities that are rooted in and expressed by organizational and strategic repertoires."[35] Religiously based groups have resources for this work that derive from theologies and liturgies of conviction, confession, forgiveness, and reconciliation. Broken relationships are seen as part and parcel of being "in this world," and sacred scriptures recognize that even those with the best intentions still often fall short. Because of these beliefs and practices, religious coalition organizations are often best suited to encourage the relational repair needed by coalition partners when suspicion and pain engulf them.

Union corruption and racism have, in particular, generated suspicion in several communities that regularly partner in living wage coalitions. "The racism and sexism of many unions, their conflicting goals [between community and labor activists] when it comes to urban renewal and other large construction projects that displace the poor without employing them, and their past indifference to service sector workers have proved an obstacle."[36] Interfaith Worker Justice spends much time nationally and locally producing documents and workshops on the "union difference" for low-wage workers. In this material, examples of which follow, a significant amount of time and talk are spent recognizing the history of racism, sexism, and xenophobia within labor unions. Starting from a theological anthropology of universal sin, accountability, forgiveness, and reconciliation, IWJ and other religious affiliates work with their constituents to rebuild "faith" in unions and to remind followers that the church has been guilty of the same sins as other coalition partners.

What about union corruption?

Unions, like religious bodies, are made up of human beings with all their flaws and frailties. There is some corruption in unions, as there is some within religious bodies. And, wherever corruption or greed is uncovered, it must be cleaned up. Most unions have rigorous procedures to combat corruption. . . . As wrong as union corruption is, it is unfortunate that union corruption receives so much front page media attention, compared to the important justice work done by unions to raise wages, benefits and working conditions for low-wage workers.

What about racism and sexism?

Racism and sexism are sins shared by unions and the religious community. The new leadership of the AFL-CIO has one of its key goals ensuring full participations for all in work, in society, and in unions. The AFL-CIO has made significant progress in making its leadership reflect its membership, although much still needs to be done.[37]

The document concludes by stating clearly that religious bodies have a responsibility to hold unions accountable, but "when unions seek justice in the workplace and the society at large, the religious community should be an ally."[38] Such repair work builds the collective identity of an economic justice movement and seeks to make the coalition of labor, religion, and community organizations more permanent.

In the end, bridge builders are developing the trust necessary for political association and agency.[39] While trust most often develops out of shared lifestyle, consumer culture, and a common educational and employment experience, religious organizations provide important alternate pathways for cultivating trust. Especially when the allies and beneficiaries of a social movement have no shared daily contexts, the confession of transcendent belief may lay the groundwork for building trust. In the words of the sociologist Christian Smith, "Learning that others one meets for the first time—at a street march, an organizer's meeting, or in jail—are, like oneself, also Catholics, Muslims, or Jews, can immediately foster a sense of ease, trust, and loyalty that greatly facilitates group communication and solidarity."[40] Religious believers' shared language and identity can often "expedite the process of coming to a shared 'definition of reality'" which is particularly helpful in the ambiguous, fluid, emergent situations that often surround disruptive activism."[41] When everything seems to be going to hell in a handbasket, a shared religious identity can make it easier to define "hell" and to decide how to get out of that basket. A shared vision helps to build and mobilize the group's collective agency. Richard Wood explains that religious networks provide "bridging social capital," which can "build an organizational culture to link diverse ethnic groups."[42]

In New Haven, Connecticut, a white, female, Yale-educated minister of a local United Church of Christ congregation and co-chair of the Board for the Connecticut Center for a New Economy (CCNE), and a black, male, nondenominational pastor who is director of the Center spoke of the deep class and race distrust in poorer New Haven neighborhoods.[43] New Haven's non-Yale elites were tired of being solicited by the university, either to be research subjects or receive charity. Another set of do-gooders was not what the people of New Haven needed. Yet conversations around the mandates of justice within their common faiths opened doors between the pastors involved in Elm City Churches Organized (ECCO) and made it possible for white clergy leaders from wealthier congregations to prove themselves as partners in the struggle. Through the CCNE and sustained grassroots conversations, white, Puerto Rican, and black ordained and lay leaders came together to foster a level of community involvement that even labor unions had not achieved. The gospel of social justice and a justice-loving God opened doors and eventually brought activists into each other's living rooms. While "people of faith" were not the whole of the movement, especially in such a strong union region, they did draw in workers who might never have taken the risk nor experienced the growth of their agency had it not been tied to their faith.

As a leader of the San Diego living wage coalition explained it, her goal for the religious organization was to build "Buber-type relationships" with all parties involved in the living wage struggle. Here she was referencing the Jewish philosopher Martin Buber's famous reflection on creating "I-Thou" rather than "I-It" relationships with others.[44] Whether the other one engaged was an ally or an opponent, she insisted on dialogical engagement that honored the spark of the divine in the other. Relationships of repair and hope were built on that foundation.

Interfaith coalition leaders help bridge divides not only among social movement organizations but also between local elected officials and unions. Especially in the South, where unions are historically weak and often suspect, religious organizing can also present worker issues in a manner that is less alienating or politically troublesome than union directed campaigns. This was particularly true in the Nashville campaign, where local unions had largely opposed the eventual mayoral victor in the Democratic primary and general election. With plenty of political resentments to go around, advisors to the mayor told leaders of the living wage coalition privately that unions could not dominate the coalition. In response, the Interfaith Committee of Middle Tennessee Jobs with Justice (co-affiliated with IWJ) took the lead in organizing, hiring two part-time faith organizers, and eventually gathering the endorsement of more than sixty Nashville religious leaders (including all the major synagogues). While unions helped fund the campaign and were present at every rally, they were not the face of the campaign. In October 2009, the first coalition delegation to meet with the mayor included five clergy (including an Orthodox rabbi), one religion professor, and the Jobs with Justice executive director. After opening with a prayer, each pastor of a congregation testified to the need and concern of their constituents for living wage jobs. By the end of the one-hour meeting, the mayor verbally agreed to raise metro worker's pay to a living wage. This was remarkable given that the mayor—based on a legal opinion he had written when he was Nashville's legal director—was the only person with the authority to establish living wage budgeting (not the Metro Council). In May 2010, the mayor submitted a budget that included living wages for all full-time Metro government employees.

Although the Nashville campaign did not resolve all the issues between the mayor and local unions, the intermediary work of an independent religious organization and their religious leaders did find some common ground on a shared worker's rights issue. Through the religious organizers' work, the unions also came to better understand where the rifts in their relationship with the mayor came from, where they stood, and where some progress could be made.

More than Crumbs: Inclusion Monitoring[45]

In addition to translating ideology and repairing relationships, religious coalition organizations also help insure that coalitions are sufficiently inclusive. By asking who is and who is not at the table, religious organizations encourage fair and productive collaborations among partners. This *inclusion monitoring* is especially crucial for new labor strategies that encourage coalitions to see and organize around the connections among multiple kinds of injustices (e.g., race, gender, class, immigrant, and environmental).[46] Religious organizations enter this mix with a unique structure and a strong ideological commitment. Structurally, their constituencies are often less defined (than labor unions, for example); they can therefore facilitate negotiations between seemingly competitive organizations in a coalition. Because they are also ideologically committed to the "most vulnerable," these religious groups often work to make sure that coalitions are inclusive and responsive to all partners. Taking their call from scriptural passages such as Exodus 22:21 (NRSV), "You shall not wrong the stranger or oppress him, for you were strangers in the land of Egypt," Matthew's promise (Matt. 6:21–36) of the Kingdom to those who welcome the stranger, and the Qur'an's summons to serve God by doing good to "neighbors who are near, neighbors who are strangers" (Qur'an 4:36), religious leaders are bound to those who may not look like allies to "politics as usual."

Low-wage workers include disproportionate numbers of African Americans and Latinos. While these workers share an economic reality, they often participate in different social groups and movements. In the workplace, they are often pitted against one another as each seeks to secure "their piece of the pie." In North Carolina's meat processing plants, for example, Latino workers reported being told by management that they had to pick up the slack of less motivated blacks; black workers were told that they would be replaced by more compliant immigrants if they didn't follow orders.[47] Black workers began to complain to local leaders,

"The Mexicans will be our undoing. Every other immigrant pushed the other up, but they are jumping us." Because of this divisive dynamic, local immigrant rights groups sometimes have tenuous relationships with local African American community groups. And, when this divisiveness mixes with historical union racism, suspicion can run high in coalitions. Or, as one Latino organizer explained to a group of activists recently, "We think we're all trying to get 'our' piece of the pie, but they've got us fighting over the crumbs!" Religious leaders of the Beloved Community Center addressed the racial/ethnic tensions in meat processing plants by working with the union and African American and Latino leaders to make sure that they coordinate their efforts. As Nelson Johnson, director of the Beloved Community Center and board chair of IWJ National, explained to these leaders, "We've got to stand with the Book! Is there *anyone* being mistreated by the company? Well, they are a beautiful child of God and we are with them." While this coordination was initially at odds with work-place culture,[48] the Beloved Community Center conducted meetings, including influential local clergy, to explain the mutual benefits of not undercutting any worker's wage security. Eventually both English and Spanish were used for almost all campaign literature and worker organizing; Black-Brown speaking teams were developed to address press inquiries.[49]

An organizer with CLUE LA described a similar experience and her organization's deep commitment to "Ephesians 2:2—We're all citizens of God's kingdom." She explained how Los Angeles hotels purposely hire almost all Latinos and almost no blacks for their wage work. This ends up stirring up black resentment of Latino workers since they see "them taking our jobs." CLUE LA decided to establish a committee with half African American and half Latino/a religious leaders to address the issue. Together they worked to include a requirement for diversity monitoring in four major hotel contracts. As the organizer explained, "We have to be careful that no group is exploitable to meet certain economic desires."[50]

In Nashville, taxi drivers organizing for representation on the Metro Taxi Commission and a fairer wage structure ran into significant problems in their coalition. The great majority of cabbies in Nashville are recent immigrants and refugees from Somalia and Ethiopia. They bring with them deep historical and religious (Christian and Muslim) differences that create significant tensions. Leadership elections in their newly formed Metro Taxi Drivers Alliance became ethnically driven and complicated strategic planning among the cabbies. Working with the

Taxi Drivers Alliance, the Interfaith Committee of Jobs with Justice and their ally Tennessee Immigrant and Refugee Rights Coalition reached out to area imams and Ethiopian ministers to help mediate conflict in the coalition. While the coalition still struggles with these issues, they did manage to coordinate a major week-long strike in the summer of 2008.

Nationally, this ideology of inclusion also guides IWJ in its efforts to integrate immigration reform into their worker justice actions. While some conservative union leaders see undocumented workers as a threat to higher wage/unionized jobs, leaders within the IWJ national network have sought to challenge this logic and nurture a more inclusive vision of the worker justice movement. Leaders such as Rev. Alexia Salvatierra, the executive director of California Clergy and Laity United for Economic Justice (CA CLUE), have focused on making sure that the stories of immigrant workers are at the forefront of worker justice campaigns. When Rev. Salvatierra opens her laptop each day, a picture of a Mexican mother being taken from her daughter in an immigration raid fills the screen. The picture is her daily reminder of the struggles these workers endure and of the family destruction wrought by immigration raids. Through a network of leadership development and media campaigns, Rev. Salvatierra works every day to guarantee that workers' voices will help in shaping the next generation of worker justice movements.

Out of this pastoral insistence on preserving the families of undocumented workers, Salvatierra and other clergy have launched a companion worker justice movement for undocumented laborers under threat of deportation. The "New Sanctuary Movement" recalls the sanctuary movement of the 1980s for refugees of the Central American wars. In the 1980s, churches and synagogues pledged themselves to be actual sanctuaries for those being deported back to the war-torn region. The new religious sanctuary movement echoes this history by supporting the victims of U.S. trade policies who have "come to this country out of desperation, worked hard, contributed to their community and yet face deportation."[51] As an act of public witness, sanctuary congregations provide hospitality and protection to a limited number of immigrant families who have a family member facing deportation (usually as a result of workplace Immigrant and Customs Enforcement raids). The movement provides legal and other forms of assistance to families, while developing public campaigns for legislation that would change their situation. Rev. Salvatierra states,

When people meet the families in the sanctuary movement and they hear the way broken laws are breaking these families the response over and over again is that this is wrong. And the Sanctuary is a way to make these invisible people visible and to give a voice to those who have no voice so that the legislators can hear and in hearing they can make wise decisions.[52]

The movement itself was launched in 2007 through a post-conference, "Building the New Sanctuary Movement," that followed the national IWJ conference in Chicago. As part of their efforts to link this new movement with the larger worker justice and living wage movement, IWJ activists produced a 112-page text "For Once You Were a Stranger" and scheduled multiple sessions on immigrant workers issues. Interfaith Worker Justice continues to train local affiliate leaders on how to include undocumented workers in organizing and leadership development for economic justice.

Religious organizations often take the lead in this kind of bridge building in coalitions because of the unique way they combine ideology, eclectic constituencies, and trust. Bridge building requires the support of other coalition organizations, but religious organizations often provide the space (sometimes literally) and the ideological impetus to further this work. Dialogue and solidarity across difference are core needs for living wage campaigns as they seek to bolster the agency and power of low-wage employees who have often been disregarded and even abused. Fighting the power of large businesses and governments, living wage campaigns require coalitions of support that bridge rather than exacerbate existing tensions among workers and their allies. What can easily divide low-wage workers must become part of the strength.

Political Participation, Leadership, and the Least of These

Internal discord and misunderstandings confront many coalitions. However, for the most vulnerable in racialized political economies, these challenges are ultimately embedded in larger issues of political participation and alienation. In the United States, higher levels of education, income, and occupation dramatically increase the likelihood of political participation (that is, activity focused on affecting government action). Resources such as skill sets, social capital, organizational affiliations, and money, which people develop by participating in nonpolitical institutions, influence their capacity and willingness to engage in political activity. In other words, the lack of resources, broadly defined, affects an individual's political agency. Low-wage workers are decidedly absent from most of the traditional pathways to increased political participation: they are simply excluded from most processes for building political agency. But according to the political scientist Sidney Verba and his colleagues, religious institutions "play an unusual role in the American participatory system by providing opportunities for the development of civic skills to those who would otherwise be resource-poor."[53] Increased religious activity is one of the only factors mitigating against the determinism associated with low socioeconomic status and low political participation (or, the equation of social stratification with political stratification). While Verba's macro-survey data focus almost exclusively on Christian churches, the findings are still provocative for interfaith organizing. For African Americans and Latinos in particular, participating in a religious organization is one of the few entry points for political development, in light of their disproportionate representation in lower educational, occupational, and income brackets.

Religious institutions enhance political agency in part because, although they certainly are stratified, they are stratified differently than workplaces. A diverse work force within a corporation usually includes persons at many income and educational levels. And normally there is a "consequent apportioning of greater skill opportunities to those at the top . . . managers organize meetings and give speeches, assembly line workers and file clerks do not" (333). Religious institutions, however, tend to be more homogenous in terms of race, ethnicity, and social class. Therefore "skill opportunities are more equally allocated across educational, income, or racial and ethnic groups because, within the congregations, there is a more limited range of people who can be chosen—or select themselves—to be active" (333). Line workers organize prayer meetings, administrative assistants write newsletters, and custodians lead the choir, developing important civic skills in the process.

While European and Latin American countries rely on labor unions and leftist parties to represent and encourage poor and working-class participation in politics, these institutions are decidedly less powerful in U.S. politics. In fact, Verba et al. find that the "average citizen is three to four times as likely to be politically mobilized in a church than a union" (388). In terms of raw capacity to activate politically disadvantaged citizens and develop their political agency, religious institutions are unsurpassed in the United States.

Of course, religious institutions and unions are not always identical in their political agendas. While unions have long been primarily oriented to representing the economic agenda of the lower middle classes in political institutions, religious institutions do not evince the same consensus on which political issues should top their agenda. In the last several decades, abortion and gay marriage have been as likely to dominate religious political mobilization as the economic needs of the least advantaged (520). As a consequence, religious institutions will probably not surpass unions as the leaders in championing the economic needs of the least advantaged in the near future (521). But they still have an enormous potential for progressive mobilization, particularly when a theological focus on the "least of these" (Matt. 25:40) or the "preferential option for the poor" intersects a systematic development of lay leadership. As their influence grows, progressive religious networks may be developing the capacity to mobilize citizens around issues of economic justice much as the religious right did in the 1980s and 1990s around conservative cultural issues.[54]

Developing Indigenous Leadership

Municipal living wage campaigns benefit directly from the political groundwork laid by churches, mosques, and temples. In terms of direct beneficiaries, clergy and even progressive business leaders, religious networks are a primary source of social capital for the activist community.[55] An organized local network of activists is vital to municipal campaign success, particularly in encouraging city and county officials to respond to local constituents. Religious organizations and their networks often become the counterweight to local chambers of commerce by providing well-trained indigenous leadership on the issues at hand.

In the Atlanta living wage campaign, led by a coalition of labor (Atlanta Labor Council), feminist (Atlanta Working Women 9to5), populist education (Project South), and quasi-religious (Georgia Citizen's Coalition on Hunger) groups, religious organizations supplied the various progressive voices that would speak for the living wage ordinance. At city council meetings, missionary Baptist workers testified on the behalf of the SEIU and their faith community; entrepreneurs and socially responsible venture capitalists from Atlanta's wealthiest Episcopal parishes followed with their call to conscience. Race, gender, and class barriers were crossed as concerned clergy spoke with each other and recruited key lay leaders in their congregations.

When the Atlanta City Council finally opened public discussion on the proposed ordinance, the packed council chamber reflected the organizing constituency and their corporate opponents.[56] In the front bank of seats sat lobbyists (almost all white and all male) from the Chamber of Commerce, a few parking lot owners, and numerous Delta airlines executives all dressed in suits and ties. The living wage coalition first anticipated little opposition from the business sector because Coca-Cola, Georgia Power, and other powerful players had no government contracts and received few subsidies. Even their initial analysis of Delta found few employees under the proposed wage. To the coalition's surprise however, Delta subcontracted large amounts of work to low-wage firms. Thus, Delta quickly became the core opposition to the Atlanta proposal and even threatened to pull its hub out of Atlanta if the ordinance passed.

The rest of the chamber that day was racially mixed—about half black and half white—and filled with the vibrant colors of union shirts (dominated by the purple and yellow of SEIU), a smattering of clergy collars, and numerous citizen supporters in casual attire. Although almost a third of the supporters of the ordinance were union members, it was only when speakers went to the public microphone for comment and asked their constituencies to raise their hands that the religious coalitional presence became more apparent. At least twenty constituents from downtown Atlanta's two wealthiest parishes, St. Luke's Episcopal Church and the Cathedral of St. Philip, came in the middle of the day to support speakers from their congregations. Potential direct beneficiaries of the ordinance and supporters from Emmaus House Episcopal Chapel (an anti-poverty mission in South Atlanta) were also present. Individuals from Congregation Bet Haverim (Jewish), the Baitul Salaam Network, Inc. (a Muslim Domestic Violence Shelter), local Unitarian Universalist, Roman Catholic, United Church of Christ, Methodist, Baptist, and Presbyterian congregations, Concerned Black Clergy, and a few religion professors ensured a prominent religious presence. All together, these religious activists constituted at least a third of the supporters in the room.

Even those congregants/workers with less education and service-sector jobs embraced the opportunity to testify publicly before the council in part because of traditions of "testifying" in their own faith communities.[57] Many of these affected workers, especially in the low-union South, had never been to a council meeting, let alone spoken at one. But through the outreach of trusted local ministers, they were initiated into another practice of political agency. As in Atlanta, in terms of both outreach networks and pools of skilled participants, religious organizations provide a base for organizing and political engagement that crosses many of the standard barriers of race, ethnicity, and class in the United States. Unfortunately, many white, middle-class organizers, particularly those representing national political parties, often recruit leaders from the same types of institutions that provided them with social capital—higher education institutions, professional business networks, and partisan political associations. Progressive organizations sustain the worker justice movement and embody their moral claims better if they recognize religious organizations not just as sites for forming individual faith—a class and education bias—but also as a base for political activation and laity leadership development.

Religious Constraints on Leadership Development and Bridge Building

No movement is without significant internal challenges, and religiously based organizations introduce their own challenges into political development and bridge building. The sociologist William Mirolla is correct that not enough research addresses the limits of what religious ideology and organizations can do for economic justice movements.[58] As we analyze religious involvement in coalitions, we must recognize how some aspects of religious hierarchy and the racialized "lifestyle enclaves" (or identities created through shared consumption or leisure activities)[59] of many congregations constrain religious participation in the living wage movement.

Religious institutions play a unique role in U.S. politics in cultivating vital civic skills among those persons with lower socioeconomic standing. While this mechanism is compelling, Verba and his colleagues document how the internal characteristics of religious organizations may affect this skill development. The polity (that is, the institutional forms) and congregational practices of churches also influence congregants' political participation. On the whole, research shows that Protestant Christians have more opportunities to cultivate and practice their civic skills than Roman Catholic Christians.[60] Since African Americans tend to be affiliated with Protestantism and Latinos with Catholicism, blacks derive a bigger political boost from their involvement in congregational life.

More specifically, research points to the role of laity leadership in fostering civic skills for political participation. Religious organizing treads on dangerous ground when it relies only on ordained clergy for political development, assuming that clergy will bring along congregational participants. Verba's research shows that being exposed to political messages (in sermons, for example) is very different from building political skills through institutional practices. In their exposure to political stimuli, Protestants and Catholics are similar: "With respect to requests for political activity or exposure to political messages . . . what is striking is how little systematic difference there is between Catholics and Protestants . . . compared to those for the practice of skills."[61] Unfortunately, sermons, prayers, and sacraments based on hierarchal standing and knowledge often mirror the institutions within which low-wage workers spend most of their lives. Intentional skill development and significant leadership sharing are needed to encourage low-wage workers into the political process. While clergy resist the "rent-a-collar" model of social movement participation, religious organizers must also resist the "rent-a-testimony" model of congregant organizing. While both models may insult participants on an individual level, clergy generally have the institutional position that insures their political participation regardless. Lower-wage workers lack these institutional options; religious polity is thus extremely important for increasing their political participation. The current distortions of political agency will persist if congregants appear merely as "the face of poverty" at political rallies.

Religious ideology can also hamper even sympathetic religious organizations from joining the living wage movement. Congregational endorsement of living wage activism can become fraught when congregations seek to affirm rather than challenge members in order to avoid conflict. Many organizers reported that "it was not unusual for a rabbi, priest, or minister to reply to a request for participation, 'Why should we put ourselves out in this way? After all, the owner of that company is a member of my congregation and a big contributor to the new building fund.'"[62] A former organizer of an IAF affiliate in the South recalled that several major member congregations slowly withdrew their support and funding as the affiliate began taking stands on key economic reforms in the city, including a failed bid for metro living wages in 2000.[63] The congregations perceived the IAF affiliate as disruptive because of their own internal class concerns. In response, crime and education rather than economic policies began to dominate the IAF agenda. Particularly in economically diverse and economically elite congregations, focusing on economic reform can highlight divisions that disrupt the unity and pastoral peace that so many congregants desire.

This desire to avoid conflict can also hide larger issues of institutionalized racism and classism within religious institutions themselves. The historical splits of major denominations around racialized economic issues (slave-holding especially) still resonate. Contemporary religious institutions largely maintain these racial divisions, understood now in terms of worship style, geographic location, and lifestyle choices. The homogeneity of these groups has double-edged implications. On one hand, it offers low-income and other persons such as blacks and Latino immigrants a unique institution, a "counterpublic" to workplace and educational systems, within which to cultivate civic skills.[64] On the other hand, though, many local congregations can insulate themselves from upsetting questions about the intersections of race, ethnicity, and working poverty because of the race- and class-based divisions among religious organizations. What enables civic skill development in one congregation allows another to see raced poverty as not "their" issue.

Because most congregations wish to maintain parishioner peace, religious endorsements of living wage campaigns come primarily from larger religious bodies (Christian denominations, Islamic organizations, Jewish movements), independent interfaith organizing networks, and smaller faith communities. Regionally based groups such as dioceses and ministerial organizations also often join and endorse municipal ordinance campaigns. While these endorsements do carry weight, they also conceal the struggles of individual churches, synagogues, and mosques to mobilize on economic justice issues without alienating some members or calling their racialized economic benefits into question.

Enhancing Moral Agency: Theological Solidarity

Even with these struggles, religious activists offer important ideological resources, mediating skills, and opportunities for political development that empower the working poor in racialized political economies. At best, they practice a form of inclusive solidarity, both as a means and an end for the movement. Reflecting on their practices of theological solidarity can help activists and their allies to sustain and develop their bridge-building and political engagement. Moreover by considering the depth of theological solidarity, particularly in the Roman Catholic and liberation theology traditions, Christians activists can hold themselves accountable to the prophetic edge of the movement, which is committed not to "grass-tops organizing" but also to a racially conscious structural empowerment of workers.

Labor and Theological Solidarity

Solidarity is a term that has significance for both labor and religious activists. Unionists often summarize labor solidarity as "The workers united will never be defeated." Through this ideal of solidarity, they help vulnerable workers gain greater control over their work lives through collective action. However, when labor solidarity is defined as union solidarity, coalition action may not extend to workers outside a union; collective bargaining agreements often only apply to workers who fund the union through money, time, and risk.[65] The legacy of union solidarity has certainly had a positive ripple effect for nonunionized workers; union organizing and lobbying have increased industry wages, benefits, and protections. But union solidarity has also sometimes meant ignoring the well-being of workers, who, because of their of race, citizenship status, or gender, were seen as not furthering the immediate interests of dominant union members. Advocates of social movement unionism, as, for example, in the living wage movement, seek to expand the concept of worker solidarity and prioritize the needs of more workers from the global labor pool.

By contrast, religious conceptions of solidarity find their origin, ground, and end explicitly in the more inclusive love of God and God's vision for the world. In the last fifty years, Roman Catholic social teachings, disseminated through papal encyclicals, have offered deep reflection on the theological nature of solidarity. While a secular or non-Christian religious perspective can certainly promote solidarity, Christian tradition places solidarity "in a context of the reign of God."[66] Many Christian activists allied with labor find these theological understandings central to their work. When San Diego ICWJ sends out their quarterly reports on "Worker Solidarity" campaigns, their idea of solidarity is not based in class or occupation, but rather in all people being "children of God" and forming the "beloved community." Theological solidarity has a different ontological grounding than union solidarity.

Ultimately, proponents of theological solidarity contend, "We are all really responsible for all."[67] In this manner, theological solidarity in multiple religious traditions begins with a decidedly inclusive understanding of allegiance. God's deep, equal valuing of each person invites followers to embody God's love by loving the neighbor through solidarity. According to papal teachings, solidarity is a virtue—or disposition of character—arising from a call to love the neighbor as one's self. As a virtue, solidarity is "a firm and preserving determination to commit oneself to the common good," which is both the good of all and each individual. Pope John Paul II explains,

> Solidarity helps us to see the "other"—whether a person, people or nation—not just as some kind of instrument, with a work capacity and physical strength to be exploited at low cost and then discarded when no longer useful, but as our "neighbor," a "helper" (cf. Gen. 2:18–20), to be made a sharer, on a par with ourselves, in the banquet of life to which all are equally invited by God.[68]

Citing the inclusive wedding banquet narrative in Luke 14:15–21 as example, God's invitation to celebrate abundant life is extending to all. Our status as children of God, God's gift of creation to all of us, and the inclusive nature of God's love all underscore the importance of the inclusive invitation for everyone's welfare. We are all guests at the table God sets for us in this world. Individual dignity is to be recognized while our collective good is cultivated and celebrated. In this way, solidarity elevates the sociological reality of interdependence discussed earlier to what John Paul II calls the "moral plane."[69] Theological solidarity reminds us that we are living in light of the renewing vision and inclusive nature of God's reign.

The realities of sin and alienation in the world also require radical correction, or preferential action, in order to move toward inclusive solidarity. Those in lower social, economic, and political conditions disproportionately experience the alienating affects of social sin, or sin embodied in institutional practices. Solidarity as struggling alongside the marginalized for justice requires a preferential rectification of these social structures.[70] Again, the inclusive love of God requires that preference be given to the needs of the marginalized, dominated, silenced, and oppressed. Matthew 25 cautions that those who do not provide for the basic needs of another ("I was hungry and you gave me no food . . . naked and did not give me clothing") or attend to their dignity ("I was a stranger and you did not welcome me . . . sick and in prison and you did not visit me") actually shun Christ himself. Passages such as these point to the centrality of preferential action in the gospels. Love realizes that the deep wounds of social sin must be addressed for and through the inclusive welfare of all persons.

In his encyclical *Laborem Exercens* (On Human Work), Pope John Paul II links the call to suffer with and struggle alongside the poor directly to an endorsement of worker solidarity as part of theological fidelity. Amplifying themes of capital and labor presented in Leo XIII's *Rerum Novarum* (Of New Things) ninety years earlier, John Paul II declares:

> In order to achieve social justice in the various parts of the world, in the various countries, and in the relationships between them, there is a need for ever new movements of solidarity *of* the workers and *with* the workers. This solidarity must be present whenever it is called for by the social degrading of the subject of work, by exploitation of the workers, and by the growing areas of poverty and even hunger. The Church is firmly committed to this cause, for she considers it her mission, her service, a proof of her fidelity to Christ, so that she can truly be the "Church of the poor." And the "poor" appear under various forms; they appear in various places and at various times; in many cases they appear as a result of the violation of the dignity of human work: either because the opportunities for human work are limited as a result of the scourge of unemployment, or because a low value is put on work and the rights that flow from it, especially the right to a just wage and to the personal security of the worker and his or her family.[71]

In this Roman Catholic view, God's inclusive love requires preferential action for worker justice. Making another person's problem one's own requires preferential attention to their experience of systematic domination and preferential action to dismantle dehumanizing structures. Ultimately, these practices of solidarity testifies that love is greater and more powerful than the alienation wrought by our sins.

Preferential Accountability

We are called to love concretely—to love an actual neighbor, not just the concept of neighborliness. Similarly, solidarity is formed and practiced in the context of real people's lives. The stories low-wage workers share during organizing remind us that there is no such thing as abstract struggles for justice; our starting point is the concrete oppressions, the systemic, systematic sufferings of specific persons.[72] Preferential accountability to those suffering under domination means being answerable to their demands for justice.[73] The Protestant ethicist Beverly Harrison explains:

> Genuine solidarity involves not mere subjective identification with oppressed people but concrete answerability to them. Solidarity is accountability, and accountability means being vulnerable, capable of being changed by the oppressed, welcoming their capacity to critique and alter our reality.[74]

Preferential accountability means alliances for change must begin with the experience of those who are suffering. Practices of solidarity begin with listening to and understanding the patterned wounds of persons and groups, seeking to prevent future wounds, and doing one's best to care for and rectify the wounds of the past.

This process requires deliberately creating physical and psychic spaces and processes to amplify the voices of those marginalized in society. In the living wage campaigns, this has meant attending not just to the issues of workers but also to the workers themselves. The move to abstraction can happen too quickly. For the religious practitioners in Baltimore's groundbreaking campaign, the impetus for a municipal ordinance came from listening intently (in one-on-one conversations, house meetings, and so on) to congregation members and to visitors to their soup kitchens. Through their concrete attentiveness, religious activists learned that low-wage jobs were proliferating, partly because of city contracts and subsidies. But because leadership teams heard stories of how low-wage workers were intimidated, they also included a protection clause for union organizing in the ordinance. In Nashville, listening attentively to low-wage workers led to a class-action wage-theft lawsuit against a local carwash, which had been one of the few sources of job opportunities for homeless persons or those with criminal convictions. In a unique campaign that included the efforts of the local interfaith worker justice committee and a diligent labor lawyer, the workers were able to negotiate a settlement that included not just $130,000 in back wages but also an air-conditioned break room and an employee manual written in consultation with the workers and faith committee. For these workers, who had almost no leverage for job mobility, wages were important but so was the dignity of negotiating an employee manual and a break room with a TV. As the labor lawyer acknowledged at their victory celebration, no judge would have agreed to the latter requests. But the ties of solidarity cultivated through listening to worker needs prioritized these goals and the workers' agency. Living wages were also about employee voice, dignity, and agency at the workplace.

Structural Conscientization

The reflective action of solidarity leads to a form of "conscientization," or an internalized critical analysis of social reality. This process enables those who are dominated to discern that something is actually amiss in their experiences of poverty, violence, and silencing. As the adult educator Paulo Freire argued, conscientization is more than simply being informed that one is marginalized by certain social forces (a form of "consciousness raising"). Freire instead focused on assisting learners in coming to their own analysis of oppression by having them analyze their own experiences through intentional dialogue. Moving from being "object" to "subject" in this work entailed linking personal stories to others in order to understand the structural nature of domination and oppression.[75] Through this educational process, marginalized persons internalize more deeply their understanding and commitment to broader social change. For example, the Nashville taxi drivers mentioned earlier knew that they were struggling financially. But it was not until these mostly new immigrants and refugees began working with area organizers that they strengthened the overall connections on how bad it was for all of them. Through interviewing and reviewing the records of more than three hundred cabbies, organizers determined that drivers were making only about $2 an hour.[76] As independent contractors, they had to buy their own cars, secure their own insurance, and cover all permits, gas, and repairs. Moreover, in order to drive in Metro Nashville they also had to pay cab companies for renting their "medallion" and dispatch services, on average $175 dollars a week. Because cab companies made their money off of renting their medallions (which cost companies just $235 a year to acquire from the city), drivers also realized that cab companies were pushing for more permits every year from the city and thus flooding the marketplace with cabs. The drivers who helped review and complete the report eventually formed the Metro Nashville Taxi Drivers Association in 2008. With more than six hundred drivers at the first meeting, they lobbied for driver representation on the Metro Taxi Commission (where only cab companies were represented) and industry regulations that would enable them to make a living wage. Through this internalized educational process, those who are suffering and impoverished can turn from relying mostly on the power and charity of more dominant persons to their own commitment and capacity to their shared futures.[77]

Without intentional processes, however, the practices of shared struggle falter in two major ways. First, the depth of the needs and woundedness of another is lost in the abstraction of "issues." Concrete answerability is lost as questions and demands are filtered primarily through more dominant voices. Second, momentum for worker justice often falters since change relies on elites who may enter and exit the realities of working poverty seemingly at will. Insights on arrangements of power lose their depth when organizing rests primarily on elite analysis; concrete processes of conscientization create agency for the long haul. Without a commitment to bridge building and relational accountability, dominated groups and persons lose significant coalitional power and may even perpetuate for others the same structures and logics of domination that once oppressed them. The Roman Catholic theologian Ada Maria Isasi-Diaz argues that

> [t]he connections among forms of oppression indicate that there must be a commonality of interests among the oppressed, which in turn points to the possibility and mutuality of the oppressed. If there is no mutuality among the oppressed, they can very easily become tomorrow's oppressors. Without real mutuality, we run the risk of not bringing about structural change but rather promoting participation of the oppressed in present structures.[78]

The goal of solidarity work is structural change for participatory justice, not using the backs of others as stepladders to power. Justice is "more than refusing to be dominated, it is also about refusing to dominate."[79] Activists who work toward robust "Black-Brown" partnerships and immigration reform within the living wage movement seek to strengthen their collective worker dignity and political power. These organizers find that connecting conversations about individual or group suffering to the stories of other dominated workers is essential for success in places like poultry and meatpacking factories or for taxi-driver alliances.

The strength of the "worker justice" frame is its capacity to hold the intersections of multiple identities together for structural change. Placing "worker" as the essential modifier for justice in living wage campaigns encourages multiple persons to see themselves as its beneficiary. "Worker" is not a single identity but one that allows for multiple identities and negotiations to form new coalitions. For example, the forty participants in a student organizing meeting in Nashville were asked to introduce themselves by sharing their worst work experience. The stories included descriptions of unsafe working conditions, sexual harassment, wage theft, and discrimination based on race and sexuality. In a group where differences in race, ethnicity, sexuality, gender, and religion (and the experiences of those categories) abounded, struggles of work opened the door for conversation and collaboration. With the growing income gap in the United States between the ultrarich and other workers, people who differ in terms of ethnicity, religious background, gender, and sexual identification are feeling the stagnation of wages, workplace abuses, and employment insecurity. "Worker justice" provides an umbrella term that can encompass many of the divides in contemporary U.S. politics, as long as the diversity of identities is preserved.

Complex Identity Recognition

While rigid categories of oppressor and oppressed can provide some insight into the patterned realities of suffering, the lived reality of injustice is often more complicated. Identities change and intersect; most people inhabit the world in multiple and changing positions of power and domination. Almost all persons are privileged in some ways and dominated in others. For example, those who enjoy privilege because of race or gender may simultaneously be vulnerable because of sexual orientation.[80] Atlanta's living wage ordinance succeeded—at least in part—because of its alliance with a domestic partnership bill that brought together constituencies that rarely see themselves as intersecting. But listening to people's concrete sufferings and privileges helps us to recall their multiple identities and to explore pathways for creative solidarity among the differences and shared sufferings.

While strategies for social change should be different based on our changing and intersecting subjectivities and our varied experiences of power and dominance, we must also remember that the suffering of many is often at the hands of a few. That black and Latino workers are disproportionately represented in low-wage jobs and working poverty is the result of a long history of racial discrimination in the United States. Years and even centuries of racialized educational barriers, poor health care, inadequate housing, neighborhood isolation, and stolen generational wealth constitute the infrastructure of the U.S. political economy. Corporations continue to profit from these racialized dynamics through such practices as prison labor for data-entry, telemarketing, and small-product production. For-profit prisons often provide extremely low-wage labor to businesses that would normally hire—for higher wages—from the same neighborhoods where many black and Latino prisoners used to live. The disproportionate number of blacks and Latinos in prison exacerbates the troubles, and the irony, of these neighborhoods: those who once contributed income to their communities are taken disproportionately from the community and displace jobs that once were in those same communities.

Shared struggles for justice must always begin with listening for the isolated and hidden sufferings. Being marginalized and dominated are often linked with being silenced; thus, listening and "hearing-into-voice" become primary efforts in building solidarity. The challenge is to listen "so hard and so carefully that my own narrative will be challenged and my behavior changed," especially for those more privileged in dynamics of power, who are used to speaking and having their voices heard.[81] This listening is personal; recognizing our interdependence helps us understand the overall dynamics of suffering. Walter Rauschenbusch, one of the fathers of the social gospel movement, described his moment of conscientization:

Single cases of unhappiness are inevitable in our frail human life, but when there are millions of them, all running along well-defined grooves, reducible to certain laws, then this misery is not an individual but a social matter, due to causes in the structures of our society and curable only by social reconstruction.[82]

Listening for connections and preferential accountability defines the task of solidarity in any specific context. We may not always inhabit the same "dominant" or "privileged" position in all dimensions of the political economy, but attentiveness to our place in any system helps us better understand the nature of our relational and preferential accountabilities.

This material analysis leads to the recognition that more persons who are defined as white are indeed involved in low-wage work. Black, brown, and white interracial awareness is thus even more necessary for building greater power for worker justice in the United States. In this context, religious activists must also help non-elite whites better understand their class identities and their roles in capitalism. In both the Atlanta and Nashville campaigns, activist researchers expressed surprise that the majority of low-wage government and government-contract workers were white: "We didn't expect that in our research, but it shows you the far reaching effects of low-wage work" and "I started analyzing the results and I decided to have my research assistant contact Metro Government to make sure we had the full database. Our Metro Council allies really appreciated this data, so the issue couldn't be written off as only the concern of black council members." While African Americans are still disproportionately over-represented in lower-wage categories, the reality of the political economy is that low-wage work is by no means confined to a certain racial or even gender demographic. Mary Hobgood, a Roman Catholic ethicist, argues, "What whites need to know is that in the system of late capitalism, empire is increasingly built on the backs of not only diverse communities of color, but increasing numbers of whites, including white men."[83] The drivers of world capitalism make more money off of minimum wages than living wages and will continue to use race tactics to divide lower-waged workers, arguing for example, that immigration, rather than unjust wage practices, is the cause of cheap labor.

Without this critical analysis and sharing of struggles, racial and immigrant scapegoating will only escalate as non-elite whites experience their disempowerment at the hands of elite whites. The theologian Sallie McFague notes, "Whites set up class, race, and other boundaries because we are terrified of how interdependent we really are."[84] Re-embracing that interdependence and understanding its concrete interrelations among all persons is essential for mutually just social change. An emphasis on "material solidarity" (i.e., how our economic interests are intertwined) may help connect the private pain of non-elite whites whose wages are declining with the larger structural dynamics of under-regulated hyper-capitalism.[85] Certainly there are more social forces that trap non-elite blacks and Latinos in working poverty. But finding connections, rather than antagonisms, with non-elite whites is important for the growth of worker justice movements and solidarity praxis.

Of course, working for radically inclusive justice is always easier said than done, particularly in light of our genuine differences and the pervasiveness of social sin. And sometimes pretensions to solidarity discourage or even wound the dominated even more. The Protestant ethicist Emilie Townes comments wisely, "Just because folks espouse solidarity does not mean they either know it or mean it."[86] In an act of self-preservation and taking an absolute stand against evil, she poetically cites June Jordan to proclaim:

> i will not rescue the killers . . .
>> when it comes to solidarity
>>> which i assume is another way to say justice
> i am not interested in them
>> except for how to decrease their numbers
>> and their power . . . [87]

While this may seem at odds with recognizing the suffering of "oppressors" (as in papal teachings), Townes is right that solidarity does not concern itself with those who cause or most benefit from the suffering and dehumanization of others. Preferential action should be the starting point of this shared struggle, countering degradation and building the participatory structures of justice is its focus.

Expansive Moral Agency

In the end, solidarity is not just about alleviating suffering but augmenting the capacity and commitment of the more dominated.[88] This is certainly not an easy road for any of the participants. Bridge-building work can be long and arduous, and making connections to state, national, and international issues are even more complex. Engaging marginalized persons and communities politically takes much sustained organizing. Religious activists (some of whom are themselves members of these communities) offer ideological resources, mediating skills, and civic development assets that help sustain these deep partnerships.

Progressive race-conscious activism requires recruitment from multiple types of civic institutions to expand worker agency. Those persons often overlooked in the lower echelons of corporations often find their voices and refine their political skills in religious institutions. Yet two major risks are associated with this turn to religious institutions: the "grass-tops" model of much religious organizing and the "identity silos" of religious institutions. Grass-tops organizing focuses on recruiting powerful clergy from the city and deploying them in strategic meetings with city councils, businesses, and the like. This organizing model is widely accepted in the living wage movement and explicitly hailed by one of the movement organizations in this study. As one lead organizer explained, "Even with a small group you can make an impact with clergy. There is power in their titles and it tends to be intimidating. They can serve as a great witness." She continued by insisting that organizers ask "What is our value added? What is it only *we* can do?" While this strategy is not problematic as one component in a multifaceted campaign for worker justice, activists who use it as a more isolated strategy miss the expansive nature of theological solidarity. In the end, struggling alongside the marginalized is not merely about distant prevention of social injustice, but cultivating their active and powerful participation within the systems that dominate them. Solidarity moves beyond charity, or even charitable justice, to participatory justice: it must cultivate the political agency of the working poor. Rev. Paul Sherry of Let Justice Roll told other organizers at a national training, "We have to prioritize poor people themselves. They have the muscle, wisdom, and strength. We need their carrying capacity to continue. As a low-wage worker once told me, 'You guys need to remember, truth comes from the bottom.' We need them as much as they need us."[89] For activists to maintain the integrity of their preferential accountability to the dominated and marginalized, the economic political agency of the working poor must remain a priority, not just an abstract issue, in the movement. Religious activists will help lead the movement's solidarity work when they prioritize broader pathways for worker empowerment while avoiding the temptation to base their organizing strategy primarily on a grass-tops use of clergy leaders.

This vision of participatory and allied struggle then calls for deepening the processes for developing indigenous leadership. Churches that wish to be sites for solidarity must analyze how their polity and practices nurture these skills. Verba and his colleagues demonstrate that clergy cannot merely resort to preaching or mentioning justice to encourage social change: participatory skills must be cultivated in congregations. While churches do not need to become radical democracies, leadership development must be intertwined with understandings of spiritual formation for social change. Moral arguments will always be an important dimension of a progressive vision for worker justice in the United States. However, religious resources in building worker solidarity will realize their potential only if religious organizations are recognized as important for bridge building and political development, and if the institutions themselves cultivate these skills among laity.

Finally, solidarity flounders when religious institutions cling to their identity silos. On the one hand, homogeneity allows many participants to gain civic skills that they could not access in other institutions. Yet it can also lead to the seeming isolation or insulation of more privileged congregants from the interdependencies of racialized political economies. Theological solidarity requires greater accountability. Networks across congregations—whether through congregation-based community organizing, religious coalitional organizations, or denominational polities—become particularly important for conscientization. Religious leaders who structurally encourage laity connections across these silos provide essential support for shared struggles and expanded capacities for social transformation. This is certainly not easy work and requires theological support and spiritual nurturance. However, this form of connecting allows believers to move closer to the incarnated solidarity that is often understood as the incarnated body of God in the world.

Sunday mornings (or Friday Prayers and Saturday Shabbat) are still the most segregated times in the United States. But the diversity of religious presence at Tuesday night council meetings or Thursday morning breakfast coalition meetings provide some hope and lessons for racial and ethnic bridge building for economic justice. In these small concrete practices, the grand concept of theological solidarity takes on life and seeks to provide healing for our ruptures and social sins.

4

"Your Daughters Will Prophesy"

Women's Labor in the Movement

The idea for the Atlanta living wage campaign came in the form of a fax. A director at the Atlanta Women's Foundation had just finished reading an article in a business magazine, "What's Wrong with Living Wages." A few minutes later, she faxed Cindia Cameron, the Atlanta-based national organizing director of Working Women 9to5. Across the top of the fax, the director had scrawled, "So, what are you gonna do?" A return fax arrived: "So, are you going to fund it?" Phones rang and a funding relationship formed. Cindia next called Rev. Sandra Robertson, the director of Georgia Citizen's Coalition on Hunger (and a Church of God in Christ minister), who responded, "It must be ordained." With another call to the head of the Atlanta Labor Council, the Atlanta Living Wage Coalition was born.[1]

The sociologist Bruce Nissen notes that three major types of organizations normally anchor living wage coalitions: (1) organized labor organizations (central labor bodies, individual unions), (2) religious bodies or religious-based social-justice organizations, and (3) poverty or low-income community organizing groups.[2] While scholars have given little attention to the contributions of religious organizations, the role of feminist organizations has gone unremarked even more. By overlooking a feminist presence, scholars have missed opportunities to analyze crucial aspects of feminist influence in the movement, including the funding of coalitions from feminist foundations, the organizing activities of feminist groups, and the importance of information supplied by feminist researchers. Moreover, scholars have ignored another intriguing story about the movement: the coalition building among feminist organizations and religiously based social justice organizations that are largely run by women.

Feminist and religious activists and organizations have systematically coordinated their efforts to counter the "feminization of poverty." But two major issues arise in relation to this work. First, both in the living wage movement and in faith-based community organizing, the disproportion-ate presence of women organizers raises stark questions about what we term the "feminization of organizing." The lack of structural support—health care, child care, retirement, and the like—for these women means that they must "sacrifice" for organizing low-wage workers. Because this structural support is lacking, women in the movement (many of whom see this as their "ministry") forego opportunities for vocational develop-ment, and they often burn out at crucial times in their careers. Second, feminist-religious organization coalitions create effective critiques of the gendered economy, but they are vulnerable to conflict around what one religious organizer called "pelvic issues." Even though the movement accepts the feminization of poverty as a core concern, the relationship of women's poverty to reproductive issues still surfaces as a stumbling block for some in the movement. In several cities, for example, the antipathy of Catholic dioceses toward feminist pro-choice organizations disrupted liv-ing wage organizing.

In responding to these issues, further theological-ethical reflection on the "sacrificial" demands of low-wage worker organizing, as well as on the capacity of Christians to reach across difference to "remember the poor," is necessary. The historically unhealthy alliance of sacrifice, service, and women both pragmatically and theologically should give movement allies pause. In addition, Galatians 2:10 reminds Christians that, even in the midst of significant doctrinal difference, aiding the poor is one ethical practice that should unite us ("They asked only one thing, that we remember the poor, which was actually what I was eager to do" [NRSV]). Against a gospel of wedge issues constructed by those in power, the Pauline text reminds fol-lowers to bridge difference in order to resist overwhelming forces of domi-nance (or empire in all its forms) and stand with the poor. The hope is that these reflections will deepen the already important connections between feminists and religiously based organizers in the movement.

Feminists in the Living Wage Movement

Even though a feminist organization was not a featured member of the original Baltimore living wage campaign, feminist organizations and feminists have been present in many other municipal campaigns since 1996, primarily through major feminist-funding networks. Over the last ten years, the Ms. Foundation has supported at least a dozen organizations, which were lead partners or coalition members in local living wage campaigns. From East Bay Alliance for a Sustainable Economy in Oakland, California, to Tenants' and Workers' Support Committee in Alexandria, Virginia, the Ms. Foundation provided grants of between $10,000 and $20,000 under their economic security program. State and municipal women's foundations, such as the one that initiated the funding of the Atlanta living wage campaign, also regularly support coalition partners. Often these gifts are the seed funds for staff and infrastructure that lead to additional local fund-raising and targeted leadership development for women. The willingness of these foundations to fund staff and infrastructure points to their understanding of the enormous human capital needed to shift conversations and action in the current political economy.

Feminist organizations are also leaders, members, and endorsers of many living wage coalitions. The Memphis Living Wage Coalition included the Memphis Area Women's Council (with member organizations such as Planned Parenthood). San Diego's coalition boasted the involvement of the National Organization of Women's local chapter, which has also endorsed municipal living wages as part of their national economic justice platform. And, as in Atlanta, both local and national levels of the feminist organization Working Women 9to5 have prioritized living wages as essential to their platforms for social justice in the workplace.

Feminist researchers have also provided the movement with vital data, including the development of state-by-state self-sufficiency standards through the national organization Wider Opportunities for Women. In this project, Diana Pearce, a social work professor at the University of Washington, partnered with local organizations in more than thirty cities to research what it actually costs to meet basics needs without any public subsidies (such as public housing, food stamps, Medicaid, or child care) or any private/informal subsidies, which are often unpaid labor (such as free babysitting by a relative or friend, food provided by churches or local food banks, or shared housing).[3] Many local campaigns use these data to set their living wage level or to establish the contrast between the wage rate they were requesting and actual needs. With this contrast in mind, coalitions can be politically pragmatic by demonstrating their willingness to compromise. The Ms. Foundation also funded the publication of *Raise the Floor: Wage and Policies that Work for All of Us* and the book's related media campaign, which featured the work of Holly Sklar, political scientist and then director of MediaVision, Laryssa Mykyta, sociologist and then-senior policy analyst for Solutions for Progress, and Susan Wefald, community development expert and then-director of institutional planning for the Ms. Foundation, all of whom analyze the economy from a feminist perspective. Sklar subsequently led the research team for the National Council of Churches' Let Justice Roll living wage campaign. Her economic analyses and editorials have been used across the nation to counter neoclassical economic arguments against raising minimum wages.

(Racial) Feminization of (Working-Class) Poverty

One reason that feminists have worked for gender-neutral living wage ordinances is because of the disproportionate number of women in working poverty in the United States. In the last several years, the "gender gap in poverty" has held steady with women 1.2 times (approximately 124%) more likely to live in poverty than men.[4] A gendered analysis of poverty has become increasingly prominent even as the single-year gender gap in income has been closing. Beginning in the late 1970s, the "feminization of poverty" became an accepted analytical term as scholars, such as Diana Pearce, observed that increased poverty rates for women and children were associated with the growth of female-headed households.[5] In 2008, 37.5% of all single female households with children under the age of eighteen fell below the poverty line (compared to 11.5% of married households with children under eighteen) whereas only 15% of all single male households with children under eighteen fell below the poverty line.[6] Monequi Dobbs, from Atlanta, speaks of these struggles.

> I am a security officer, but I am also a mother. At times my job has caused stress that prevents me from being the type of mother I would like to be.

> I have worked in security for [Atlanta] City Hall for five months. Prior to working at City Hall I was employed by the airport where I also did security. . . . I choose to work in security because it is an important job to society. My job is to secure City Hall. We keep the building safe so that events such as September 11th don't happen here.

I currently live with my grandmother who is disabled and my two-year-old daughter. I am the only wage earner in my house. I have to live with my grandmother because it is the only economically feasible option. Otherwise I would have to live in the "projects," which is no place to raise a child. I can't afford a car and as a result I take [public transportation] to work. This can take as long as an hour and a half. The hours I work are especially hard when it comes to spending time with my daughter. I am not able to put her in day care because I have to leave some mornings too early and come home too late some evenings. I also find myself missing all the important times in her life. I had to miss her second birthday because I was stuck working all day. I have trouble making ends meet on $7 an hour. I am currently in debt because I can't afford to buy necessary items and as a result end up using my credit cards.[7]

While the increased numbers of female-headed households is still considered a factor in the feminization of poverty, debate continues about the root causes of the feminization of poverty.

Many feminist economists and sociologists find that the low-wage jobs held disproportionately by women are a stronger factor in the feminization of poverty than single motherhood. In 2009, 63% of the workers who earned the federal minimum wage were women.[8] Women also predominate in the lowest-wage occupations, which, according to the U.S. Bureau of Labor Statistics, are: (1) food preparation, serving, and related occupations; (2) buildings, grounds cleaning and maintenance; and (3) personal care and service.[9] In her analysis of gendered poverty in seventy American cities, Sarah Lichtenwalter concluded that the percentage of females employed in low-wage occupations, not single female-headed households, is "the primary determinant" of the feminization of poverty.[10]

Although wage growth has been greater overall for women than for men since 1970, feminist researchers caution that the picture is more complicated than simply "closing" the gender wage gap.[11] Women's earning power over time is important if we are to notice the myriad ways that unpaid labor curtails women's lifetime earnings. Currently, the U.S. Bureau of Labor Statistics calculates the gender wage ratio for a single calendar year of full-time earnings. The ratio compares male and female wages in the same occupations during a one-year period. However, if women's earnings are analyzed cumulatively and longitudinally (as, for example, over the course of a fifteen-year period in the "Panel Study of

Income Dynamics"), the gender income gap is even more pronounced, due to the lower number of hours that women work over a working life and their years without pay due to family care.[12] The economists Stephen Rose and Heidi Hartmann maintain that when earnings are analyzed longitudinally, women in their "prime working years"—between the ages of twenty-six and fifty-nine—earn only 38% of what men earn during the same period.[13] Because women still bear most of the burden of unpaid home-based labor, including child and elder care, the majority of women—52%—will miss one full year of earnings in their prime earning years; only 16% of men will. Education and experience do not protect women from this significant income loss over the life span. Women overwhelmingly hold the lowest paid jobs in the United States; combined with this, women's unpaid labor, particularly in caring for children and the elderly, puts them at greater risk for working poverty if they divorce or never marry, especially if they have children.[14]

Even in closing the single-year gender wage ratio, the story is one of gain through loss. Particularly for those in working poverty, closing the single-year gap is tied to the fact that men in the lowest income brackets are generally paid minimum wage, which has been falling in real dollar value for decades. For the working poor, gender equity in wages is illusory, in part because low-wage men are struggling so much in the labor market.[15] This is also where gender equity interacts markedly with race. In 2008, the average median annual income of white women was approximately 79% of what white men earned. Latinas earned 89% of what Latino men earned, and only 60% of white men's earning.[16] Similarly, black women earned approximately 89% of what black men made, which equaled 67% of white men's income.[17] These statistics underscore what the American studies professor Phyllis Palmer called the "racial feminization of poverty."[18] Minority women—black, Latina, and Native American—are simply at greater risk for falling into poverty than are white women.

Ultimately, scholars of the feminization of poverty track not only income inequality but also the "inequalities and biases within households, labor markets, legal codes, and political systems throughout the world" that make women more vulnerable to poverty.[19] Women in the United States are more vulnerable to working poverty as compared with other industrialized countries due to low levels of child support from fathers combined with inadequate welfare payments, family allowances, and child-care support.[20] Comparisons of industrialized Western countries show that the largest gap between female and male poverty rates is in the

United States.[21] As the sociologist Martha Gimenez notes, "[F]or men, poverty is often the consequence of unemployment and a job is generally an effective remedy, while female poverty often exists when a woman works full-time. . . . Virtually all women are vulnerable—a divorce or widowhood is all it takes to throw many middle-class women into poverty."[22] Gimenez also reminds readers that it can be misleading to see gender as the most important variable leading to poverty: "Gender matters among those whose social class location reduces them to the need to work for their economic survival."[23] "Propertyless women" are most at risk of becoming poor, what Gimenez calls the "feminization of working class poverty."[24] When weighing public policy programs to support the populations most in need, it would be a mistake to assume that all women are equally at risk of becoming poor. Class, gender, and race are the powerful co-conspirators of poverty; government policies must be made to reduce their effect.

Although minimum and living wage laws are technically gender neutral, they affect working-class, and particularly minority, women in critical ways. Raising absolute wage growth is the vital concern of both male and female working poor. Although feminist movements were slow to recognize how much gender-neutral wage floors mattered to wage growth for women of the working poor, their current "family-friendly workplace" campaigns regularly include living wages as the starting point for reform.[25] For this and other reasons, feminist organizations and feminists within religious organizations have become important, but often underrecognized, leaders in organizing for low-wage workers.

Feminization of Grassroots Organizing

Even as the feminization of poverty brings feminist organizations to living wage campaigns, another gendered phenomenon arises in the campaigns themselves. The political scientist Richard Wood reports that more than half of all community organizers are women, and half of their board members are women as well: "This is unlike any other sector."[26] Women are also the principal face of low-wage worker organizing, particularly in religiously based groups. Women, many self-identifying as feminists, also make up the preponderance of paid staff and board members of the religious organizations in the movement. In fact, the campaigns in Atlanta, Nashville, Memphis, and San Diego, which are central to this study, were all headed or co-chaired by women, many of them ordained. Organizers in Atlanta were pleased that half of the volunteers from their endorser organizations were men, although they also noted that "women did the hard work" in the campaign. At the national level, 59% of the local IWJ chapters in the nation are headed by women; the national network office, itself founded and run by a religious laywoman, is currently staffed predominantly by ordained and laywomen. At least within religiously based organizing, a *feminization of organizing* has seemingly occurred. Why is this so and what are its implications?

One of the important things to remember about religion in the United States is that women are overrepresented in congregational attendance, accounting for at least 59% of religious attendees. But because of the long-standing patriarchal practices of religious traditions, women are much less likely to be paid clergy in some congregations. Only 8% of U.S. Christian congregations have a female clergy leader and only 5% of Christian church-goers attend a congregation led by a woman,[27] while women make up about 30% of all students in Christian theological higher education overall.[28]

Social service has been a time-honored alternative for women excluded from clerical leadership. Those with "callings" were often encouraged to work for "charities" or take on roles as diaconal ministers (deacons who serve at the intersection of "church and society" and have ministries of "word and service" but normally not "word and sacrament"). But the political nature of social justice ministries has moved them far from this traditional charity work. In social justice ministries and organizations, organizers analyze local power, develop indigenous leaders, build advocacy networks, lobby political leaders, and raise funds to maintain their organizations. Even though direct service may sometimes be involved, organizers focus primarily on building political agency with and on behalf of the working poor and their allies.

The number of women leading religiously based, social justice organizations opens doors for collaborations with feminist organizations. In 2003 the Washington-based IWPR started a project investigating "the values that motivate and guide women's public activism around social justice issues" in order to "build stronger ties between women social justice activists, particularly in religious and interfaith organizations, and the women's movement."[29] With funding from the Ford Foundation and the Sisters Fund, the project coordinators have produced two major books, convened a Working Group on Women's Public Vision, and presented at feminist and interfaith conferences around the country. In 2007 IWPR led a day-long, pre-conference at the National Interfaith Worker Justice Conference focused on "Strengthening Women's Leadership in Organizing." Additionally, the Ruth Ray Hunt Memorial Fund of the New York Women's Foundation sponsors "Faith, Feminism, and Philanthropy," a multiyear initiative in several cities that brings women from diverse secular and religious backgrounds together for conversation and collaboration around economic self-sufficiency.[30]

These programs are important because they expand the processes of political engagement that often overlook women with limited economic, educational, and occupational advantages. Individuals develop resources (e.g., skill sets, social capital, organizational affiliations, and money) through participation in various nonpolitical institutions; these resources influence their capacity and willingness to engage in political activity. Increased church activity is one of the only factors mitigating the determinism associated with low socioeconomic status and low political participation.[31] Women's presence in this political activism holds even more importance because women are also generally less politically active than men. Although women often vote more than men, they are less likely to be affiliated with political organizations or contact their representatives on issues.[32] Compared to 53% of men, only 46% of women think they can influence local politics.[33]

Amy Caiazza reports in her study of women interfaith community organizers that the most common barrier to political activism is the fear of taking on public roles. This is amplified for women of color, particularly when they come from low-income or immigrant backgrounds. One Latina immigrant reported, "I remember my father saying to me, 'Don't even look at someone eye to eye. It's disrespectful. You lower your sight, you don't stare at someone.' So, the whole idea I would be taught how to confront was terrifying."[34] Some women, particularly minorities and immigrants, also fear physical and political retribution if they speak out. The history of political violence against African American women in the United States can cause some to avoid political participation. Latina immigrants report being told to shun politics to avoid retributive firings or even deportation. Muslim women activists describe how the increased surveillance and violence since 9/11 can discourage them from politics.[35]

Overcoming these barriers to women's political activism takes special efforts. Based on her observations, Caiazza concludes that interfaith religious organizations do this best when they not only provide the space for women to confront their fears and their anger, but gently push women into greater leadership roles, build alliances across race and class, and develop intentional mentoring programs. Kim Bobo of IWJ national explains it this way:

> We do training, both in group settings and individually, around, how do you present stuff in a way that you'll be taken seriously? How do you run a meeting so that you're taken seriously? And how do you deal with the problem people you're going to have? . . . Women will say, oh, I don't know anything, I couldn't possibly do that. . . . You don't have confidence? Fine. Pretend for awhile. And you'll eventually get some.[36]

In this way, women-dominated religious organizations help model political engagement and political leadership for other women. This feminist intentionality is important and crucial for broadening women's political agency. As one young woman described her experience in religious organizing, "I'm like government actually works! People actually get stuff done! I was just so excited to be a part of that. So I've been involved the last four years . . . I've snowballed into a better activist . . . I'm just trying to do as much as I can, because I think the more people who get involved, the more we can change our country."[37] The ubiquitous presence of women in religious community organizing can contribute to this sense of empowerment and efficacy.

Yet for many women of faith, new opportunities in economic justice organizations come with significant concerns and costs. When religious women take leadership roles in campaigns for living wages, they are once again committing themselves to work that pays them little and demands enormous personal and familial sacrifice. In fact, faith-based activism could be seen as a new sector of underpaid and unpaid women's work in the United States.

At an IWJ pre-conference in 2007, about one hundred professional organizers, almost all women, gathered to reflect on the challenges and contributions of women to organizing. One of their first tasks was to list the challenges they faced in organizing. In small groups, they shared their stories and struggles. As the groups posted their paper sheets at the front of the room, the facilitator noted similar themes: "Overworked"; "Health care"; "Child care"; "Money"; "Respect." But when the facilitator read out "Refusal to Name the Problem" on one of the sheets, participants expressed their affirmation particularly loudly.

As the women unpacked their comments, several critical themes emerged that echoed conversations I had heard elsewhere. First, organizing requires enormous flexibility in work schedules. Work on nights and weekends, and travel (even if locally) are almost always necessary. Finding child- and elder-care support is extremely difficult for those with significant family commitments, which still fall heavily on women and increase with the growth of women-led households. As a female Nashville organizer bemoaned, "I feel like I'm always late for someone. My babysitter, a worker, my kids. My days and weeks change so much that I'm always having to scramble to get child care. People have just had to get used to me dragging them along. But you should see some of these union guys when I bring my kids along to a meeting." Social justice organizations are not big enough to offer on-site care, and the unconventional work hours place many women organizers outside of the normal day-care system. Many professional organizers testify that young women continually enter the field and then drop out because they need regularized routines and dependent care. A male volunteer with a Chicago IWJ affiliate noted regretfully, "Yeah, we just churn and burn 'em. . . . We get these great women in their early twenties, they work so hard for about three or five years and then have to leave us when they want to start families. Some of them come back to volunteer in their late thirties, but we lose so much talent and momentum . . . and they can't stay in their calling."[38] The Nashville organizer quoted earlier had "retired" for several years after her children were born because of the demands on time and money. Maintaining a career in organizing is challenging financially: salaries are low, few organizers receive family health care coverage, and even fewer have retirement plans. As a religious organizer said to a union organizer at an IWJ national conference, "Well, at least you all have benefits! I think ours is the 'consider the lilies of the field' plan," a reference to the biblical assurance that God would provide if one has faith.[39]

In addition, movement work consists largely of organizing male-dominated sectors of clergy and labor. While women's leadership has expanded in both sectors, stories abound of disrespect, underevaluation, and being discounted. "Don't get me started on how many times I've been asked to take minutes for meetings—that I'm leading!"[40] "A union organizer recently asked me if I'd ever really been a worker . . . because I was too attractive to have worked my way up to be an organizer."[41] There are plenty of strategies for strengthening women's activist work (e.g., "provide space to embrace their anger," "develop mentoring programs," "meet women where they are"[42]), but few religious organizations address organizing as a sustainable occupation. Unions are beginning to address these problems with proposals for sharing lead organizing jobs and upgrading benefits.[43] But, again, few of these proposals have been implemented in unions, let alone in the arena of religiously based organizers beyond the FBCO affiliate networks (IAF, PICO, DART, and Gamaliel).

Enhancing Moral Agency: Sacrifice and Structural Supports for Organizing

Religious traditions widely value and even sanctify—confirm the holiness of—sacrifice, but many contemporary feminist theologians and ethicists regularly criticize this stance. Although sacrifice for the good of others is often revered in religious traditions, women have historically borne both the expectation and practice of sacrificing their lives to the needs of their children, husbands, and community. Even early suffragists questioned the prioritizing and sanctifying of sacrifice as the primary Christian virtue. In 1893 the Methodist minister and suffragist Anna Howard Shaw argued that "The greatest defect in the religious teaching to and accepted by women is the dogma that self-abnegation, self-effacement, and excessive humility were ideal female virtues."[44] In 1960 the pioneering feminist theologian Valerie Saiving Goldstein criticized the influential Christian ethicist Reinhold Niebuhr for construing the human condition from "a masculine standpoint."[45] Niebuhr, like many Protestants, understood *agape* (the love of God) as idealized in Jesus' wholly other-regarding sacrifice on the cross.[46] He argued that in contrast to God's self-sacrificing love, humans were naturally prideful and needed humility to offset this sin (or spiritual brokenness). Goldstein countered that women's primary sin is not pride but self-abnegation. Particularly because women are charged with nurturance, they more often neglect their own development as persons and need instead to emphasize autonomy and self-realization in their spiritual journey. The Christian ethicist Barbara Andolsen later summarized this as the core problem with sacrifice as a religious virtue: "Men have espoused an ethic which they did not practice; women have practiced it to their detriment."[47] Women, and religious women in particular, often do not properly balance self-regard and self-love with other-regard and love of neighbor.

Even if not directed solely at women, the strong religious tradition of sacrifice in service to the poor also complicates the practice of women organizers. In Catholic traditions, especially in mendicant orders and lay associations such as Catholic Worker communities, voluntary poverty is prized as a spiritual practice. The value put on voluntary poverty, combined with the gendered history of service, can have a particularly strong impact on religious women organizers. In their calling to help the poor, their sacrifices of material gain are often seen as worthy and necessary.

Yet Catholic traditions see "voluntary poverty" as a special calling, not the path for all persons of faith or everyone who works with the poor. Solidarity with the poor is foundational to the nature of the church and the practice of all discipleship. In contrast, voluntary poverty is part of the "evangelical counsels" intended for those few seeking a path of perfection in this life. Those called usually take vows of poverty under the supervision of a religious order that holds possessions in common, provides health care, and secures retirement benefits. Even in these orders, poverty is not the final goal or virtue but is rather a clearing away of worldly attachments and distractions for complete devotion to God. While salutatory in the church's view, voluntary poverty is not required of the whole church, or even of all ministers.

In stark contrast, many Protestant traditions explicitly resist the specialized call to voluntary poverty, arguing that God does not require it of anyone. The Westminster Confession of 1647, recorded in the contemporary *Book of Confessions* of the Presbyterian Church (USA), explicitly states,

> No man may vow to do anything forbidden in the Word of God, or what would hinder any duty therein commanded, or which is not in his own power, and for the performance whereof he hath no promise or ability from God. In which respects, monastical vows of perpetual single life, professed poverty, and regular obedience, are so far from being degrees of higher perfection, that they are superstitious and sinful snares, in which no Christian may entangle himself.[48]

While a historical anti-Catholic tone certainly frames this statement, it is still seen as guiding the contemporary reformed church.[49] It also underscores that even if everyone is called to reduce poverty, no one is required to go into poverty to minister to people who are poor.

Most of the women of faith who are movement organizers are not the nuns or mendicants who take vows of celibacy and, in their simplicity, are supported by the health care, housing, and retirement system of a centralized church. They are women with dependents, not living in parsonages; many cannot even buy into group family health care, let alone receive retirement contributions. Clearly, women find organizing—particularly among low-wage workers—extremely hard to sustain in the long term.

On one hand, the feminization of religious organizing is one example of a sociological phenomenon: disproportionate numbers of women taking on social service and political work that has low societal power and prestige. On the other hand, in acknowledging their burnout and the need to exit periodically from this work, women organizers also display a feminist resistance to being trapped in roles that are sacrificially structured. In many ways, women organizers are caught between conflicting ethical frameworks—one that espouses women's self-regard and another that espouses radical "sacrifice" to serve the poor. Combine this with the reality of scarce funding for organizing, and women organizers are indeed caught in a kind of paradox: the cause ignites their passions, yet working for it rapidly burns them out.

People of faith and churches need to reflect carefully on organizers' resistance to institutionalized voluntary poverty. Are we requiring working poverty of those serving the working poor? And why do women continue to carry this burden disproportionately? New approaches to funding relationships for sustaining organizers and their long-term vocational agency may offer some solutions. Organizers themselves suggest developing retention committees for women organizers. These committees would not necessarily supervise but rather reflect on what it takes for women organizers to thrive in the environment (consider sabbaticals, flex time, etc., for organizers). Others suggest the financing model of FBCOs where congregations pay annual fees by congregation size to join the network, and the network actually pays the salaries and benefits for longtime organizers who are trained by the network. (However, others counter that this model operates so heavily on congregational self-interest that it not likely to work for low-wage issue organizing.)[50]

In addition, ecclesial institutions might open their ordination tracks and benefits programs more fully to women of faith who are organizing the poor. Denominations need to explore the barriers and supports for those desiring a ministry in faith-based organizing. Even if ordination is not possible (e.g., Roman Catholic, Southern Baptist, Presbyterian Church of America, Eastern Orthodox, etc.), religious institutions could consider helping organizers buy into group health care and benefits plans. Feminist foundations have taken the lead in experimenting with funding solutions by directing their gifts to infrastructure and staff financing, something that is rare in the foundation world. Most other foundations prefer to fund innovative "programs" that provide little margin for "overhead," or staff salaries. Yet organizing is an intensive relational process that requires building trust across time and boundaries of race, gender, and class. When foundations fund "new" programs at the expense of staff time, women organizers have little opportunity to build the organizing networks that identify possible participants and funds for maintaining the organization's gains.

Although feminist theologians and others have challenged the ideology of sacrifice as a virtue, much more is required to divorce this ideology from the institution of organizing. A preferential option for the poor invites those who fund professional organizers to reconsider how we might make this ministry a sustainable priority rather than an optional, and rare, exceptional calling for select people of faith. Ed Chambers, heir to the community organizer Saul Alinsky and founder of the Industrial Areas Foundation training school, stated, "Creating the profession of organizing included a lot more than quality training. Decent salaries had to be paid. Health benefits and retirement plans had to be created. Proper vacations and sabbaticals had to be arranged. Most importantly, the needs and well-being of organizer's marriages and families had to be taken seriously. All these steps went in the opposite direction of the post–World War II culture of *machismo*."[51] Only a few FBCOs have been able to establish Chambers's vision. But sustainable organizing of low-wage workers requires a faithful, feminist reordering of our organizing institutions and their funding, a transformation far beyond the feminization of organizing.

Coalition Fissures: Production and Reproduction

In facing the challenges of working poverty and sustaining women organizers, feminists and faith-based women activists are deepening their relationships and linkages through involvement in living wage coalitions. In their shared concerns for economic justice, these activists have identified and developed sources of power and potential. But as feminist and religiously based organizations work together in the living wage movement, wedge issues have also brought serious cracks to the surface of their partnership, which are most likely to appear when partnering organizations differ on the issues and may increase as the movement matures and links to other economic justice issues.

The wedge issue most often evident was abortion: Would abortion foes collaborate on a non-abortion issue? The National Organization for Women, Planned Parenthood, and the Roman Catholic Church have all endorsed living wage ordinances in multiple cities; in others, their abortion-based conflict has blocked coalition work and endorsements. For example, the Atlanta Living Wage campaign nurtured a broad range of organizational support, with over 101 supporting organizations. Noticeably absent from their endorsees and coalition partners at their public announcement in 2001 was the Catholic Archdiocese of Atlanta. With Catholic social teachings providing much of the foundations of the historical and contemporary living wage movements, this absence was glaring. A coalition leader explained it this way: because of her feminist ties, NOW and Planned Parenthood were among the first endorsers of the living wage ordinance in Atlanta. With these signers in place, the leader's Archdiocese connections informed her that they could not sign on to a coalition that included pro-abortion organizations even though they supported the measure privately. Although this did not derail the Atlanta Living Wage Coalition (and several Catholic congregations endorsed the ordinance individually), the negotiations did illuminate the limits of religious ideology in a coalition where abortion foes have a particularly bitter history. In other cities, religious groups act preemptively, not even seeking funding from feminist networks. In one of these cities, the campaign director commented, "We have a very conservative diocese here, I wasn't about to upset them." Part of their funding came from Catholic sources and the bishop had endorsed the ordinance.

Enhancing Moral Agency: Remembering the Poor

One cannot underestimate the importance of anti-abortion stances for many Christians and particularly the Roman Catholic Church. Although many people of faith also are pro-choice, abortion is a wedge issue that is hard to resolve. The Vatican doctrinal note on Roman Catholics' participation in politics in fact underscores the centrality of their "seamless garment of life" convictions for political participation:

John Paul II, continuing the constant teaching of the Church, has reiterated many times that those who are directly involved in law-making bodies have a "*grave and clear obligation to oppose*" any law that attacks human life. For them, as for every Catholic, it is impossible to promote such laws or to vote for them. As John Paul II has taught in his Encyclical Letter Evangelium Vitae regarding the situation in which it is not possible to overturn or completely repeal a law allowing abortion which is already in force or coming up for a vote, "an elected official, whose absolute personal opposition to procured abortion was well known, could licitly support proposals aimed at *limiting the harm* done by such a law and at lessening its negative consequences at the level of general opinion and public morality."[52]

Yet even within this doctrinal note, the Vatican states that attention to one issue cannot undo commitments to other core social commitments of the faith. Under the direction of Cardinal Ratzinger, now Pope Benedict XVI, the guidance continues:

> The Christian faith is an integral unity, and thus it is incoherent to isolate some particular element to the detriment of the whole of Catholic doctrine. A political commitment to a single isolated aspect of the Church's social doctrine does not exhaust one's responsibility towards the common good.

Even in a document emphasizing the importance of the Catholic Church's anti-abortion platform, the holistic vision of the common good is most essential to Catholic political engagement.

The U.S. Council of Catholic Bishops argues, "For Catholics, the defense of human life and dignity is not a narrow cause, but a way of life and a framework for action."[53] And that way of life includes support for the dignity and rights of workers. In their advice on faithful participation in politics, the Council underscores that stance:

> Church teaching on economic justice insists that economic decisions and institutions be assessed on whether they protect or undermine the dignity of the human person. We support policies that create jobs for all who can work with decent working conditions and adequate pay that reflects a living wage. We also support efforts to overcome barriers to equal pay and employment for women and those facing

unjust discrimination. We reaffirm the Church's traditional support of the right of workers to choose to organize, join a union, bargain collectively, and exercise these rights without reprisal.[54]

Commitment to worker dignity is integral to the whole of Christian political engagement. Especially when a signature of support for living wages has no explicit relationship with the endorsement of abortion, the diocese arguments for abstention seem weakened.

Certainly, Catholic leadership worries that joining a coalition with pro-abortion organizations might imply endorsement of other agendas. Reflection on scriptural sources may add another perspective to these discussions. For even when they were divided by deep theological issues, the early Christian church united around poverty as a cause that demonstrated the power of the gospel. In Galatians 2:1–10, Paul recounts his visit to the Jewish Jerusalem church leaders in order to make his case that non-Jewish followers of what was to become "Christianity" did not need to convert to Judaism first, be circumcised, and follow Mosaic Law.[55] Many scholars note the bitterness between the factions on that controversy, a significant one in the early church.[56] Paul had not returned to Jerusalem for fourteen years, and many of the "circumcision faction" even broke off table fellowship with the non-Jewish followers.[57] Paul recounts to the Gentile Galatians the rigorous debate of the Jerusalem meeting, even claiming the presence of "false brothers" and "spies" in its midst. He continues, "Those who were supposed to be acknowledged leaders . . . contributed nothing to me." This strong statement can be read either as Paul's statement of independence or as testimony that the Jerusalem leaders ultimately imposed no restrictions on his work.[58] But either reading still leads to the conclusion of the passage. In agreeing to abide their differences, the Jerusalem leaders ask only one thing of Paul: that he "remember the poor" (Gal. 2:10, NRSV). The Jerusalem leaders acknowledge that even if Paul's mission is not theirs, his mission is important as well. After extending the hand of fellowship, their sole admonition of Paul is to "remember the poor."[59]

Paul certainly meant this passage to testify to the legitimacy of his "gospel to the Gentiles." But considering that Paul worked throughout the Roman Empire, we might add another layer of interpretation. The biblical scholar Brigette Kahl notes that identity with the Roman Empire and worship of the god of Caesar largely defined unity in Paul's time.[60] The Galatians were a conquered people who went through civic rehabilitation and incorporation into the Roman Empire by participating in the imperial religious cult, making offerings and sacrifices to Roman gods, and hosting banquets and public events in the emperor's honor. Jews, by contrast, were ambiguous figures in the Roman Empire. Rome reluctantly categorized them as a legal religion exempted from the cultic practice of the imperial religion. But Paul does not want a limitation on the diversity of practicing Christian communities or ritual conformity because of Rome's influence. Rather than worshipping the Roman Empire or conforming to its religious category of proper "others," Paul argues that fellowship across this difference can and should abide. Giving into an exclusive "gospel of circumcision" ultimately would submit Christians to the imperial gospel of power and status.[61]

In our contemporary context, Christian ethicists often identify the economic, cultural, political, and military dominance wielded by the United States in the world as the "American empire." In the Catholic ethicist Thomas Massaro's explanation, "To employ the label 'empire' is to make a claim about domination, about asymmetrical power relationships between a hegemon and its less powerful neighbors."[62] With its political, cultural, and military power, the United States spreads and supports it interests—often economic—around the world.[63] In an even more nuanced argument, contemporary empire is located not just in American hands but also in the power of neoliberalism worldwide. Elsa Tamez, a liberation theologian and biblical scholar, suggests, "Freedom from the present evil age" (Gal. 1:4, NRSV) has more resonance with "today's market economy . . . guided by neoliberal policies which are not oriented by the criterion of life for all people."[64] The gospel (and law) of the contemporary empire is the efficiency and good of the neoliberal market.

This pervasive neoliberal view of the political economy means that religious persons must work hard to envision and enact alternatives. This imperial power would much rather have religious communities defined along a range of personal morality wedge issues. Roman Catholics, white evangelicals, and the like are much more easily contained when they are associated primarily with anti-abortion and anti-gay political activism. Reductionism serves the politics of interest groups and the power play that defines empire, and it upholds a competitive neoliberal market. The gospel of wedge issues slowly submits religious belief and practice to the reductionist power of contemporary empire and the logic of the "free" market.

The Galatians text invites resistance to the gospel of wedge issues. Moreover, the text invites believers to share the anti-imperial ethic of "remembering the poor." Rather than seeing the Galatians either in the Roman Empire or as a small sectarian—and easily contained—community, Paul holds firm to an expansive vision of the gospel, a vision marked by attention to the poor who are without status. Kahl explains that "Material solidarity with the poor is the seal of 'being in Christ,' the social embodiment of the 'handshake of the community' between Paul and the Jerusalem leaders." Across their doctrinal difference, Gentile and Jewish Christians shared a commitment to the poor. This form of spiritual, economic, and political solidarity both in Paul's time and in ours ultimately "subverts and contradicts the imperial order."[65]

The Pauline text does not suggest that remembering the poor will solve deep doctrinal or ethical differences. But it does invite Christians to think about how their "othering" serves the Roman Empire and what brings unity in the gospel. In living wage coalitions, the biblical text invites coalition participants to move beyond religious practice defined, and thus confined, by wedge issues, particularly when those issues are not the work of the coalition. Solidarity in the form of remembering the poor subverts the contemporary empire in myriad ways.

Sustaining Coalitions for Working Women

By partnering together in the living wage movement, religious and feminist organizations bring a remarkable focus to the burden of working poverty borne by so many women in this country. But feminist analyses of these coalitions also highlight the feminization of organizing and the conflict over reproductive issues in the movement. Structural reform and maintaining diversity in remembering the poor are starting points for strengthening these coalitions over time. Especially around issues of reproduction and the political economy, there is much more to be said. Birthing and raising children, women bear myriad unpaid costs that support those in the paid economy. This disproportionate burden is only one of the reasons many feminist organizations view reproductive freedoms as part of economic sustainability packages. But at minimum, Christian traditions must offer ways forward for collaboration and recognize the important coalition work that can be done, even amid grave differences. As with Paul, we must remember our common ethical ground, and the structural support it requires, if we are to challenge the dominance of neoliberalism.

5

"Where Two or Three Are Gathered"

Ritualizing Moral Agency

Memphis, Tennessee, is best known for blues, barbeque, and Elvis. But among religious activists, it is also known for fasting. As part of the efforts of Workers' Interfaith Network (WIN) to enact citywide living wage legislation in 2006—efforts that were successful—and subsequently to expand the ordinance's reach, forty-hour fasts have become a mainstay of coalition activism. The organization, led by an ordained female United Methodist minister, draws on the long tradition of religious fasting both to sharpen devotion to the sacred and to bring attention to injustice. The 2008 fast was timed to fall within Lent (the traditional forty days of fasting and repentance from Ash Wednesday to Easter), and to coincide with the forty-year interfaith remembrance service for the Memphis Sanitation Worker's strike where Martin Luther King Jr. had spoken and marched shortly before his death. Hosted by a local Methodist congregation, the service included workers sharing their stories in the midst of scriptures, prayers, and hymns. Like an altar call near the end of the service, participants were asked to place a blue commitment card in the offering plate (monetary offerings could also be made). Activists were encouraged to abstain from solid food for forty hours ("as a sign of sacrifice and solidarity with workers whose jobs do not pay enough to meet their families basic needs"), to pray ("about the morality of our economy"), and to write politicians urging them to expand living wages.[1] The accompanying "The Fast for a Living Wage" guide included theological justifications for fasting.

> People of faith must be especially concerned about whether workers are sharing in the fruits of their labor. Whether it is Islam's teaching on the importance of worker's receiving 'the benefit of what they earn,' or Judaism and Christianity's shared story about a king who

forces people to build him a palace without just pay, our faiths teach us that we should pay workers a wage that does not leave them destitute . . . .

During the Fast for a Living Wage, we will lift up a cry for justice with working poor people in our community and our nation. We will repent of our communal sin of allowing workers to be ground down by poverty. We will pray for our elected officials, at local and national levels, to hear the call for a living wage. We will urge our elected officials to act for a living wage.

Four suggested prayers were also offered for evening, morning, midday, and evening during the fast. At 11 a.m. on Saturday morning at another area church, clergy helped participants end the fast with a formal "breaking of the bread" and a simple meal.[2]

Choosing to fast, pray for affected workers, and write local politicians over a forty-hour period is just one way that religious activist organizations invite people of faith to see their religious practices as political practices for economic justice. Through the use of familiar rituals, refashioned and resituated in the political economy, religious activists draw on the practices of faith to deepen and enhance the moral commitments and agency of participants.

The Multiple Roles of Ritual in Living Wage Activism

Religious rituals are potent practices that have united persons in common action since the beginning of recorded history. Thus we are not surprised to see them when people are struggling with issues of survival, basic fairness, and political authority. The ethicist David Craig argues that "Ritual [i]s a semiscripted performance, the formal structure and frequent repetition of which helps make participants' desires into meaningful expressions of identities, bonds, and purposes upheld by a . . . community or a[n] . . . association."[3] Religious rituals regularly serve as a way for people to participate in collective meaning making and to claim their agency. Through these practices, people claim their capacity to "do" something in light of their faith, gratitude, joy, doubt, suffering, and yearning.

In the political arena, religious rituals have been employed to shore up political regimes, promote oppression, and demonize opponents. But they also can offer an alternative, collective power that disrupts dominant norms and expectations with a different moral vision for a society. Religious rituals, when enacted by religious activists in the living wage movement, are meant to stop politics as usual and, even if only momentarily, present economic relationships that are more just and compassionate.

Religious rituals help form the *collective identity* of an activist group and offer a *low risk* type of activism. Moreover, performing religious rituals in protest of the current political economy also contests the boundaries of the *sacred and profane,* boundaries that often benefit the powerful. Drawing too on *embodied testimony,* religious activists *remember the sacred,* or expand the numbers of persons and places that should be included in sacred care for greater justice. Together, these symbolic activities enhance the moral capacity and commitment of those who engage in religiously based activism.

In the face of this demonstration of moral agency, opponents frequently challenge religious activists' use of religious ritual. Critics of living wage activism often claim that unions "dupe" the clergy and, even more pointedly, "use" religious rhetoric and practice for partisan political ends. Some of this complaint may be frustration at the activists' seeming monopoly on moral resources. But religious organizers must also recognize the temptation of using theology and ritual instrumentally to short-term political effect. In the end, connection to enduring communities of worship (congregations, intentional communities, and so on) is necessary for keeping these rituals *lithe and authentic,* renewing the *whole context of faith* that makes sense of political work, and providing a longer-term vision of the *liturgical nature of activism* itself.

Collective Identity

Research has shown that people do not join social movements based on simple cost-benefit analyses.[4] Sociologists who study social movements have begun to focus on the movements' cultural practices, looking at how activists mobilize and construct identities in service of their political work.[5] While we all have multiple identities (sister, teacher, sports fan, etc.), social movement activists specifically cultivate vital *collective identities* in order to encourage participation, to bond persons for greater risk-taking, and to offer a source of power for those less dominant in society.[6] The sociologist Sharon Nepstad notes that "Not all collective identities have equal moral weight . . . for committed people of faith, however, religious identities have great moral significance."[7] For those whose collective identity is shaped in religious traditions, religious ritual often offers connections to a compelling form of meaning making and life sustenance. Or, as Christian Smith explains it, "*Homo oeconomicus* . . . is often joined, carried, and sometimes overridden by *homo ritualis, homo affectus, homo significans,* and *homo symbolicus.*"[8] In activist movements, these religious rituals have a powerful thrust; a reductionist "rational actor" explanation misses the point.

Here is one example. At four o'clock in the afternoon in busy downtown Chicago, an anxious worker stood among the IWJ picketers at a sidewalk protest. She had recently been fired for union organizing and protesting the wage structure at her hospital. She was present that day to tell her story over the bullhorn. Her story was compelling, but what happened next brought her and those around her to tears. At the end of her testimony, the director of IWJ called on the clergy present to lay hands on the woman and pray for her courage and continued journey. While the hands of eight clergy touched her, prayers also went out over the bullhorn. Passersby stopped, the picket line slowed, and sounds of "Yes . . . yes" and "Amen" filled the air. The woman began to cry. A powerful connection was made not only with the woman's individual story but also with the cause of worker justice itself. As the one hundred or so activists filed onto buses later, conversations continued about the power of that moment, with comments of "That's what our work is about."

The worker's story was certainly important in the rhythm and focus of the protest. Participants encouraged her with clapping and head nodding as she told it. But something else happened in the religious ritual that followed. Whether it was in claiming and being claimed by the laying on of hands, the power of extended touch that offers healing or commission, or the physical acknowledgement of sacred solidarity, a collective identity, based in worker justice, emerged in that moment. And radical individuality faded in that same, shared moment. The worker's value and pain were acknowledged beyond her "usefulness" to the movement. And, the words and actions of other participants resonated with and extended the religious foundations of their activism in solidarity with her risk.

Sociologists routinely note that religious rituals produce emotion that can form and enliven a group. The emotion of ritual practice often serves to consolidate group identity and weave commitments among participants. Nepstad states that as individuals embark on ritual practice—their movements and language synchronize with one another—their attention is drawn to a mutual focus. This fosters unity and an awareness of shared moral beliefs. Feelings of isolation dissipate as one develops a sense of belonging to the group. Rituals move people beyond their individual existence to a collective existence.[9]

The physicality, shared focus, and emotion serve to forge the collective identity necessary for the solidarity and sustenance of a movement. Moreover, emotion in a social movement can produce spiritual insight, healing, and strength, all of which activists deeply value in and of themselves—not just for the political ends pursued.

Lower Risk

Participating in the laying on of hands on a sidewalk is not a high-risk protest action. In the United States, religious activists are unlikely to be arrested or harmed for this kind of public ritual. Police told the picketers to keep moving; but on *that* day, they did not tell the clergy to keep walking when they laid hands on the worker. In a public, politicized space, the religious ritual was practiced without much fear. In many ways, this *lower risk* is part of the power and efficacy of religious ritual in U.S. living wage activism. Religious rituals are low risk in two ways: they rarely lead to arrest or violence, and they offer new activists a familiar form for participating. Thus, they widen opportunities for persons of faith to participate in the movement.

Since they are a form of norm breaking, protest and activism involve some risk.[10] But sociological research indicates that new activists rarely undertake high-risk protest activities. Seeking arrest, agreeing to jail time, and risking the deprivation of one's income and life normally require significant socialization, a slow transformation of self, and significant "biographical availability" (such as flexible work, lack of family constraints, etc.).[11] Low-risk activism grows out of attitudinal affinity and, especially, a direct invitation to join. In addition, opportunities to "play at being an activist" are a "prerequisite to becoming one."[12] In this process, some recruits will engage in higher risk activism—such as interrupting work at an unjust work site or filing a lawsuit—but only a few activists in the United States ever move toward high-risk activism in any social movement.

Familiar forms of religious activity invite people of faith to participate and provide them with opportunities for trying on a new activist identity. The fasting in Memphis was a largely familiar and low-risk practice for participants. But it also prepared participants for the slightly higher-risk activity at subsequent protests. Later that year, WIN activists invited some of their children to lead them into city hall with red wagons filled with living wage petitions. The targeted city council members, however, refused to come down to receive the signatures. So WIN activists began to sing "We Will Not Be Moved." The song itself originated as a spiritual, declaring, "I will not be moved . . . I'm on my way to glory, I shall not be moved"; in the late nineteenth century it was adapted as a labor song and then, in the early twentieth century as a black civil rights anthem. For forty-five minutes they sang. Finally, the council members conceded and came down to accept thousands of signatures for the living wage law. Standing in a government building singing certainly entails increased risk—there is a chance of forcible removal, loss of social capital with city leaders, and possible arrest. But religious singing, with your children, is certainly not as threatening to its intended audience as chanting or shouting. The hymn itself is familiar, invites participation (sometimes from casual observers), and holds audience attention, even when that audience is besieged politicians.[13]

Understanding the importance of these activities, organizations such as IWJ have spent significant time and money reviving and expanding the use of religious rituals related to labor issues within congregations themselves. The national IWJ program "Labor in the Pulpit/on the Bimah/in the Minbar"[14] specifically seeks to incorporate labor concerns into the worship weekend before Labor Day through prayer, scripture, song, and ritual.[15] Since 1996, thousands of local religious communities have participated. The successful San Diego living wage campaign was actually launched through the 2001 Labor in the Pulpits weekend with eighty different services in thirty-nine congregations, reaching 15,000 members.[16]

At a Labor Day worship service in Nashville, the altar included tools of labor: a drill, a keyboard, pruning sheers, blood pressure cuff, and so on. Hand drumming set the stage for a worship service focused around the hands of labor in the congregation. A local taxi driver testified about the injustices in the Nashville taxi system. Later in the service, congregants meditated on their own hands, the numerous hands that make our lives possible, and God's hand in the world, leading to this blessing of hands:

Blessed be the works of your hands,
O Holy One.
Blessed be these hands that have touched life.
Blessed be these hands that have nurtured creativity.
Blessed be these hands that have held pain.
Blessed be these hands that have embraced with passion.
Blessed be these hands that have tended gardens.
Blessed be these hands that have closed in anger.
Blessed be these hands that have planted new seeds.
Blessed be these hands that have harvested ripe fields.
Blessed be these hands that have cleaned, washed, mopped,
    scrubbed.
Blessed be these hands that have become knotty with age.
Blessed be these hands that are wrinkled and scarred from doing
    justice.
Blessed be these hands that have reached out and been received.
Blessed be these hands that hold the promise of the future.
Blessed be the works of your hands,
O Holy One.[17]

Worship planners borrowed this prayer of blessing from the IWJ resource for Labor in the Pulpits. The blessing reminds us all of the work our hands do, of our identity as workers, and of how many workers' hands make our lives possible. At the close of the service, volunteers were recruited for local actions. The agential feeling of "I can do this"—fast, bless hands, sing a song—is meant to open a pathway to greater participation and collective movement identity.

Remaking Sacred and Profane

Singing hymns in the council's chamber and even placing the tools of labor on an altar signals another effect of religious ritual: contesting the boundaries *between the sacred and the profane*.[18] For secularists, cross-pollinating religion (sacred) and politics (profane) disrupts the separate categories of private (religion) and public (politics). Even for those who regularly blur these boundaries, the dominant "incursion" of religious belief and argument into politics in the last twenty years has been on issues of "personal morality," defined primarily by abortion and same-sex relationships. In contrast, the living wage movement brings religious symbolism, ritual, and argument to the political sphere in order to contest the purportedly amoral workings of the economy. In making this challenge, religious activists are encouraged to express their power even in seemingly "other" spheres.

Take, for example the actions of CLUE LA activists. In the midst of particularly difficult contract negotiations with the hotel sector, religious activists decided to practice "Java for Justice."[19] Wearing their various vestments (collars, prayer shawls, etc.), they entered the restaurants of hotels that had rejected a new union contract guaranteeing living wages and other benefits. After being seated and ordering coffee, one of the clergy would stand up at the table and deliver a short, two- to five-minute homily on worker justice from his or her religious tradition. They then left the restaurant, leaving behind shocked diners, angry supervisors, and—occasionally—applauding employees.

By standing up at a restaurant table in a clerical collar and delivering a homily, the clergy claimed the restaurant as sacred space and connected what is seemingly profane, or at least mundane—workers' wages—with the desire and gaze of God. Questions of how theology relates to labor practices or religious institutions to hotel restaurants were dramatically answered in fifteen minutes. Religious practice and argument spilled over the boundaries of polite society, and capitalist society in particular.

Or, take the example of the San Diego IWJ affiliate members. Each week for several months during the public comment section of the city council meeting, a different clergy member and worker brought a symbolic present for the council (an apple pie, a employee's paycheck), spoke about the need for living wages, and closed with the passage from Micah 6:8: "He has told you, O mortal, what is good; and what does the Lord require of you but to do justice, and to love kindness, and to walk humbly with your God?" (NRSV)—at least until someone found out that the mayor's favorite verse was "But let justice roll down like waters, and righteousness like an ever-flowing stream" (Amos 5:24; NRSV). As one councilman noted, "Seeing [my] bishop at the hearing and listening to his comment left [me] no choice but to support the ordinance."[20] The affiliate also took advantage of more "secular" celebrations to deliver their public messages. African American ministers and various workers personally delivered "Have a Heart" living wage Valentine's Day cards to each council member. Rev. Willey Manley, pastor of the Greater Life Baptist Church, had this to say:

Today we are bringing you Have a Heart messages in honor of Saturday's holiday, which celebrates love, kindness and compassion. Each card has been hand-made by members of the Interfaith Committee for Worker Justice . . . On each Valentine, you will find a story of real individual who works in San Diego and whose life would be improved by a living wage. We encourage you to read these stories carefully and consider [the] struggles faced by people who work so very hard, and who receive so little. . . . As religious leaders and people of faith, as members of the Interfaith Committee for Worker Justice and the San Diego Living Wage Coalition, we ask you again, to "Have a Heart" this Saint Valentine's Day and vote yes for a living wage.[21]

On Mother's Day, ICWJ also delivered a written eulogy to the mayor's assistant, which recalled the sacredness of a mother's love and mourned the loss of family time by mothers who must work multiple jobs to cover basic necessities. Eventually, assistants to the mayor and the council sent a message to the organization: "Please tell the religious people not to come anymore."[22] Perhaps even more powerful was the organization's planned action during Holy Week. Kneeling outside city hall, twelve Christian clergy washed the feet of workers making less than a living wage. The rabbis then distributed horseradish root, "an important part of the Passover Seder meal that symbolized the bitterness of slavery."[23] In many ways, the relevance of religious ethical commitments to public politicized space was ritually announced to those in power. At their final living wage rally before the city council's vote, Rabbi Laurie Coskey, San Diego ICWJ's director, closed the prayers and testimonials of other ministers with this final declaration before the crowd of nearly one thousand: "The San Diego Chamber of Commerce is over there doing a press conference because they can't get hundreds of people to stand out in the sun to support their position. We are the people, and the city belongs to us."[24] Through several years of coordinated organizing and careful attention to ritual practice, San Diego had declared their relevance, and God's, to the decisions made by the city council.

Whether through the recitation of scripture in the San Diego council chambers, foot-washing outside City Hall, a homily in Los Angeles hotel restaurants, or the presence of clergy in vestments protesting outside a Nashville car wash, the boundaries of normally separate spheres of activity were being contested.[25] Religious ritual claims work as a sacred concern and resists counterclaims about the amorality of the market. These public, political religious practices resist the colonization of our lives by values of efficiency and reclaim the goods of justice, dignity, and humanity in every sphere of life.

This form of activism also declares that the specific time-space of a proceeding (such as a city council meeting) is not limited to that historical moment but is connected to transcendent meaning and communities that precede and exceed the present action. The sociologist Pierrette Hondageneu-Sotelo reminds us that "Religious-based rituals and collectively enacted rites invoke the legacies of ancestors and ancient traditions."[26] Memphis WIN's "Fast for a Living Wage" guide stated, "For centuries, people of faith have practiced fasting as a means of seeking justice." When a religious ritual is enacted, the presence of the divine is acknowledged along with the generations of communities who have practiced these rituals before and which surround persons globally in practicing their faith. The immediate community is enlarged just through participating in a ritual that connects to others across time and space.[27] Further, summoning the divine in normally nonreligious spaces extends and transcends the immediate moment to ask more ultimate questions. In this way, religious ritual makes the short-term outlook of most political decisions less determinative; there is a longer range, metaphysical timeline to be considered as well.

Embodied Testimony

While many of the rituals described so far rely heavily on some form of "talk," or verbal testimony, religious ritual also introduces others forms of communication into talk-dominated politics. By both placing bodies at the center of political contestation and using symbols that move beyond verbal speech, religious activists regularly introduce *embodied testimony* into public policy debate. Rev. Robert Ard, an African American minister and former Republican candidate for the California Assembly stated in his support for San Diego's living wage ordinance, "Some see numbers. We see *people* who are working, poor people whose lives will be changed for the better."[28] People and, more specifically, their bodies are foregrounded when clergy on a Chicago street lay their hands on the shoulders and head of a fired worker to acknowledge, bless, assure, and commission a person and a community. Everyday speech is made more physically present when rabbis in San Diego distribute horseradish root to the city council to symbolize the bitterness of slavery. Verbal debate is transcended and transformed in Los Angeles when religious activists thank hotel managers who sign union contracts with gifts of milk and honey, and lament those who are stalling or rejecting contracts by delivering bitter herbs.

These practices are normally paired with a talk-based explanation of the symbolic action or bodily presence; still, these rituals open up a space inside political conversation for contestation that is not just expert-centered talk. Two things are significant about this form of testimony. First, it allows those who are not as linguistically skilled (whether because of language barriers, education, or disability) to participate in political action. Considering that low-wage workers disproportionately fall into these categories, alternative forms of political participation are important for building moral agency. Not everyone can give an eloquent testimony or argue the intricacies of municipal wage policy, but they can kneel in prayer or wash other workers' feet. Ritual provides an avenue for presence and persuasion in the political realm beyond skilled talk.

Second, religious ritual augments bodily presence in the political realm, stopping the political process to focus, not just on words but on physical presence. When someone kneels to pray inside a city council chamber or holds their hands before them in meditative prayer, there is an invitation to pause and notice that person's body. In this moment, the often heavily burdened bodies of low-wage workers become more visible in a world that designs myriad ways (back hallways, third shifts) to make them disappear. Boundaries are transgressed when low-wage workers are seen and celebrated. David Craig notes that ritual can "re-perform . . . norms *bodily*, redirecting the space of public debate from trading of principles to the training of people."[29] In this ritual performance, activists perform their vision of communities of worker justice, not simply talk about them.

Re-membering the Sacred

In these myriad ways, religious rituals reconstitute our understandings of the sacred and expand the time, spaces, and people that are included in the sacred canopy. Car washes, city council chambers, and hotels are places where the sacred is present and desiring of justice. Undocumented workers, restaurant servers, taxicab drivers become holy concerns and sacred testimonials. In this manner, membership in the sacred is expanded, and we are reminded of its breadth.

Perhaps the most literal example of this *re-membering of the sacred* came in Los Angeles when CLUE LA decided to stage a symbolic marriage of religious and labor organizations on one of the main tourist avenues. Its members marched with clergy and labor leaders, surrounded by the varied wedding accoutrements of different religious traditions.[30] The multifaith wedding procession, with some participants adorned by the henna tattoos typical in Hindu traditions and other couples walking under a Jewish chupah and breaking a glass at the end of the march, sought to symbolize the depth of commitments between these two constituencies. Tired of being called the pawns of unions, religious activists drew on a ceremony that underscored a covenantal relationship between two parties. Certainly the ritual was intended partly as an eye-catching spectacle: it was Los Angeles after all, and tourists duly took pictures. But the wedding procession was also meant to convey the depth of trust necessary for their coalitional work and a visual announcement of the reach of the sacred.

In Nashville, the growing number of Muslim immigrant taxi drivers meant that the primarily Christian clergy of the Interfaith Committee of Mid TN JwJ had to signal their inclusion and concern more directly. At their first Interfaith Rally for Living Wages, two young Muslim women wearing hijabs passed out bulletins at the door, the education director from the Nashville Islamic Community Center sang one of the opening prayers, and Muslim cabbies were specifically recruited for attendance. This intentionality was meant not only to signal sacred concern for the taxi driver's work and community contributions, but also to ritually symbolize the re-membering of Nashville's religious community and to welcome Muslim activists specifically to the organization.

Whether in grand displays like CLUE LA's ritual marriage or in smaller and subtler ways as in Nashville, religious activists around the country are transcending boundaries to reconstitute the coalitions of sacred care for low-wage workers. In doing so, they underscore the expansive concerns of the divine and the range of people—poultry workers, meat packers, janitors, servers, undocumented and documented workers, small business owners, union members, and varied people of faith—who join in those concerns.

Enhancing Moral Agency: Renewing Religious Roots

Religious ritual appears in multiple ways in the living wage movement, from starting a committee meeting with prayer to washing workers' feet before a city council. These practices support and enhance participants' moral agency, or commitment and capacity to discern and work for the needs, rights, responsibilities, and the flourishing of oneself and others. But the use of religious ritual is also vulnerable to becoming a form of theater for political expediency, losing its larger meaning and legitimacy. In order for religious ritual to maintain its integrity, power, and meaning— for participants and observers—religious activists must build and maintain connections with other, more continuous, worshipping communities.

Most of the religious rituals developed by activists in the movement are innovations. While echoing familiar forms, the space, words, and symbols of the movement's rituals are just different enough to signal a new compelling message. Yet the new meaning of these altered rituals ultimately relies on the cultural and theological meanings of their former contexts. The street marriage of faith and labor under a chupah makes sense because of the chupah's ongoing use in Jewish religious communities. When activists are involved in more continuous communities of worship, they know a ritual's original context and can better imagine an innovation that will echo the original while speaking to the new.

Religious activists need to nurture their connections to ongoing communities of worship for three major reasons: (1) to keep rituals lithe and authentic, (2) to place politics in the whole context of faith, and (3) to provide a longer-term vision of the liturgical nature of activism itself. In the end, while social movements can often be a form of church (or ecclesia) for many participants, the depth of movement practices rely on the power of these rituals in communities of weekly and daily worship. A dialectical relationship between movement communities and ongoing communities of worship revives, invigorates, and actualizes the fullness of a progressive faith. In other words, a mutually nourishing relationship between the priestly and prophetic functions of *both* congregations and social movement organizations helps to deepen and sustain the practice of faith for religious activists.[31]

Lithe and Authentic Religious Ritual

The first concern for maintaining the *litheness and authenticity* of religious ritual in protest is, perhaps, the most pragmatic. For those familiar with the interactions of religious rhetoric and political organizing, it is obvious when someone who is less shaped by a religious tradition "uses" it to political purpose. Here, for example, we consider a recent presidential candidate's awkward testimonies about his faith in Jesus ("He was a person who set an extraordinary example that has lasted 2,000 years, which is pretty inspiring when you think about it") or about his favorite book in the New Testament being Job.[32] In the end, the politician's comments testified more to his discomfort than anything else. More meaningful use of religious language and practices of religious ritual come from ongoing immersion in religious rhythms. Without this practice, religious ritual becomes stiff and arthritic. Moreover, meaningful innovation can only come from knowing a practice well. When immersed in ongoing communities of faith and ritual practice, activists become more nimble as their ritual muscle memory deepens and allows for flexibility and originality. In these moments, religious ritual is not just something left over or a one-time loan from faith communities but grows out of the ongoing practice of people of faith.

In Nashville, planning an interfaith service for living wages showed the need for ritual knowledge and for humility from activists who were less formed in religious traditions. Hosted by the church of a supportive councilman, the interfaith service sought to bring religious leaders together to launch the campaign and release a living wage study for Nashville. Hoping for maximum stakeholder participation in the service, the organizers soon realized that the program was packed. Two Christian clergy who reviewed the program immediately noted that it had nothing close to an order of worship. The program was more rally than religious service. Consulting with clergy, the organizers reshaped the program to reflect a more regular service with its attendant emotional and theological rhythms (in this context, particularly Protestant Christian). This was not a rally held in a church, but a worship service honoring workers and commissioning a community on their behalf.

Many secular organizers and activists are uncomfortable in these contexts of faith expression. But the more secular (or "spiritual" as opposed to "religious") organizers in Nashville realized their need to listen and learn from those who participated regularly in communities of faith. In Nashville, several community organizers also met regularly with an ordained Presbyterian clergywoman and former IAF organizer to learn more about the Bible and progressive justice theology. When Mid TN JwJ hosted interns from IWJ's "Seminary Summer" program, they made sure there were theological mentors in addition to organizing mentors for their summer interns.

As with the Nashville service, connection to ongoing communities of faith contextualizes religious rituals in the larger life of a religious community. In the Christian tradition, weekly (and often daily) gathering for worship reminds people of the complexity of human life—its joy, its brokenness, and God's presence in all. Confession is linked with assurance of forgiveness, and both are tied to celebration, proclamation, and intercession; gathering in is always paired with sending forth. In these rhythms are the testimony of lives lived in interdependence, accountability, solidarity, and celebration. Connection with concrete communities of ongoing worship practice also reminds activists that demands for employer repentance must be coupled with openness to reconciliation and words of assurance. Reminders of our own finitude summon people of faith not to demonize opponents but to intercede on their behalf, yearning for the fullness of life blessed by a justice-loving God.

At their best, ongoing worship communities remind activists of the internal goods intended by each religious ritual.[33] While religious ritual can certainly be effective for political purposes, foot-washing is not for mere visual impression or even political efficacy but for honoring the dignity of another and forming us in humble service to another. Religious ritual ultimately retains its power because of its ties to authentic practice and a holistic system of faith. When activists do not attend to and nurture ties to ongoing communities of faith and the internal goods of religious practice, the risks are great. Without these ties, religious ritual may eventually be running only on fumes in the long journey toward justice.

The Whole Context of Faith

Returning to the fullness of faith is particularly important when activists have to endure and make sense of political losses. The realization that a campaign is not going to succeed can be deeply disheartening, especially when workers' quality of life hangs in the balance. While our focus overall is on learning with the successes and ongoing challenges of the living wage movement in the United States, there have been losses as well.

Almost every campaign goes through significant compromises in route to a final agreement. In Atlanta, the powerful lobbying of Delta Airlines forced the pro–living wage mayor to design a taskforce to encourage "reconciliation" between the two sides on a living wage ordinance applicable to city contractors. Delta and the Chamber of Commerce had already gone to the state legislature and won a provision to outlaw all mandatory local living wage ordinances—effectively nullifying Atlanta's ordinance even before it could be enacted.[34] The Atlanta City Council's eventual resolution exempted airport contractors and implemented a bonus-points process in the contract bidding process (that is, business received additional bid points for paying $10.50 an hour, paying employee health care, family health care, and domestic partner benefits). Living wage activists, as of 2010, are still working on overturning the state ban on local living wage ordinances.

The Nashville campaign experienced a bittersweet moment (more bitter by most accounts) in June 2010 when the mayor included living wages for full-time employees in his new budget and which the Metro Council subsequently passed. Fierce debate on the Metro Council floor indicated that while the raises affected a small number of workers, fiscal conservatives were warning, "Mark my word, this is opening the door for more wage mandates down the road. Not this term. They're too politically savvy for that. But next budget, we'll see something for contractors and then something for all of Davidson County." While this principled victory was important, as was Mayor Dean's *Tennessean* editorial defending it, the Metro School Board—which has autonomous control of the specific spending of its general budget allocation—simultaneously outsourced seven hundred custodial jobs to a private contractor and which in turn dropped all of them below the living wage.

How do religious activists make sense of these setbacks or losses? In Atlanta, the campaign shifted its focus to overturning the state law and raising the minimum wage at the state level. They also created, with SEIU, a "working families platform" for Atlanta council-member candidates. Fourteen of the sixteen candidates endorsing that platform won their elections. Thus, the Atlanta campaign responded to loss by designing a significant concession, setting a new pragmatic goal, and starting again at the state level. In Nashville, where the campaign is the most recent among all those described here, the reality of the recent recession meant that it was not even fully functional to respond to the new developments. With changes in foundation and private funding, the major sponsoring organization in Nashville had to stop paying their part-time faith organizers in late 2009 and then their full-time director in early 2010. While volunteer work continues, the economic downturn hurt staff and the campaign environment overall. At these junctures, a new pragmatic goal is not enough; other kinds of reflective work are needed as well.

At a gathering honoring the outgoing Nashville director in February 2010, union organizers, labor lawyers, immigrant rights organizers, and faith leaders came together to say a final thank-you. As clergy members spoke, their comments about learning "practices of love" and "seeing God in more faces" intertwined with congratulations for achievements and good wishes for next steps. In that moment, clergy leaders were voicing an important message about religious activism: it's not all about politics. Formed in ongoing communities of worship, these religious leaders spoke in theological terms that were not about political expediency. The mystery of meaningful encounters, relationships of repentance and transformation, laughter, and experiencing the presence of God were central. While a sense of loss was pervasive, a larger framework for hope, thanksgiving, and commitment was also palpable.

Certainly, these meaningful insights do not require immersion in ongoing communities of worship. But the larger life and rhythms of congregations or intentional communities (like the Catholic Worker movement) can help remind religious activists of the whole context of their faith. Two important convictions, at least, may arise from this immersion: (1) faith is more than politics, even though it certainly includes politics; and (2) within and beyond the highs and lows of politics is God's desire and love for us and all of creation still endures.

Liturgical Activism

The journey toward greater economic justice is long. Mentoring students in summer training programs over the past four years, I have watched them struggle with the great need and few resources for low-wage worker organizing. Organizing hours are often long and unpredictable. Campaigns have highs, lows, and a lot of mundane work that is seldom praised. And burnout comes with organizing; of the directors observed, several previously have taken a leave from organizing, and others are considering sabbaticals.

In this context of struggle, the liturgy of religious communities also offers lessons for the organizing life itself. Most communities of faith have a liturgical calendar with a yearly cycle. These yearly seasons (e.g., Advent, Christmas, Ordinary Time/Epiphany, Lent, Holy Week/Triduum, Easter, Ordinary Time/Pentecost) remind us of the stories of our faith and the seasons of our lives. Through a liturgical year, religious communities have days of anticipation (of new birth, rites of passage), great celebration (of miracles, of resurrection), purposeful discipline (repenting of sins, fasting for devotion), and even "ordinary time" (where daily life is lived outside of the great seasons). This cyclical calendar can provide assurance for the varied nature of work for justice. In activism too there are times of heightened anticipation, perhaps of a vote, a rally, or an organizing drive. But there are also times of great lament and brokenness, where the call to repentance comes to both the targets of activism and to activists themselves. With victories, there is wild celebration and hope that the world is being transformed, if only slightly. And there are ordinary times, when the mundane tasks of database entry, grant writing, and so on can be isolating. Ongoing relationships to religious traditions and communities of worship help remind religious activists that there are seasons to every journey, and that we must learn to live fully into each season without rushing to find another. Each part of the liturgical year teaches us something about the goods and wisdom of that part of the faith journey. Perhaps it can even teach us of the differing ways God is present in the rhythms of organizing.

% 6 %

Conclusion

"Come, Walk with Us, the Journey Is Long"

A t the IWJ national conference in 2007, one of the first tasks of the opening plenary was learning a song. IWJ's energetic, music-loving, executive director Kim Bobo usually chooses a song for every national conference and leads the assembled activists in its initial singing. Gathered in the large multifunctional performing arts/meeting space, hundreds of IWJ local affiliate staff and volunteers, union leaders and organizers, and students followed the piano, guitars, and Bobo's enthusiastic musical direction. The song would be sung at the beginning of all plenaries during the three-day conference and on the way to a group protest. That year's chosen song was South African in origin, with words provided in English and the final arrangement done by Bobo.

1. Come, walk with us, the journey is long.
Come, walk with us, the journey is long *(repeat)*
The journey, the journey, the journey is long.
The journey, the journey, the journey is long *(repeat)*
2. Share our burden, and join in the song.
Share our burden, and join in the song *(repeat)*
The journey, the journey, the journey is long.
The journey, the journey, the journey is long *(repeat)*
3. Come, uplift us, and bring us new life.
Come, uplift us, and bring us new life *(repeat)*
The journey, the journey, the journey is long.
The journey, the journey, the journey is long *(repeat)*
4. Give us peace when the journey is done.
Give us peace when the journey is done *(repeat)*.
The journey, the journey, the journey is long.
The journey, the journey, the journey is long .*(repeat)*[1]

As voices joined together, the song's pace, rhythm, and words evoked many dimensions of IWJ's and the living wage movement's work. Hopeful and joyful in tone, the song also presents a wise realism and fierce perseverance. The song's composers pair the expansive metaphor of "the journey" with the optimistic, determined yet patient "is long." The whole of the song is sung like an active prayer, encouraging and inviting people to live faithful action.

"Come, Walk with Us" is not timid, naïve, or narrow in its view of the journey. Rather, it reflects the role of living wage campaigns in the larger ecology of the worker justice movement in the United States. Municipal living wage ordinances—what Paul Sonn of the National Employment Project calls "traditional living wage laws"—are at a low point as a political strategy across the country.[2] In 2010 fewer municipal ordinance campaigns were ongoing than in 2005. Many of the cities with current active campaigns are especially challenging cases, such as Nashville, where city charters disallow direct wage mandates by metro councils. Many cities, like Atlanta, Memphis, and Nashville, have also had to take valuable organizing time to fight statewide bans on municipal living wage laws (passed in Georgia, withdrawn in Tennessee). So what's next for the living wage movement?

The Living Wage Gateway

In many ways, the living wage movement should be seen as an important gateway to other worker justice and community accountability struggles such as raising state and federal minimum wages, developing and enforcing anti-wage theft laws, demanding fair treatment of undocumented workers, and negotiating community benefit agreements. While wage standards are primary to many of these developments, they also are nested in a larger emphasis on worker dignity and community standards for economic development. Religious activists are also finding their home in these larger struggles.

The most common next step for living wage coalitions has been to expand the coverage of municipal ordinances and to work for their enforcement. Activists work to extend coverage of these ordinances to more employees of the city (who may be under different payroll and benefits boards), direct contractors, and businesses receiving tax subsidies. In Memphis, for example, WIN has successfully expanded the coverage of their ordinance twice since its initial passage. But even with these legislative successes, a number of cities have not enforced their laws effectively. As the political scientist Stephanie Luce documents, many living wage coalitions have had to make great efforts to insure the implementation of ordinances.[3] Some have established more "insider" channels such as enforcement advisory boards that work with the city to make sure that its contractors are complying with the law; San Diego ICWJ has adopted this approach. Other coalitions use more "outsider" channels of contacting media and filing grievances and lawsuits to bolster enforcement (for example, in Miami, Baltimore, and Madison, Wisconsin).[4]

These enforcement efforts have connected activists to the larger struggle of wage enforcement campaigns across the nation. Researchers for the New York University Law School's Brennan Center for Justice have documented that "wage and hour violations have become endemic in scores of low-wage industries."[5] Violations occur regularly around lack of prompt payment, failing to pay overtime, paying less than minimum wage, forcing employees to clock in and out when business is slow, and requiring them to work off the clock. IWJ's director Kim Bobo's 2008 book, *Wage Theft in America: Why Millions of Working Americans Are Not Getting Paid—and What We Can Do about It*, has also signaled a shift in the policy focus of the IWJ network. In their 2010 national strategic plan, IWJ listed "living wages and benefits" as the organization's second core "value," but municipal living wage campaigns were not named among the organization's strategic priorities. Instead, goals such as passing "wage theft" legislation at local and federal levels were central. Again, in Memphis, WIN has taken on this task with vigor, negotiating with and, when necessary, protesting against employers who are "stealing wages," as well as proposing a local law that would classify nonpayment of wages as criminal theft. At their protests and rallies, they carry signs designed by national IWJ that state simply "Thou Shall Not Steal—Stop Wage Theft Now." Indeed, IWJ, guided by Bobo, is also working with the Department of Labor to increase wage enforcement.

Living wage organizing and wage enforcement has also knit tighter connections among labor, faith, and immigrant worker organizations. With the overrepresentation of documented and undocumented immigrants in low-wage industries, worker justice issues sit near the center of many immigration concerns. In its most recent tool kit on immigration reform, IWJ notes,

There is no denying that the immigration system in the U.S. is broken. More than 11 million undocumented people are living here, including children raised as Americans and workers who have become an integral part of the U.S. economy.

Without legal status, immigrant workers are victims of every kind of labor abuse and cannot protect their rights without fear of deportation. The continuation of a debased class of workers, whom employers can and do underpay, overwork, and violate their legal rights, contributes to a downward push on wages and working conditions for all workers in the United States.[6]

Concern for immigrant workers has moved IWJ to organize for an "unbreakable fire wall" between the Department of Labor and the Immigration and Customs Enforcement agency for the enforcement of wage laws for undocumented workers, for a "fair and reasonable" process to normalize the status of undocumented workers, and for the issuance of visas based only on the needs of the U.S. economy, not on "race, ethnicity, or country of origin."[7] IWJ's activist literature and protests are grounded in citations from Exodus 22:21, "You shall not wrong a stranger or oppress him, for you were strangers in the land of Egypt" (NASB) and Leviticus 19:33–34, "When an alien resides with you in your land, you shall not oppress the alien. The alien who resides with you shall be to you as the citizen among you; you shall love the alien as yourself, for you were aliens in the land of Egypt: I am the Lord your God" (NRSV). Once again, religious activists combine moral and theological arguments with pragmatic economic arguments, this time about the enormous financial contributions immigrants make to the U.S. economy and the interdependence of all low-wage workers.

Living wage coalitions also realize even the limited impact of strong municipal living wage ordinances. Paul Sonn and Stephanie Luce note that "In small cities, the number of workers covered could be fewer than 100. While in large cities like New York the number could be as high as 60,000, even that figure reflects just a small portion of the city's low-wage workforce."[8] Local organizing for living wages has uncovered the general population's support for raising minimum wages across the board, including all workers. Many local living wage coalitions therefore see their next step as passing wider legislation, pressing for sector-specific (e.g., "big-box" retailers, in Chicago; hotels, in Los Angeles; and security guards, in Washington D.C.), citywide (New Orleans and Santa Fe) and statewide minimum wages. The statewide approach was particularly salient when the federal minimum wage was stagnant for nearly a decade at $5.15 an hour. By lobbying legislatures and sponsoring ballot initiatives, activists effectively moved thirty-three state minimum wages higher than the federal level by 2006 (272). After activists' victories at the state level and years of living wage organizing at local levels, Democrats made increasing the federal minimum wage central to their platform for congressional candidates in 2006 (274). With their recapturing of Congress, the federal minimum wage was finally raised to $7.25 in 2009. Almost as soon as that legislation was signed in 2007, Let Justice Roll and other national organizations began working with Senator Ted Kennedy and others to raise the wage to $10 by 2010, with the goal of restoring to the minimum wage the meaning and utility it last held in 1968.

The localized character of living wage coalitions feeds particularly well into a reexamination of local economic development processes as a whole, or "the set of policies that cities and counties use to stimulate and shape new job and business growth in their communities" (280). Activists in Los Angeles have been at the forefront of negotiated "community benefit agreements" (CBAs) when major developments, such as sports arenas, airports, housing developments, or convention centers, are being planned for a community. Typically, CBAs are contracts with private developers that guarantee workers living wages, priority for local hiring, environmental protections, and may even extend to union neutrality, childcare facilities, and other needed worker benefits. These agreements help private developers speed through city zoning, permits, and subsidy processes and give them an edge when bidding against others for city-controlled land (280). This approach is more effective in highly competitive downtown development markets, but CBAs point to the growing edge of activists linking living wage concerns with overhauls of city economic development systems (281).

In the end, the tireless organizing of the living wage activists has effectively placed "the concerns of the working poor back on the national agenda" (284). Sonn and Luce conclude in their "New Directions for the Living Wage Movement":

> As this movement has grown in its organizing capacity and policy vision, living wage activists are successfully promoting new approaches for raising the minimum wage, for improving enforcement of wage protections, especially for immigrant workers, and

for making economic development programs a vehicle for creating good jobs above the minimum wage floor. . . . In this fashion, the living wage movement is beginning to generate a more comprehensive public policy agenda responding to the growing problems of low-wage work and widening inequality in our economy. (285)

Through living wage activism, activists have created myriad new coalitions, strengthened existing relationships, benefited numerous low-wage workers monetarily, and changed the vocabulary of the political economy. Have they reduced poverty in the United States significantly? Not yet. Compromises abound on legislation, and no single public policy is a magic bullet to end working poverty. Evaluating the living wage movement requires a good reality check. Rev. Paul Sherry of the Let Justice Roll campaign concedes, "We are working with rough justice. As our friend [Protestant theologian] Reinhold Niebuhr used to say 'What is possible?' With fear and trembling, we have to make political decisions."⁹ But what these campaigns do well is expose the complicity of government in poverty production, demytholigize the "free market," provide an opportunity for expanding political engagement beyond the typical players, and extend sacred care for workers. For the approximately 96 million people (as of 2008) who live below 200% of the poverty line in the United States, this work is essential.

Developing Moral Agency

In order to build the living wage movement's depth and power in these next stages, it is important to remember the movement's complex work that we have discussed so far. Religious activists in the movement have already demonstrated varied and evolving approaches to counter the economic and political poverty of the working poor. With each of their practices, we learn important lessons about building moral agency and we encounter key challenges to inform future work. By reviewing the depth and breadth of their activities, we remember that the movement is not just about a policy but about the range and quality of organizing practices and the moral discussions they undertake to foster greater economic political agency for the working poor and their allies. As we close, therefore, let us reiterate some of the most salient arguments about the strengths and growing edges of the movement we discussed throughout.

Using the words of the IWJ mission statement, religious activists seek "To educate, organize, and mobilize the religious community in the United States on issues and campaigns that will improve wages, benefits, and conditions for workers, and give voice to workers, especially workers in low-wage jobs."[10] To amplify the voices of workers, these activists undertake a constellation of activities designed to counter the sociodemographic barriers that exclude the working poor and their concerns from public policy making. Good moral arguments (or *framing*), however important, must be combined with effective practices for social change to enhance the moral knowledge, judgment, motivation, and power of the working poor. Robust economic political agency for the working poor and their religious allies entails parallel work in *bridge building, alternative political development, gendered leadership*, and *ritual renewal*. Moral agency becomes, therefore, a multidimensional concept dependent on significant institutional work and continual cultural nurturance.

The living wage movement arose in the midst of the efforts and failures of "urban renewal" in the early 1990s. Despite a significant infusion of development funds, a high percentage of full-time workers and their families languished in urban poverty. As ministers and lay activists in Baltimore explored this phenomenon, they identified the local government as a collaborator and purveyor of low-wage (or poverty-wage) jobs. The government's own system of outsourcing and low-bid contracts rewarded poverty-level job creation. Few wage or job-quality standards were in place for private businesses receiving tax abatements and other subsidies provided by the city. Simultaneously, local government was outsourcing higher paying (often unionized) jobs to private low-wage contractors in order to cut budgets. Through activists' careful analysis and innovative organizing, BUILD criticized the government's generation of low-wage jobs and launched an alternative vision for municipal wage policies.

The BUILD program and the many living wage coalitions that followed countered the intersecting nature of political and economic poverty, and made the supposedly invisible hands of the economy visible. Combining the strengths of workers, unions, poor-people's groups, and religious organizations, they broke open some of the myths of local political economies and proposed a constructive policy highlighting the moral nature of wages. In diffusing the municipal strategy and honing the living wage frame, activists wrote one of the great movement success stories of the past two decades in the United States. Activists revived a largely dormant term—living wage—and transformed the rhetorical landscape of poverty reduction and worker justice with its use. Tellingly, a database search of newspaper and wire services for "living wage" between 1970 and 1990 produced only 870 hits; between 1991 and 2009, more than 29,000 articles included the term. The concept of the living wage has become a mainstay in popular discussions of the political economy. Throughout this story of diffusion, religious activists and organizations have steadily partnered, and often anchored, living wage organizing.

At the 2007 IWJ national conference, Rev. Alexia Salvatierra of CA CLUE stated that religious activists "want to say it is possible . . . we have the power to stop making people invisible."[11] While cultivating this power could be seen primarily as an exercise in building political efficacy, we better grasp the entirety of religious organizing when we see political efficacy as one dimension under the umbrella of moral agency. Moral agency cannot be reduced to political efficacy and, at important points, political efficacy is not the exclusive or primary goal of religious activists' work. Certainly the blessing of a laborer's hands in a Labor Day worship service has political implications, but recognizing the presence of God in another and sharing sacred connections are also related to pastoral care and discipleship (whether or not they are politically "effective" in the secular sense). Religious living wage activists reveal the multiple ways religious networks, theologies, and practices can build the commitment and capacity of people to discern and "do something" for the needs, rights, responsibilities, and flourishing of low-wage workers. Most of this work is focused on changing political structures, but the goal of worker dignity transcends public policy measures and seeks a larger shift in moral understanding and active commitment to creating the sacred care all workers deserve.

Moral Framing and Interdependence

Religious activists remind all people of faith of the abiding importance of clear, compelling, and resonant moral arguments—even when it comes to the seemingly expert-dominated talk of the economy. The capacity for new moral action relies, in part, on helping people deconstruct the "natural" or "necessary" occurrence of social structures and the impact they have on their lives. Activists seek to reexamine "what is" in order to imagine "what could be." *Framing* work contributes to this process by creating and diffusing alternative interpretive categories and visions of the social world. Religious activists bring significant gifts to this process because of their immersion and training in traditions of moral argument.

Social movement–framing theorists tell us that compelling frames must accomplish two primary tasks: *punctuating* (that is, announcing something as unjust) and *attributing* (identifying responsible parties and responsive action). Religious activists punctuate the injustice of current wage structures with phrases such as "A job should keep you out of poverty, not in it." But these pronouncements are followed with three vital dimensions of attribution: diagnosis, prescription, and motivation. Activists diagnose the problem of working poverty as an issue of the erosion of the minimum wage as well as the inversion of the relationship between worker productivity and worker earnings. They point to the dramatic change in sociopolitical priorities in the last thirty years. During this period, in contrast to the positive correlation between increased worker productivity (104%) and increased minimum wages (103%) between 1947 and 1973, worker productivity and wages seem to have no connection (the inflation-adjusted minimum wage actually fell 24% from 1973 to 2004 while productivity increased 78%).[12] Religious activists trace this erosion and reversal to political decisions. Challenging the claim that economic rewards are "naturally" distributed, they focus not only on the greed of many businesses but also on the conscious neglect and collusion of government with corporations in creating poverty-wage jobs. After identifying tangible targets, they propose policies such as municipal living wage ordinances as political means to insure greater economic equity and democracy. They ramp up the motivation to enact this prescription by emphasizing that living wages are both "ethically and economically right."

Importantly, religious activists speak repeatedly about prioritizing the moral nature of the issue. In a time when utilitarian cost-benefit analyses often dominate discussions of the political economy, successful religious activists remind us all to "stick to the moral high ground and don't get caught in debating numbers." Yet they do not shy away from economic arguments, using them as an important ancillary support for their central moral claims. In so doing, they not only recast the economy in moral terms but also engage people who regularly are left out of the insider policy making.

How religious activists draw on long-standing theological and economic streams to do this reframing is often overlooked or underestimated. Theirs is a reclamation and translation of historical traditions on the moral nature of wages, the moral responsibilities of government, and the priority of the poor. As activists regularly assert, "Wages are a bedrock moral issue." These arguments can be traced back to Fr. John Ryan's early twentieth-century argument that divine ownership of all creation means that all God's children have the right to sustenance. For Ryan as well as the contemporary living wage activists, wages should reflect the ethical value of labor, not just the economic calculus. Like Ryan, Rauschenbusch, and Martin Luther King Jr. before them, contemporary activists also hold government morally responsible for insuring economic rights and responsibilities. Dr. King argued in the 1960s that government should not just be a "watchmen" protecting only negative rights (of incursion) but also a guarantor of positive action to meet people's basic needs. In the end, these claims are also buoyed by a focus on the preferential option for the poor as embedded in Hebrew and New Testament scriptures, and articulated particularly in Catholic and liberation theology. A preferential option for the poor shifts the focus of poverty discussions from individual failure onto the social structures that produce inequity and deprivation, and calls for a reordering of society to provide justice, not just charity.

Recognizing the connections of contemporary frames to these rich moral traditions is important because this lineage provides a measure of caution and accountability to public moral argument. For example, some religious activists make the case that living wages will move workers away from dependence on government subsidies. This claim resonates strongly with the social-equity strand (versus neoliberal strand) of neoclassical economics, which argues that government should intervene in the economy to secure basic economic needs and stimulate the economy through relief to lower and middle economic classes. But residing in this claim is also a dangerous idealization of independence from government. While popularized Keynesian-style economic reasoning acknowledges the need for occasional government interventions, its advocates still idealize independence from government. This is not practically, morally, or theologically sound for living wage activists. From a practical standpoint, all of us depend on government in myriad ways everyday (from roads to food safety to mortgage tax credits). Prizing independence for low-wage workers falsely stigmatizes their interactions with government while the middle and upper economic classes rest easily in their myth of independence. Prioritizing independence from government also undermines the good of interdependence, which is supported by theological convictions on the social nature of the self and the sociality of God. Particularly in Christian traditions, people are seen as created in and for relationship by a relational God. Healthy interdependence is a more salient theological good for religious activists concerned with institutional reform. For Catholics and many others, interdependence is a moral category that drives us to commit to the common good because "We are *all* really responsible *for all.*" Political orderings (those created by governments, for instance) can systematize forms of mutual support that are consonant with the theological purposes of sociality.

In the end, recognizing the historical legacy of contemporary frames pushes us to contextualize moral reasoning in larger constellations of ethical thought. The priority of "wages as a moral bedrock" is tied historically to arguments about the responsibilities and good of government as well as such theological ideals as interdependence. While these conversations may not take center stage in popular framing, they are important backstage discussions that help people of faith resist neoclassical economic sacralization of independence. As many theologians argue, government is not a necessary evil but an institution permitted by God for the good of humanity. Healthy interdependence should define our relationship to it.

Bridge Building and Theological Solidarity

Effective public arguments draw carefully on our rich shared traditions in order to encourage us to work together for social change. But compelling moral arguments are only part of the successful dynamics of the living wage movement. The coalitional strength of the movement also produced a collective identity and collective agency that surprised many in light of the recent declines in the labor movement. By building strong relationships among union, religious, and community coalitions, the living wage movement changed the nature of municipal politics across the country. Religious activists contributed to the strength of these coalitions, in part, by their bridge-building work.

This work is needed, in part, because of the racialized landscape of working poverty in the United States. While 9.2% of whites fell below the poverty threshold in 2008 (and dominate the face of poverty by sheer numbers), African Americans and Latinos are disproportionately represented in low-wage labor sectors and poverty statistics: 24.7% of blacks and 21.2% of Latinos fell below the poverty line while they were only 12.8% and 15.4% of the population respectively. The percentages of those in working poverty are even higher with 48.4% of blacks, 52.1% of Latinos, and 29.4% of whites falling below 200% of the poverty threshold in 2008.[13] This landscape is even harder for recent immigrants from Mexico and Central America (documented and undocumented) who make 44% less their U.S.–born Latino neighbors.[14]

In the midst of a political economy that seeks to divide these groups from each other, religious organizations help provide the space for mediating those very tensions that could divide the movement. By offering a key site for the political mobilization of the working poor and building bridges among racial/ethnic identities, religious organizations counter the dominant patterns of political participation in the United States.

The resources that people develop in nonpolitical settings (for example, skill sets, social capital, affiliations, and money) lay the groundwork for their political participation. Yet, low-wage workers are decidedly absent from traditional pathways to political participation. The racial segregation of religious life in the United States contains an irony, however. While religious life is stratified economically and racially, these divisions play out differently from workplaces. Because congregations and religious organizations tend to be more homogeneous demographically, opportunities for civic skill development are distributed more evenly: janitors lead prayer meetings, waitresses run committee meetings, and so on. In this way, active participants in religious organizations are often prepared for civic engagement in ways that outstrip their socioeconomic demographics. In fact, religious organizations are three to four times more likely to mobilize a person politically than a union.[15] Religious networks are a primary vein of social capital for social movements and key sites for the political development of low-wage workers.

Those who are more socioeconomically marginalized are not, however, primarily moved to participation because of political speech (for instance, a sermon). Civic skill development is what matters—running meetings, speaking publicly, developing networks. The more involved a person is in the varied activities and leadership of an institution, the greater their political participation. This also points to the danger of an elite focus, or grass-tops organizing, in some religious organizations. Because of their homogeneity and intentionality around leadership development, religious institutions are some of the very few spaces in the United States that can nurture the political capacity and agency of low-wage workers. When worker justice organizing focuses primarily on clergy recruitment and messaging, they replicate many low-wage workers' experience of hierarchy in their job sites and in American political recruitment. To move toward greater participatory justice, people of faith must examine our organizing and polity practices as well as our messages.

Religious organizations also fight the deleterious effects of the racialized political economy on the political power of the low-wage workers by undertaking key bridge-building tasks. Drawing on their theological commitments and unique structural location, religious activists focus particularly on *ideology translation, relational repair*, and *inclusion monitoring*.

When diverse groups try to work together toward intersecting goals, their various cultures and ideologies can create barriers to collaboration; this is why ideology translation is so necessary. In the midst of these cultural conflicts, religious leaders bring particular strengths derived from their training and experience in translation work. By interpreting the varied vocabularies of communities and coordinating role exchanges among clergy, union leaders, and low-wage workers, religious organizations regularly cultivate pathways for better communication and strategic resonance.

When longer histories of conflicts or deeper distrust exist among groups, religious activists pursue relational repair among the groups. In part, because religious facilitators ground themselves in traditions that recognize humanity's brokenness, they are often unfazed when they see it and more prepared to facilitate its healing. Theologies and practices of confession, forgiveness, and reconciliation become particularly important in light of the labor movement's own history of racism, sexism, and xenophobia. But rather than condemning unions for their mistakes, IWJ and other religious activist groups note the church's "sins" in these areas as well. From this place, they seek ongoing accountability and practical ways forward on these issues.

Much of the relational repair in the living wage movement focuses on "Black-Brown" solidarity and connects with religious activists' attention to inclusion monitoring. Employer policies and practices regularly exacerbate Black-Brown suspicion in low-wage jobs by threatening workers with cheaper replacements, and deportation. In these hostile environments, religious coalitional organizations are in a unique structural position—largely independent of a particular union or immigrant constituency—both to mediate conflict and to insure inclusion of more vulnerable workers. This combination of relative structural autonomy and a theological commitment to the "least of these" is also why IWJ and other leading religious organizations in the movement have linked immigration reform closely with their living wage work. Securing living wages is even harder when an entire demographic of the low-wage sector cannot safely report their wage abuse even while they are scapegoated as the reason for other minorities' low-wages. Religious activists resist this purposeful division of low-wage workers by providing the psychic and physical space for bridge building.

In the end, the practice of religious activists in the living wage movement illuminates and concretizes the multiple dimensions of *theological solidarity*. Theological solidarity differs in its ontological grounding from union solidarity, which is based on occupational or worker status. It is grounded rather in the inclusive love of God and is meant to be a glimpse of the reign of God. Thus, theological solidarity resides in continual relationship to the brokenness of this world. This juxtaposition requires preferential accountability to those wounded by the structural brokenness; in the living wage movement, it requires accountability to low-wage workers. This preferential accountability to the vulnerable and broken summons us to love concretely, to love actual persons and not just the concept of neighborliness, listening to and tracking the patterned woundings of the world in order to be part of its healing. Through this concrete attentiveness, we also encounter the complex identities of persons, with their multiple and changing relationships to power, and garner greater opportunities for creative alliances (as, for example, between domestic partnerships and living wages in Atlanta). Ultimately, theological solidarity seeks not only to alleviate suffering but also to build the agency of all involved; it envisions participatory justice as part of God's desire for the world. The efforts, successes, and challenges of religious activists in the living wage movement reflect, in many ways, the deeply challenging journey of faith that is theological solidarity.

Women's Leadership and Structurally Remembering the Poor

The practices of theological solidarity not only lead religious activists to analyze and resist the racialized dynamics of the low-wage economy, but its gendered dynamics also. They join feminist organizations and activists in criticizing the *feminization of poverty*. Women in the United States are 124% more likely to live in poverty than men.[16] Moreover, in 2008, 37.5% of single female households with children under the age of eighteen fell below the poverty line, whereas only 15% of single male households with children in the same age group fell below this same line.[17] While some early feminist researchers identified single motherhood as the primary risk factor for poverty, more recent feminist research identifies low-wage jobs as the strongest determinant of women's poverty in the United States. Whether in food service, custodial, or personal care, women predominate in the lowest-wage occupations.[18] Combine this with an analysis of women's earning over the course of their careers and the results are even starker. Because of the lower number of hours women work and the years without pay for family care, women earn only 38% of what men do during the prime working years of (age twenty-six through fifty-nine).[19] The United States is *last* of all industrial nations in levels of child-care support from fathers, welfare payments, and child-care subsidies.

From this evidence, we begin to see the gendered impact of seemingly gender-neutral, living wage organizing. Responding to this reality, feminist activists, feminist funders, feminist organizations, and feminist researchers have been important, but underappreciated, partners in the living wage movement. In fact, women—many of them feminists—are the principal face of low-wage worker organizing, particularly in religious organizations. The predominance of women in these roles has led not only to collaboration between feminist and religious organizations but also reflection on the *feminization of organizing*.

Women's leadership in living wage coalitions is particularly important because women, in general, are less politically active than men and view themselves as less influential in politics. Seeing women in political roles and mentoring them into leadership then becomes even more important for enhancing their political agency. But professionals working in low-wage worker organizing face significant challenges. As an occupation, community organizing requires great flexibility in scheduling; coordinating child and elder care, which still falls to women disproportionately, becomes very difficult. These women are normally paid only modest salaries and many organizations cannot afford family health care, let alone retirement benefits. Religious low-wage organizers are also organizing in sectors—labor and religious institutions—that are still male-dominated. The combination of these stressors results in burnout for many women organizers by their late twenties to early thirties.

As women organizers identify these issues themselves, people of faith who support their work must ask some hard questions of themselves. Do the structural demands we place on these activists unduly require and even sanctify their sacrifice? Historically, women have not properly balanced self-love and their personal development with love of and service to the neighbor. Unfortunately, traditions of women's service have intersected too easily with misunderstandings about assuming voluntary poverty in order to serve the poor. But serving the poor, particularly in Christianity, is the responsibility of the church as a whole; radical financial sacrifice should not be automatically required for those who undertake this ministry full time. In this way, feminist and religious women organizers challenge us to rethink our theological and institutional models. Without this reconsideration, we are in danger of making faith-based activism a growing sector of underpaid women's work in the United States.

In addition to bringing our attention to the strengths and challenges of women in low-wage worker organizing, the collaborations of feminist and religious activists also bring ideological fissures around reproductive issues to the surface. While these coalitions cannot resolve the issue of abortion easily or quickly, the breadth of Catholic social teaching about political engagement and deeper reflection on scriptural texts such as Galatians 2:1–10 should challenge these divisions. The Galatians passage argues for a new focus in the contentious relationship between the Jewish and non-Jewish followers of what was to become Christianity. In many ways, the Galatians would have been safer if they had followed the Roman imperial religious cult or been part of the already (although tenuously) recognized, exempted religion of the circumcised Jews. But rather than worshipping the Empire or agreeing to its constructed category of proper religious "others," Paul chose a third way. He argued that fellowship and identity across religious difference can and should abide. "Remember[ing] the poor" becomes the seal of fellowship for the diverse and divergent communities and a stand against the Roman Empire.

In our contemporary context, the word "empire" is often understood as the political dominance of neoliberal economics in the market economy. Resisting this form of empire also requires escaping the reductionism that it often imposes on religious practice. Neoliberalism is less threatened when religious communities are constructed along the lines of personal morality wedge issues such as abortion and same-sex marriage. Paul sets forth an expansive vision of religious practice, a vision that unites Gentile and Jewish Christians across differences in a shared commitment to the poor. This spiritual, economic, and political solidarity ultimately subverts the power of empire; the coalitional work of feminists and religious organizations for the working poor can do the same.

Rituals and Renewing Faithful Activism

Religious activists in the living wage movement continually invite people of faith to understand their religious practices as political practices for economic justice. Perhaps this is most true when activists refashion and resituate religious ritual in the midst of the political economy. In creating and practicing rituals, living wage activists are forming the *collective identity* of the group through a *low-risk* form of activism that contests the boundaries of the *sacred and profane* and draws on *embodied testimony* to *re-member the sacred.*

Collective identities are necessary to encourage people to take collective action. Religious identity is a particularly powerful resource for this collective identity work. When clergy lay their hands on the hospital worker in Chicago in the midst of sidewalk protest, her story and even the practice of the clergy transcends radical individuality and forms a group identity and solidarity. Rituals, through their physicality and emotion, help produce and sustain the collective identity essential for movement activism.

Rituals also offer a low-risk entry point for people of faith to join collective action for social change. In order to expand a movement, people need accessible entry points to activism. Religious ritual in political protest offers this accessibility both because it trades on largely familiar forms of practice and because the rituals themselves are rarely seen as threatening. Singing "We Shall Not Be Moved" or washing the feet of workers in front of the city council will likely not result in dramatic repercussions for participants. The accessibility of this form of public action informs IWJ's commitment to offering religious rituals for faith communities around the country and the development of "Labor in the Pulpit/on the Bimah/in the Minbar" as one of their signature annual events.

The use of religious ritual ultimately contests the contemporary boundaries between the sacred/private (religion) and the profane/public (politics). Whether delivering a worker justice homily in a hotel restaurant or delivering horseradish to council members, religious activists use religious ritual to declare the seeming mundane or profane as relevant to the sacred desires of God. Contesting the boundaries of capitalist society, these rituals resist the colonization of our lives by the values of efficiency and monetary bottom lines. These rituals also testify that the present historical moment is connected to more transcendent meaning and communities; there is a metaphysical timeline to be considered as well.

Religious activists also contest the expert-dominated talk of most of political life and the way that talk excludes both the less linguistically skilled and actual bodies from politics. Particularly in a movement that includes persons who, because of language barriers, education, or disability are not considered skilled language users, the embodied nature of religious ritual enables their participation in ways that are important for building moral agency. In addition, religious ritual focuses not only on the words, but also on the physical bodies of those present in protest. This is particularly important for a movement that is highlighting the heavily burdened bodies of low-wage workers, which are often hidden from sight, through back hallways, utility closets, and third shifts. Religious activists' rituals, then, perform an alternative vision of worker dignity for the political economy.

In all these ways, religious rituals reconstitute and expand the arenas and persons that are included in sacred care, not only for political efficacy but also for theological integrity. In the midst of this work, religious activists must also recognize the temptation to instrumentalize religious ritual for short-term political effect. By maintaining connections to more enduring communities of worship, rituals will remain more *lithe and authentic*, renewed by the *whole context of faith* that is seen in the *liturgical nature of activism* itself.

Religious rituals' meaning and significance relies on their echoing of original contexts and purposes. The use of a chupah in a religion-labor marriage in Los Angeles derives its meaning from the chupah's ongoing use in Jewish religious communities. Pragmatically, knowing and being immersed in ongoing communities of worship provides activists both with a greater range of knowledge of rituals and greater skill in meaningful innovation. Theologically, strong connections to ongoing communities of worship also help contextualize these rituals in terms of the whole practice of faith and the complexity of human life. In the Christian tradition (as in many others), confession is linked with forgiveness and is tied to celebration, proclamation, and intercession; gathering is always paired with sending forth. To emphasize only one ritual or one dimension of religious practice is to lose the vision of the whole. Through a more holistic practice, reminders of our own brokenness may help us not to demonize opponents but to pray for them and ultimately to offer reconciliation. Moreover, connections to ongoing communities of worship also remind us of the internal purposes and goods that these rituals intend. They are not just about political efficacy or political theater; faith is more than politics (although it certainly has political implications). A blessing of a worker's hands is first about blessing and connection to God. Politics flows in, from, and around the practice, but its transcendent purpose should not be lost. Finally, in the midst of the highs and lows or the organizing life, the yearly liturgical calendar of religious traditions also reminds us of the cycles of life and their spiritual significance. Days of anticipation, great celebration, purposeful discipline, mourning, and even "ordinary time" provide important assurances about the varied nature of the work for justice. The liturgical calendar invites us to learn the lessons and meanings in each season without rushing to the next. Through attention to the whole practice of faith, and its context in ongoing communities of worship, we may even learn more about the myriad ways God is present in the lifecycle of organizing.

God's Labor and Ours

In the end, religious activists in the living wage movement have helped to change the nature of the conversation in municipal and ecclesial settings around the nation. As of this writing, every major Protestant denomination (excluding Southern Baptists), as well as Reformed, Conservative, and Reconstructionist Judaism, have joined Roman Catholics in endorsing living wages as part of their social policy statements. But even these endorsements push beyond a specific policy. Religious activists are changing the theological conversation about work and worker justice across the nation. And, in the context of this changed theological conversation, groups like IWJ are focused on preparing a new generation of religious activists for this organizing work.

In a large classroom in the basement of a Chicago convent, about forty college and seminary students gathered to hear an interfaith panel on worker justice organizing. The students were part of IWJ's annual summer internship program, which matches students with affiliates, unions, and worker centers across the nation. After hearing from a Methodist minister about his long history of worker justice activism and from a Muslim woman with Interfaith Youth Core, a young local rabbi leapt up to begin his presentation. In an animated style, the rabbi began by asking if anyone could recite the fourth commandment. The students exchanged quizzical looks, and a few ventured their guesses. "Honor your father and mother?" "No" the rabbi answered, "That's the fifth." "You shall have no other gods before me?" "That's the first—try again." A few more guesses and few more corrections, and finally a student said, "Oh! Remember the Sabbath!" The rabbi replied, "Good, but that's only the very beginning. What's the next part of the commandment?" A few mumblings from students and the rabbi started, "Remember the Sabbath day, to keep it holy"—dramatic pause—" Six days shalt thou labour, and do all thy work" (Exod. 20:8–9. TaNaK).

After a round of "Oh, yeah," the rabbi analyzed the text. He argued that the commandment was about work as well as Sabbath. "Yes, the Sabbath is holy and sacred unto God. But God commands us to work." He continued by declaring that the passage spoke to the sacred requirement to work as well as to God's work during the six days of creation. Work is something God participates in, as something that is under the purview of God's commands. Ultimately, the rabbi argued, work was not to be seen as "divine punishment" but as part of the holistic nature of God and of human flourishing. In this context, the cause of worker justice finds its deepest grounding and accountability. After a thoughtful pause, the rabbi closed with the questions, "What does your tradition teach about work? How must we honor work? What will you teach about work?"

The living wage movement places these questions squarely before people of faith. Living wage activists provide concrete actions to accompany theological answers around "justice," "dignity," and "hope"—whether it be through reframing issues, connecting communities, recruiting new leaders, supporting women organizers, or renewing rituals. By engaging and evaluating religious activists' practices, we are invited to continue the struggle. In that spirit, "Come, Walk With Us, The Journey is Long" invites the hearer to join the rhythms of realism, celebration, and anticipation that are needed to sustain contemporary worker justice activism and the anti-poverty work of progressive religious activism.

Notes

NOTES TO THE INTRODUCTION

1. The Industrial Areas Foundation was founded by Saul Alinsky in the 1940s and is now the national hub of fifty-seven multi-ethnic and interfaith organizational networks working primarily in low- and middle-income communities. The IAF "has a radical belief in the potential of the vast majority of people to grow and develop as leaders, to be full members of the body politic, to speak and act with others on their own behalf. And IAF does indeed use a radical tactic: the face-to-face, one-to-one individual meeting whose purpose is to initiate a public relationship and to re-knit the frayed social fabric." www.industrialareasfoundation.org/iafabout/about.htm.

2. Deborah M. Figart, *Living Wage Movements: Global Perspectives*, Advances in Social Economics (London: Routledge, 2004), 72.

3. Stephanie Luce, *Fighting for a Living Wage* (Ithaca, NY: Cornell University Press/ILR Press, 2004), 19. In the 1980s, Urban Development Actions Grants (UDAGs) offered an alternative form of federal funding with interest-free grants to developers to redevelop and restart seemingly stagnant urban economies. New York, Detroit, and Baltimore were the highest users of this form of urban renewal. Because few guidelines accompanied UDAGs, developers mostly built convention centers, hotels, marinas, and high-end condominiums instead of mixed-income housing or other social infrastructures. The sociologist Andy Merrifield argues that these grants were soon "hastening, not ameliorating, social polarization, since few of the goodies seemed to trickle down to needy people." Andy Merrifield, "The Urbanization of Labor: Living Wage Activism in the American City," *Social Text* 18, no. 1 (2000): 32.

4. Janice Fine, "Community Unionism in Baltimore and Stamford: Beyond the Politics of Particularism," *Working USA* 4, no. 3 (2000–2001): 64. The UDAG program was cut entirely in 1987, but much of their strategy was localized to cities that had utilized such programs before. This cut in federal funding also heightened competition among cities to cut expenses by privatizing and court business with tax breaks.

5. Marc. V. Levine, "Downtown Redevelopment as an Urban Growth Strategy: A Critical Reappraisal of the Baltimore Renaissance," *Journal of Urban Affairs* 9, no. 2 (1987): 103-23.

6. A study by the Chicago Institute on Urban Poverty found similar results for the privatization of government employees. For example, entry-level workers had lowered compensation levels ranging from 25% to 46% when they were outsourced to private firms. This wage loss disproportionately affected female minority workers because "government agencies disproportionately hire" these workers. Jared Bernstein, "The

Living Wage Movement: What Is It, Why Is It, and What's Known About Its Impact," in *Emerging Labor Market Institutions for the Twenty-First Century*, ed. Richard B. Freeman, Joni Hersch, and Lawrence Mishel, 112 (Chicago: University of Chicago Press, 2005).

7. Fine, "Community Unionism in Baltimore and Stamford," 64.

8. Ibid.

9. William P. Quigley, "The Living Wage Movement," *BLUEPRINT for Social Justice* 54, no. 9 (2001). www.loyno.edu/twomey/blueprint/vol_liv/No-09_May_2001.html

10. Ibid., 121.

11. Fine, "Community Unionism in Baltimore and Stamford," 67.

12. Ibid., 65.

13. Oren M. Levin-Waldman, *The Political Economy of the Living Wage: A Study of Four Cities* (Armonk, NY: M. E. Sharpe, 2005), 143.

14. Figart, *Living Wage Movements*, 804.

15. Fine, "Community Unionism in Baltimore and Stamford," 65.

16. Ibid.

17. Ibid.

18. The prevalence of part-time work, somewhat limited the number of city workers the ordinance lifted out of poverty. Merrifield, "Urbanization of Labor," 45; Christopher Neit et al., "The Effects of Living Wages in Baltimore," (Washington, DC: Economic Policy Institute, 1999), *epi.3cdn.net/63b7cb4cbcf2f33b2d_w9m6bnks7.pdf*; Mark Weisbrot and Michelle Sfroza-Roderick, "Baltimore's Living Wage Law: An Analysis of the Fiscal and Economic Costs of Baltimore City Ordinance 442" (Washington, DC: Preamble Center, 1996).

19. Fine, "Community Unionism in Baltimore and Stamford," 65.

20. Ibid.

21. Ibid., 68.

22. Ibid.

23. www.buildiaf.org

24. Stephanie Luce, "'The Full Fruits of Our Labor': The Rebirth of the Living Wage Movement," *Labor History* 43, no. 4 (2002): 408.

25. ACORN statistics quoted in S. Laurel Weldon and Harry Targ, "From Living Wages to Family Wages," *New Political Science* 26, no. 1 (2004): 77.

26. www.acorn.org

27. Quoted in Luce, "'Full Fruits of Our Labor,'" 409.

28. Isaac Martin, "Dawn of the Living Wage: The Diffusion of a Redistributive Municipal Policy," *Urban Affairs Review* 36, no. 4 (2001).

29. Ibid., 82.

30. The anonymity of participants in any meetings that were closed to the general public are protected in this study. I do not assume participant anonymity for public meetings or rallies, but because of many workers' (and even activists') vulnerability I do not attribute quotes to person's that were not on the formal agenda for an event (or if I later learn these persons have been subject to management retaliation). I do attribute all quotes to specific persons who were documented in an organization's official records or were reported in the news.

31. Stephanie Luce and David Reynolds (political scientists), Robert Pollin and David Neumark (economists), and Bruce Nissen and Isaac Martin (sociologists) have

already begun to map this territory well. See Luce, *Fighting for a Living Wage*; David Neumark, *How Living Wage Laws Affect Low-Wage Workers and Low-Income Families* (San Francisco: Public Policy Institute of California, 2002); Bruce Nissen, "The Effectiveness and Limits of Labor-Community Coalitions: Evidence from South Florida," *Labor Studies Journal* 29, no. 1 (2004): 67–89, and Nissen, "Living Wage Campaigns from a 'Social Movement' Perspective: The Miami Case," *Labor Studies Journal* 25, no. 3 (2000): 29–50; David B. Reynolds, *Taking the High Road: Communities Organize for Economic Change* (Armonk, NY: M. E. Sharpe, 2002).

32. Many scholars provide ethical analyses that more specifically address the economic impact of living wage ordinances from both religious and humanist perspectives. See particularly Christine Hinze and Marvin Mich (Christian ethicists), Jill Jacobs and Aaron Levine (Jewish ethicists), Jerold Waltman and William Quigley (political scientists), Jared Bernstein, Donald Stabile, Deborah Figart, Robert Pasch and Falguni Sheth, James Buss and Arthur Romero (economists). See also Figart, *Living Wage Movements*; Bernstein, "Living Wage Movement"; William P. Quigley, *Ending Poverty as We Know It: Guaranteeing a Right to a Job at a Living Wage* (Philadelphia: Temple University Press, 2003); Jerold L. Waltman, *The Case for the Living Wage* (New York: Algora Publications, 2004), and Waltman, *Minimum Wage Policy in Great Britain and the United States* (New York: Algora Publications, 2008); Thomas O'Brien and Scott Paeth, *Religious Perspectives on Business Ethics: An Anthology, Religion and Business Ethics* (Lanham, MD: Rowman and Littlefield, 2007); Quigley, "The Living Wage Movement"; Donald Stabile, *The Living Wage: Lessons from the History of Economic Thought* (Cheltenham, UK: Edward Elgar, 2008); Deborah M. Figart, Ellen Mutari, and Marilyn Power, *Living Wages, Equal Wages: Gender and Labor Market Policies in the United States*, Routledge Iaffe Advances in Feminist Economics (London: Routledge, 2002); Robert E. Pasch and Falguni A. Sheth, "The Economics and Ethics of Minimum Wage Legislation," *Review of Social Economy* 57 (1999): 466–87; Marvin L. Krier Mich, "The Living Wage Movement and Catholic Social Teaching," *Journal of Catholic Social Thought* 6, no. 1 (2009); Christine Frier Hinze, *Radical Sufficiency: The Legacy and Future of the Catholic Living Wage Agenda* (forthcoming), and Hinze, "What Is Enough? Catholic Social Thought, Consumption, and Material Sufficiency," in *Having: Property and Possession in Religious and Social Living*, ed. William Schweiker and Charles Matthews, 102–88 (Grand Rapids, MI: Eerdmans, 2004),; Jill Jacobs, "The Living Wage: A Jewish Approach," *Conservative Judaism* 55, no. 3 (2003): 38–51; Hinze, "Social and Economic Ethics," *Theological Studies* 70, no 1 (2009): 159–76.

33. IWJ national conference, 2007.

34. Gary J. Dorrien, *Social Ethics in the Making: Interpreting an American Tradition* (Malden, MA: Wiley-Blackwell, 2009), 2.

35. Dorrien, *Social Ethics in the Making*, 2.

36. My understanding of "class" connects with Weberian traditions on the varied life opportunities connected to the resources and skills one brings to the marketplace. In short, class is one's place in the economic system of owning means of production (capitalist class), owning skills and credentials (middle class), and owning "unskilled" labor power (working class). The connection between class and group status is perhaps best seen in the construction of the working poor as a group that

deserves more surveillance than participation in political processes. I also find the Marxian concept of exploitation to be important to understanding the "inverse inter-dependent welfare principle" of class. Gains made by those who are dominant in the economic system often come as a result of losses to the less economically powerful. Particularly in the current U.S. economy, the history of economic inequality tracks this assumption well. See *Encyclopedia of Social Theory*, s.v. "Social Class" (by Erik Wright), ed. George Ritzer (Thousand Oaks, CA: Sage Publications, 2005).

NOTES TO CHAPTER 1

1. Interfaith Worker Justice, "Rally Song Book" (Chicago: Interfaith Worker Justice, 2005), 11. Bobo's fifth stanza originally reads "Oh Congress, won't you raise the minimum wage" but can be altered for local activism.

2. For a recent version of the original, see Bruce Springsteen, *We Shall Overcome: The Seeger Sessions* (Sony Records, 2006). In the early 1900s, Joe Hill and Ralph Chaplin wrote songs based on religious hymnody for social movement organizing. See, for example, Hill's "Preacher and Slave" set to the tune of "In the Sweet Bye and Bye" and Chaplin's "Solidarity Forever" to the tune of "The Battle Hymn of the Republic."

3. Aldon D. Morris, *The Origins of the Civil Rights Movement: Black Communities Organizing for Change* (New York: Free Press, 1984) defines a "movement halfway house" as "an established group or organization that is only partially integrated into the larger society because its participants are actively involved in efforts to bring about a desired change in society" (139). These organizations "develop a battery of social change resources such as skilled activists, tactical knowledge, media contacts, workshops, knowledge of past movements, and a vision of a future society" (140). Morris identifies the American Friends Service Committee, the Fellowship of Reconciliation, the War Resister's League, and the Highlander Folk School as examples.

4. Richard L. Wood, *Faith in Action: Religion, Race, and Democratic Organizing in America*, Morality and Society Series (Chicago: University of Chicago Press, 2002), 6.

5. Luce, "'Full Fruits of Our Labor,'" 403.

6. Ibid.

7. Merrifield, "Urbanization of Labor," 33.

8. Luce, "'Full Fruits of Our Labor,'" 408.

9. Heidi Swarts argues that ACORN was the most important national organization in the diffusion of the movement while also conceding that the local nature of organizing (including faith communities) was essential to the movement as well. Heidi J. Swarts, *Organizing Urban America: Secular and Faith-Based Progressive Movements*, Social Movements, Protest, and Contention (Minneapolis: University of Minnesota Press, 2008), 74.

10. Jon Gertner, "What Is a Living Wage?" *New York Times*, January 15, 2006.

11. Swarts, *Organizing Urban America*, 74ff. For example, the New Party helped a coalition called "Progressive Milwaukee" win the first citywide and countrywide living wage ordinance for direct city workers indexed to inflation in 1995 and Twin-cities New Party and ACORN also helped Minneapolis-St. Paul pass their ordinance in 1997. Merrifield, "Urbanization of Labor," 33.

12. Kim Bobo, "Citizen Wealth: Forty-Year Organizing Veteran Wade Rathke Has Plenty of New Ideas," *Religion Dispatches* (2010), www.religiondispatches.org/books/politics/2732/acorn_founder_writes_on_saving_working_families/.

13. Most of my research was also concluded before the major ACORN scandals of 2009 and therefore not affected by the ensuing controversies and de-funding. My Nashville involvement is ongoing, but the small ACORN affiliate that was launched in Nashville in late 2008 was (a) still organizing their funding base, (b) not directly involved in the living wage coalition, and (c) closed after the controversy emerged.

14. Gertner, "What Is a Living Wage?"

15. "Jen Kern on Peri's Living Wage Research and the Grassroots Movement" (2008), www.peri.umass.edu/kern/.

16. Bernstein, "Living Wage Movement," 132.

17. In my research cities, San Diego had the endorsement and organizing power of a local FBCO network San Diego Organizing Project (SDOP) behind it, which was affiliated with PICO. Atlanta received the endorsement of Atlantans Building Leadership for Empowerment (ABLE), a Gamaliel affiliate, but did not rely on them for organizing. While Nashville previously had an active IAF affiliate called Tying Nashville Together (TNT), they were going through a time of realignment during the 2008–10 living wage campaign and were not active in the city. Memphis also did not benefit from the organizing of a FBCO.

18. Margaret Levi, David Olson, and Erich Steinman, "Living-Wage Campaigns and Laws," *WorkingUSA* 6, no. 3 (2002): 115.

19. Fifth principle of San Diego Interfaith Committee Worker Justice, "Mission Statement," November 2007.

20. San Diego Interfaith Committee Worker Justice "Mission Statement," November 2007.

21. Bobo, "Citizen Wealth."

22. M. Douglas Meeks, "The Economy of Grace: Human Dignity in the Market System," in *God and Human Dignity*, ed. R. Kendall Soulen and Linda Woodhead, 196–214 (Grand Rapids, MI: Eerdmans, 2006).

23. George Lardner, "Business Gets Cold Feet on Subminimum Wage," *Washington Post*, March 20, 1981.

24. Jonathan Wiseman, "House Passes Increase in Minimum Wage to $7.25," *Washington Post*, January 11, 2007.

25. 2.8 million workers made below the $7.25 minimum wage, and 1.6 million workers received spillover benefits for firms attempting to maintain their existing wage structure hierarchies. Lawrence Mishel, Jared Bernstein, and Heidi Shierholz, *The State of Working America 2008/2009*, An Economic Policy Institute Book (Ithaca, NY: ILR Press, 2009).

26. Kai Filion, "Minimum Wage Issue Guide" (Washington, DC: Economic Policy Institute, 2009), epi.3cdn.net/9f5a60cec02393cbe4_a4m6b5t1v.pdf.

27. Heidi Shierholz, "New 2008 Poverty, Income Data Reveal Only Tip of the Recession Iceberg" (Washington, DC: Economic Policy Institute, 2009), www.epi.org/publications/entry/income_picture_20090910.; Mishel, Bernstein, and Shierholz, State of Working America 2008/2009, 209.

28. Robert Pollin, *A Measure of Fairness: The Economics of Living Wages and Minimum Wages in the United States* (Ithaca, NY: ILR Press, 2008), 12.

29. Ibid.

30. Ibid.

31. Ibid.

32. Mishel, Bernstein, and Shierholz, *State of Working America 2008/2009*, 124.

33. Carmen DeNavas-Walt, Bernadette D. Proctor, and Jessica C. Smith, "Income, Poverty, and Health Insurance Coverage in the United States: 2007," ed. U.S. Census Bureau, Current Population Reports, P60-235 (Washington, DC: U.S. Government Printing Office, 2008).

34. Filion, "Minimum Wage Issue Guide."

35. DeNavas-Walt, "Income, Poverty, and Health Insurance Coverage."

36. Ibid.

37. Holly Sklar and Rev. Dr. Paul H. Sherry, *A Just Minimum Wage: Good for Workers, Business and Our Future* (Cincinnati: Friendship Press, 2005), 11.

38. Robert Pollin and Jeannette Wicks-Lim, "Economic Analysis of Nashville Living Wage Proposal" (Amherst, MA: Political Economy Research Institute (PERI), University of Massachusetts–Amherst, 2009), 7.

39. Willis J. Nordlund, *The Quest for a Living Wage: The History of the Federal Minimum Wage Program*, Contributions in Labor Studies (Westport, CT: Greenwood Press, 1997), xv.

40. Ibid.

41. Neumark explains that "employers were [also] viewed as having disproportionate bargaining power over such workers, and the minimum wage was intended to ensure they received a 'fair' wage for their work." David Neumark and William L. Wascher, *Minimum Wages* (Cambridge: MIT Press, 2008), 1..

42. Ibid., 32.

43. Irene Andrews, "Minimum Wage Comes Back!" *American Labor Legislation Review* 23, no. 2 (1933): 103. Quoted in Nordlund, *Quest for a Living Wage*, 33. Nordlund notes that backers of the FLSA also thought the reduction in work hours would lead to improved employment numbers as more persons were needed to work the same amount of hours.

44. U.S. Bureau of Labor Statistics, "Record of the Discussion before Congress of the United States on the Fair Labor Standards Act of 1938," (Washington, DC: Government Publications Office,1938), 1. Nordland argues, following W. E. Boles [Walter E. Boles, "Some Aspects of the Fair Labor Standards Act," *Southern Economic Journal* 6, no. 4 (1940).], that the rhetoric around "morals" (as in protection from prostitution for women, excessive drinking for men, and time for worship for all) that was part of the early living wage movement was not present in the congressional debate about the FLSA. Nordlund, *Quest for a Living Wage*, 32.. This however does not mean "morality"—as in worker dignity, etc.—was not in play during the debates.

45. The FLSA that was eventually agreed upon was much weaker than the original version desired by Roosevelt. The administration had started with a minimum of forty cents per hour, but the final legislation started at twenty-five cents with five-cent increases each year until it reached forty cents. The bill did also not include any automatic adjustments and exclude numerous workers in agriculture, state, and

local governments, retail, hospitals, education, and domestic services. Stephanie Luce argues that the concept of the "living wage" was also dropped in this process as the minimum wage became a wage floor to "protect workers from ruinous competition" but not provide a wage capable of sustaining a family. But activists continued to rally around increases in the minimum wage to make it a fuller "family wage," and its value did rise more steadily particularly after World War II. Luce, "'Full Fruits of Our Labor,'" 402.

46. Pollin, *Measure of Fairness*, 17.

47. M. P. Taylor, "Budget Blues," *Dallas Morning News*, March 9, 1993.

48. Human Nutrition Information Service Consumer Nutrition Division, "U.S.D.A. Family Food Plans, 1983: Low Cost, Moderate and Liberal," ed. U.S. Department of Agriculture (Washington, DC: Government Printing Office, 1983).

49. Arloc Sherman, *Wasting America's Future: The Children's Defense Fund Report on the Costs of Child Poverty* (Boston: Beacon Press, 1994), 6 and 8.

50. For more detailed explanation, see www.bls.gov/cpi/home.htm

51. U.S. Bureau of Labor Statistics, "Consumer Expenditure Survey 1998" (Washington, DC: Government Printing Office, 1999).

52. Constance F. Citro and Robert T. Michael, "Measuring Poverty a New Approach" (Washington, DC: National Academy Press, 1995), www.census.gov/hhes/povmeas/methodology/nas/files/ack.pdf.

53. Robert Bray and Max Toth , "Winning Wages: A Media Kit for Successful Living Wages Strategies" (San Francisco: Tides Foundation and SPIN Project Independent Media Institute, 2003), www.spinproject.org/article.php?id=95.

54. Pollin, *Measure of Fairness*, 23.

55. Mishel, Bernstein, and Shierholz, *State of Working America 2008/2009*.

56. DeNavas-Walt, "Income, Poverty, and Health Insurance Coverage," 13.

57. U.S. Census Bureau, "S1703. Selected Characteristics of People at Specified Levels of Poverty in the Past 12 Months" (Washington, DC: Government Printing Office, 2009).

58. Shierholz, "New 2008 Poverty."

59. U.S. Bureau of Labor Statistics, "Characteristics of Minimum Wage Workers: 2008," in *Labor Force Statistics from the Curren Population Survey* (Washington, DC: Government Printing Office, 2009).

60. Author's calculations from U.S. Bureau of Labor Statistics, "Table 10: Distribution of wage and salary workers paid hourly rates, by hourly earnings and selected characteristics, 2008 annual averages" in "Highlights of Women's Earnings in 2008" (Washington, DC: Government Printing Office, 2009), 48–49.

61. Ibid.

62. Bray and Toth, "Winning Wages."

63. Mishel, Bernstein, and Shierholz, *State of Working America 2008/2009*, 124. Derived from the authors' analyses of U.S. Bureau of Economic Analysis (2008), Bureau of Labor Statistics (2008d), and the Current Population Survey (2008) data.

64. Clare DiSalvo, "Working Hard, Falling Short" in *Serving Witness: Religious Leader's Stories of Workers Who Lack a Living Wage* (San Diego: San Diego Interfaith Committee for Worker Justice, 2004), 2.

65. Mishel, Bernstein, and Shierholz, *State of Working America 2008/2009*, 121.

66. Bray and Toth, "Winning Wages," 65.

67. UNICEF Innocenti Research Centre, "A League Table of Child Poverty in Rich Nations," in *Innocenti Report Card No.1* (Florence, Italy: Innocenti Research Centre, 2000), www.unicef-irc.org/publications/pdf/repcard1e.pdf.

68. IWJ National Conference, 2007.

69. Including such standoffs as a refusal to raise the minimum wage if Reagan judicial nominees were not approved. Nordlund, *Quest for a Living Wage*, 185.

70. Rick Wartzman, "Falling Behind: As Officials Lost Faith in the Minimum Wage, Pat Williams Lived It—Historic Shift in Washington Left a Louisiana Worker Struggling to Pay the Bills—a Program That Ike Liked," *Wall Street Journal*, July 19, 2001.

71. Lardner, "Business Gets Cold Feet on Subminimum Wage." Strategically, this comment emerged in the context of the Chamber's reversal of support for Sen. Orrin Hatch's youth differential amendment to the FLSA (which would have lowered the required minimum wage for persons under twenty years of age in order, arguably, to decrease youth unemployment). The Chamber opposed any amendment to the FLSA because opening it up would likely lead to an increase in the minimum wage as well. Nordlund, *Quest for a Living Wage*, 178.

72. Welfare cuts by Reagan in 1981 also increased the numbers of those in working poverty and undermined workers' capacity to organize in a suddenly expanded labor pool. Luce, *Fighting for a Living Wage*, 17.

73. Merrifield, "Urbanization of Labor," 43.

74. Pollin and Wicks-Lim, "Economic Analysis of Nashville Living Wage Proposal," 7.

75. Arkansas IWJ organizer on 2007 Let Justice Roll tele-meeting.

76. Laura R. Olsen, "Whither the Religious Left? Religiopolitical Progressivism in Twenty-First-Century America," in *From Pews to Polling Places: Faith and Politics in the American Religious Mosaic*, ed. J. Matthew Wilson, 53 (Washington, DC: Georgetown University Press, 2007).

77. Alan Cooperman and Carlyle Murphy, "Religious Liberals Gain New Visibility: A Different List of Moral Issues," *Washington Post*, May 20, 2006.

78. Robert P. Jones, *Progressive & Religious: How Christian, Jewish, Muslim, and Buddhist Leaders Are Moving Beyond the Culture Wars and Transforming American Life* (Lanham, MD: Rowman and Littlefield, 2008), 14.

79. Olsen, "Whither the Religious Left?," 54; Mark O'Keefe, "Religious Left Makes a Political Push," *Christian Century*, September 21, 2004, 12; Rebecca T. Alpert, *Voices of the Religious Left: A Contemporary Sourcebook* (Philadelphia: Temple University Press, 2000), 2. This slogan "God is not a Republican or a Democrat" is Sojourner's ubiquitous bumper sticker in the progressive religious movement.

80. Jones, *Progressive & Religious*, 15.

81. Ibid., 16.

82. This is meant to be an illustrative, not exhaustive, list. David Heim, "The Divided Mind of the Religious Left: Voters and Values," *Christian Century*, August 8, 2006, 26; Olsen, "Whither the Religious Left?," 59.

83. O'Keefe, "Religious Left Makes a Political Push," 13. In 2004, several progressive religious organizations took out a full-page ad in the *New York Times* and coordinated conferences and protests during the Republican Convention.

84. Heim, "Divided Mind of the Religious Left," 26. See also Jim Wallis, *The Great Awakening: Reviving Faith and Politics in a Post-Religious Right America* (New York: HarperLuxe, 2008).

85. E. J. Dionne, *Souled Out: Reclaiming Faith and Politics after the Religious Right* (Princeton, NJ: Princeton University Press, 2008).

86. C. Melissa Snarr, "Challenging Electoral Hegemonies: The Ethical Potential of (Religiously Attuned) Community Organizing" (paper presented to the American Academy of Religion conference, Chicago, November 1–3, 2008).

87. John Greene, Robert P. Jones, and Daniel Cox, "Faithful, Engaged, and Divergent: A Comparative Potrait of Conservative and Progressive Religious Activists in the 2008 Election and Beyond." (Washington, DC: Public Religion Research, Ray C. Bliss Institute of Applied Politics, 2009), www.uakron.edu/bliss/docs/ReligiousActivistReport-Final.pdf.

88. Ibid.

89. Charles F. Hall, "The Christian Left: Who Are They and How Are They Different from the Christian Right?" *Review of Religious Research* 39, no. 1 (1997): 31.

90. Mark Gabrish Conlan, "San Diego Passes Living Wage Law 5–4," *Zenger's Newsmagazine*, April 13, 2005.

91. Olsen, "Whither the Religious Left?," 57.

92. Jones, *Progressive & Religious*, 16. See also Charles M. Blow, "Rise of the Religious Left," *New York Times*, July 2, 2010.

93. Isa. 43:19 states "I am about to do a new thing; now it springs forth, do you not perceive it? I will make a way in the wilderness and rivers in the desert" (NRSV).

NOTES TO CHAPTER 2

1. Rev. Paul Sherry, former leader of the National Council of Churches' Let Justice Roll campaign, presentation at Interfaith Worker Justice national conference, June 2007.

2. Robert Bellah built on Rousseau's and Durkheim's work on civil religion to define American civil religion as "an institutionalized collection of sacred beliefs about the American nation," as witnessed in the founding documents and public rituals such as presidential speeches and public spaces, which become almost sacred such as the Washington Mall. Robert Bellah, "Civil Religion in America," *Daedalus* no. 96 (1967): 1–21.

3. Craig Jenkins and Charles Perrow, "Insurgency of the Powerless: Farm Worker Movements," *American Sociological Review* 42 (1977): 249–68; Anthony Oberschall, *Social Conflict and Social Movements*, Prentice-Hall Series in Sociology (Englewood Cliffs, NJ: Prentice-Hall, 1973); John McCarthy and Mayer Zald, "Resource Mobilization and Social Movements: A Partial Theory," *American Journal of Sociology*, no. 82 (1977): 1212–41.

4. This is also known as "micro-mobilization," defined as "the range of interactive processes devised and employed by social movement organizations to mobilize or influence various target groups with respect to pursuit of collective or common interests." David Snow et al., "Frame Alignment Processes, Micromobilization, and Movement Participation," *American Sociological Review* 51 (1986): 464–81.

5. Aldon D. Morris and Carol McClurg Mueller, *Frontiers in Social Movement Theory* (New Haven, CT: Yale University Press, 1992).

6. David Snow and Robert D. Benford, "Master Frames and Cycles of Protest," in *Frontiers in Social Movement Theory*, ed. Aldon D. Morris, 139 (New Haven: Yale University Press, 1992).

7. James M. Jasper, *The Art of Moral Protest : Culture, Biography, and Creativity in Social Movements* (Chicago: University of Chicago Press, 1997), 65, quoted in Sharon Erickson Nepstad, *Convictions of the Soul: Religion, Culture, and Agency in the Central America Solidarity Movement* (Oxford: Oxford University Press, 2004), 8.

8. Martin Luther King Jr., *Where Do We Go from Here: Chaos or Community?* (New York: Harper and Row, 1967), 179.

9. Snow and Benford, "Master Frames and Cycles of Protest," 137. The authors actually use the term "prognosis" rather than "prescription" for determining a line of action. Prescription is chosen here to emphasize the agency (rather than the predictive ability) of the actor in determining future action.

10. Rev. Elizabeth Miller, "Raise the Minimum Wage," *Morning Call*, 2005, quoted in Sklar and Sherry, *Just Minimum Wage*, 7.

11. Rev. Robert W. Edgar, "NCC General Secretary's Statement Asking Minimum Wage Hike" March 7, 2000, quoted in Sklar and Sherry, *Just Minimum Wage*, 8.

12. Ibid., 13.

13. Ibid., 11.

14. Originally developed by Supreme Court Justice Louis Brandeis in the 1933 case *Ligget Co. v. Lee* (288 U.S. 517, 558–559), the term developed as a counter to the "race for efficiency." The race to the bottom results when states or nations compete to outdo each other in offering deregulation, tax incentives, etc., to attract businesses, often at the expense of worker rights and wages.

15. Testimony before San Diego City Council. Copy provided by ICWJ.

16. Ibid.

17. Sklar and Sherry, *Just Minimum Wage*, 35.

18. Ibid., 38.

19. Atlanta Living Wage Coalition, "Short-Changed: The High Cost of Working Poverty for Communities and Families" (document as testimony to the Atlanta City Council by Working Women 9to5, 2003), 2.

20. Rev. Dr. James A. Forbes Jr. in Sklar and Sherry, *Just Minimum Wage*, ii.

21. www.iwj.org/issues/living_wage.html.

22. Rev. Rebekah Jordon, executive director of Mid-South Interfaith Network for Economic Justice, "Fight Poverty: Pass living wage ordinance," *Commercial Appeal* (Memphis, TN) January 22, 2004, quoted in Sklar and Sherry, *Just Minimum Wage*, 27.

23. Resolution on Living Wage Campaigns, General Assembly, Union of American Hebrew Congregations, December 1999, quoted in Sklar and Sherry, *Just Minimum Wage*, 8.

24. Ibid., 48.

25. Training Session, Interfaith Worker Justice National Conference, Chicago, IL: June 2008.

26. Sklar and Sherry, *Just Minimum Wage*, 40.

27. Ibid., 15.

28. Conlan, "San Diego Passes Living Wage Law 5–4." Interestingly, Ken Cramer's son, George, had previously spoken against the ordinance before the council.

29. Sklar and Sherry, *Just Minimum Wage*, 1.

30. United Church of Christ, Worker Justice button.

31. Christian Smith, *Disruptive Religion: The Force of Faith in Social-Movement Activism* (New York: Routledge, 1996), 238. The San Diego ICWJ pressed this "experiential credibility" deeper by not only using worker testimonies before the city council but inviting members on a "Working Poor Job Shadow Experience." Along with religious leaders, city council members would spend time working with a low-wage earner and understanding what it took to survive on "poverty wages."

32. Donatella Della Porta and Mario Diani, *Social Movements: An Introduction* (Oxford: Blackwell, 1999), 75.

33. Kim Bobo, "Kim Bobo on Alan Wolfe," *Interfaith Worker Justice Blog*, October 30, 2007, interfaithworkerjustice.blogspot.com/2007/10/kim-bobo-on-alan-wolfe.html. Bobo is the founder and executive director of Interfaith Worker Justice.

34. The farm worker activist César Chávez was not invoked in the participant observation, with the sole exception being a cover quote for a "Labor in the Pulpit" church service in Nashville. "Labor in the Pulpits /on the Bimah /in the Minbar" refers to the IWJ and the AFL-CIO co-sponsored program every Labor Day weekend in the United States. The program focuses on the shared goals of the faith community and the union movement for worker justice. Often union members will serve as guest speakers in congregations to speak out about their faith, work and the union movement.

35. Also read to the city council by the executive director of San Diego's ICWJ in 2004.

36. Ann Swidler, "Culture in Action: Symbols and Strategies," *American Sociological Review* 51 (1986): 273–86.

37. Laura Murphy, "An 'Indestructible Right': John Ryan and the Catholic Origins of the U.S. Living Wage Movement, 1906–1938," *Labor: Studies in Working-Class History of the Americas* 6, no. 1 (2009): 57.

38. Ibid., 58.

39. John Augustine Ryan, *Economic Justice: Selections from Distributive Justice and a Living Wage*, ed. Harlan Beckley, 113 (Louisville, KY: Westminster John Knox Press, 1996).

40. Murphy, "An 'Indestructible Right,'" 57.

41. Ryan, *Economic Justice*, 114.

42. Ibid., 114.

43. Ibid.

44. Ryan, *A Living Wage: Its Ethical and Economic Aspects* (New York: Macmillan, 1906), 71–72.

45. Ibid., 115.

46. Oral history of Frances Perkins, "Reminiscences." *New York Times* Oral History Program, Columbia University Oral History Collection, pt. 3, no. 182, book 7, 26–27 (Glen Rock, NJ: Microfilming Corporation of America, 1976).

47. Ryan, *Economic Justice*, 122.

48. Sklar and Sherry, *Just Minimum Wage*, 1.

49. San Diego Interfaith Committee on Worker Justice mission statement.

50. Testimony before the San Diego City Council, 2004.

51. *The Book of Resolutions of the United Methodist Church* (Nashville: United Methodist Publishing House, 2000), 55.

52. Ryan, *Economic Justice*, 116.

53. Denis Grasska, "'Living Wage' Gets Push from Religious Community: Workers Will Receive Increases over Three Years," *Southern Cross*, May 12, 2008.

54. Walter Rauschenbusch, *Christianizing the Social Order* (Boston: Pilgrim Press, 1912), 152.

55. Rauschenbusch, *Christianity and the Social Crisis* (New York: Macmillan, 1907), 380.

56. Michael Long argues that King embraced a vision of social democracy rather than liberal democracy and looked to Sweden as an exemplar of this kind of government. Michael G. Long, *Against Us, but For Us: Martin Luther King, Jr. and the State*, (Macon, GA: Mercer University Press, 2002). Douglas Sturm defines a social democracy as one that "is solidaristic and relational in its basic social theory. It promotes a politics of participation. Its doctrine of rights is affirmative: one's rights are to be empowered and enabled to find fulfillment within an encompassing community of fellow citizens. In their respective doctrine of rights [liberal democracy] is primarily concerned with freedom of speech and association, whereas [social democracy] is concerned, as well, with education, meaningful employment, and housing." Douglas Sturm, "Martin Luther King Jr. as Democratic Socialist," *Journal of Religious Ethics* 18, no. 2 (1990): 82–83.

57. Long, *Against Us, but For Us*, 136.

58. Martin Luther King Jr., "Revolution and Redemption," unpublished closing address at the European Baptist Assembly in Amsterdam (August, 16, 1964), King Center Letters Archive, 9.

59. Joseph A. McCartin, "Building the Interfaith Worker Justice Movement: Kim Bobo's Story," *Labor: Studies in Working-Class History of the Americas* 6, no. 1 (2009): 89.

60. Deut. 24, Ps. 34:6, and Prov. 21:13, for example.

61. Walter Brueggemann, "Entitled Neighbors: A Biblical Perspective on Living Wage," *Witness* 85, no. 5 (2002): 18.

62. Ibid., 19.

63. Conferencia General del Episcopado Latinoamericano, "Puebla: Evangelization at Present and in the Future of Latin America" (Washington, DC: National Conference of Catholic Bishops, 1979), sec. 733. Pope Paul VI discussed the "preferential respect" due the poor in 1971 in *Octogensima Adveniens (Justice in the World)* declaring "the Gospel instructs us in the preferential respect due to the poor and the special situation they have in society: the more fortunate should renounce some of their rights so as to place their goods more generously at the service of the poor." Pope Paul VI, *Octogesima Adveniens* (1971), www.vatican.va/holy_father/paul_vi/apost_letters/documents/hf_p-vi_apl_19710514_octogesima-adveniens_en.html. While this statement signaled a significant shift toward solidarity compared to *Rerum Novarum*'s 1891 emphasis on giving to the poor out of surplus, later encyclicals, U.S.

Catholic Bishop statements, and especially liberation theologies would extend the concept even farther. The U.S. Council of Catholic Bishops explained in their 1986 landmark economic treatise *Economic Justice for All* that "As followers of Christ, we are challenged to make a fundamental 'option for the poor'—to speak for the voiceless, to defend the defenseless, to assess lifestyles, policies, and social institutions in terms of their impact on the poor. This 'option for the poor' does not mean pitting one group against another, but rather strengthening the whole community by assisting those who are most vulnerable. As Christians, we are called to respond to the needs of *all* our brothers and sisters, but those with the greatest needs require the greatest response." United States Conference of Catholic Bishops, *Economic Justice for All: Pastoral Letter on Catholic Social Teaching and the U.S. Economy* (Washington, DC: U.S. Catholic Conference, 1986), x–xi.

64. Rev. Paul Sherry, IWJ National Conference, 2007.

65. For an introduction to the moral assumptions of this economic history, see Rebecca Todd Peters, *In Search of the Good Life: The Ethics of Globalization* (New York: Continuum, 2004).

66. Ibid., 51.

67. Ibid., 45.

68. Ibid., 72.

69. Sklar and Sherry, *Just Minimum Wage*, 33.

70. Peters, *In Search of the Good Life*, 59.

71. United Methodist Church (U.S.), *The Book of Discipline of the United Methodist Church, 2004* (Nashville: United Methodist Publishing House, 2004).

72. In a previous version of this chapter, I pointed to two other possibility problematic assumptions within even the social equity strand of neoclassical economics: (1) its focus on consumption as the economic driver of the economy, and (2) its tolerance for inequality as long as basic needs are met. These are still important concerns that have been taken up by others and deserve more pursuit in another context. I focus on independence in this version because movement activists can most realistically address this within their present work. C. Melissa Snarr, "Waging Religious Ethics: Living Wages and Framing Public Religious Ethics," *Journal of the Society of Christian Ethics* 29, no. 1 (2009).

73. IWJ National Conference, June 2007.

74. It should be noted that the mortgage tax break is the leading welfare program for the U.S. middle class. Claude S. Fischer, *Inequality by Design: Cracking the Bell Curve Myth* (Princeton, NJ: Princton University Press, 1996).

75. By identifying interdependence as a lived reality and theological good, I do not imply that every form of interdependence is equally good. Certainly there is evaluation involved in assessing the quality of interdependence. Not all interdependencies are equal. A worker may need a job to survive, and the employer may need the worker to produce a product (a form of interdependency), but if one is trapped in a job that pays inadequately or subjected to demeaning conditions, this interdependency is to be judged negatively. Interdependent well-being as an ideal is not merely the capacity to leave a job or fire a worker whenever a relationship does not meet one's goals (or a negative limit); rather an interdependent relationship of respect, accountability, and mutual well-being is the positive ideal.

76. Martin Luther King Jr. and James Melvin Washington, *A Testament of Hope: The Essential Writings of Martin Luther King, Jr.* (San Francisco: Harper and Row, 1986), 254.

77. H. Richard Niebuhr, *The Responsible Self: An Essay in Christian Moral Philosophy* (New York,: Harper and Row, 1963), 71.

78. C. Melissa Snarr, *Social Selves and Political Reforms: Five Visions in Contemporary Christian Ethics* (New York: T&T Clark, 2007), xviii.

79. Amy Caiazza, *Called to Speak: Six Strategies That Encourage Women's Political Activism, Lessons from Interfaith Community Organizing* (Washington, DC: Institute for Women's Policy Research, 2006), 7. Caiazza's research included many of the leaders that were in my participant observation as well (particularly from Atlanta and the National IWJ board). For this reason I draw from her interviews, which were completed before my more formal research began.

80. Pope John Paul II, *Solilicitudo Rei Socialis* (1987), www.vatican.va/edocs/ENG0223/_INDEX.HTM.sec. 38. Emphasis in the original.

81. Margaret Farley, "New Patterns of Relationship: Beginnings of a Moral Revolution," in *Women: New Dimensions*, ed. Walter Burkhardt, 627–46 (New York: Paulist Press, 1976).

82. M. Douglas Meeks, *God the Economist: The Doctrine of God and Political Economy* (Minneapolis: Fortress Press, 1989), 111. Meeks and the entire stream of social Trinitarianism is deeply indebted to Jürgen Moltmann's work, particularly *The Trinity and the Kingdom: The Doctrine of God* (New York: Harper and Row, 1981).

83. Joy Ann McDougall, *Pilgrimage of Love: Moltmann on the Trinity and Christian Life*, Reflection and Theory in the Study of Religion (Oxford: Oxford University Press, 2005), 10. The literature here is vast, but some mapping of its terrain can be seen in Kathryn Tanner, *Jesus, Humanity and the Trinity: A Brief Systematic Theology*, (Minneapolis: Fortress Press, 2001); Sarah Coakley, "Why Gift? Gift, Gender and Trinitarian Relations in Milbank and Tanner," *Scottish Journal of Theology* 61, no. 2 (2008): 224–35. ; and John Milbank, *Being Reconciled: Ontology and Pardon*, Radical Orthodoxy Series (London: Routledge, 2003). Tanner is sharp in her criticism of equating Trinitarian and human relationships particularly when it comes to issues of difference in the Trinity. She argues that short of a moving to tri-theism, we risk losing human difference and agency when we emphasize the unity of the Trinitarian action and being. For example, our finitude means we do not act when our beloved does, nor do we ever know her completely in our relation to her. Kathryn Tanner, "Kingdom Come: The Trinity and Politics," *Princeton Seminary Bulletin* 28, no. 2 (2007): 129–45. But following McDougall, Johnson, and Coakley, I think there is much more room for real difference in varied forms of God's activity within the Trinity, and metaphorically it still holds great weight for encouraging reflection, at least, on the good of interdependence for Christian ethicists. Elizabeth A. Johnson, *She Who Is: The Mystery of God in Feminist Theological Discourse*, 10th anniversary ed. (New York: Crossroad, 2002).

84. Daniel L. Migliore, "The Trinity and Human Liberty," *Theology Today* 36, no. 4 (1980): 490.

85. McDougall, *Pilgrimage of Love*, 160.

86. Snarr, *Social Selves and Political Reforms*, 114.

87. Della Porta and Diani, *Social Movements*, 75.

88. Pope Benedict XVI, *Caritas in Veritate* (2009), www.vatican.va/holy_father/ benedict_xvi/encyclicals/documents/hf_ben-xvi_enc_20090629_caritas-in-veritate_ en.html.

89. Caiazza, *Called to Speak*, 7.

NOTES TO CHAPTER 3

1. The main title of this chapter references Matthew 25:35 (NRSV). The Mississippi Poultry Workers for Equality and Respect organization is affiliated with the IWJ workers' center network, and this story was told at IWJ's national convention in 2007.

2. See generally, William Mirolla, "Religious Protest and Economic Conflict: Possibilities and Constraints on Religious Resource Mobilization and Coalitions in Detroit's Newspaper Strike," *Sociology of Religion* 64, no. 4 (2003): 443–61.

3. Jeremy Brecher and Tim Costello, *Building Bridges: The Emerging Grassroots Coalition of Labor and Community* (New York: Monthly Review Press, 1990).

4. Sidney Verba, Kay Lehman Schlozman, and Henry E. Brady, *Voice and Equality: Civic Voluntarism in American Politics* (Cambridge, MA: Harvard University Press, 1995).

5. This term comes from Aldon Morris's work on the black civil rights movement and the movement's cultivation of black leaders through alternative social institutions. Morris, *Origins of the Civil Rights Movement*, 282–86.

6. U.S. Census Bureau, "Annual Social and Economic (Asec) Supplement, 2007" Current Population Survey, 2007 (Washington, DC: Government Printing Office, 2008). U.S. Census Bureau, "S1703. Selected Characteristics of People at Specified Levels of Poverty in the Past 12 Months." Official racial categorization in the U.S. Census is "White, not Hispanic" and "Black, only" and the ethnic designation of "Hispanic, any race." I use Latino throughout for consistency and because many Latinos associate "Hispanic" with colonization by Spain and also with lighter-skinned elites in Latin American countries.

7. U.S. Census Bureau, "Pov01: Age and Sex of All People, Family Members and Unrelated Individuals Iterated by Income-to-Poverty Ratio and Race: 2008," Annual Social and Economic Supplement (Washington, DC: Government Printing Office, 2009).

8. U.S. Census Bureau, "Annual Social and Economic (Asec) Supplement, 2007"; Sylvia Allegreto, "Basic Family Budgets: Working Families' Incomes Often Fail to Meet Living Expenses around the U.S.," (Washington, DC: Economic Policy Institute, 2005), www.epi.org/index.php/phpee/redirect/bp165; Annette D. Bernhardt, The Gloves-Off Economy: Workplace Standards at the Bottom of America's Labor Market, Labor and Employment Relations Association Series (Champaign: Labor and Employment Relations Association, University of Illinois at Urbana-Champaign, 2008).

9. U.S. Census Bureau, "S1703. Selected Characteristics of People at Specified Levels of Poverty in the Past 12 Months."

10. Daniel Dockterman and Gabriel Velasco, "Statistical Portrait of Hispanics in the United States, 2008" (Washington, DC: Pew Hispanic Center, 2010), pewhispanic.org/factsheets/factsheet.php?FactsheetID=58.

11. Testimony read by Rev. Willie Manley at a San Diego City Council public comment on February 19, 2004.

12. Jeffrey S. Passel, "The Size and Characteristics of the Unauthorized Migrant Population in the U.S. Estimates Based on the March 2005 Current Population Survey" (Washington, DC: Pew Hispanic Center, 2006), pewhispanic.org/files/reports/61.pdf

13. Manuel Pastro Jr. and Enrico Marcelli, "Somewhere over the Rainbow? African Americans, Unauthorized Mexican Immigration, and Coalition Building," *Review of Black Political Economy* 31, no. 1 (2003): 125–55.

14. Rakesh Kochhar, "Sharp Decline in Income for Non-Citizen Immigrant Households, 2006–2007" (Washington, DC: Pew Hispanic Center, 2008), pewhispanic.org/reports/report.php?ReportID=95.

15. Kochhar, "Latino Labor Report 2006: Strong Gains in Employment" (Washington, DC: Pew Hispanic Center, 2006), i.

16. Ibid., ii. pewhispanic.org/reports/report.php?ReportID=70.

17. Heidi Shierholz, "Immigration and Wages: Methodological Advancements Confirm Modest Gains for Native Workers," (Washington, DC: Economic Policy Institute, 2010), 2, www.epi.org/publications/entry/bp255/.

18. Dockterman and Velasco, "Statistical Portrait of Hispanics."

19. Brecher and Costello, *Building Bridges*, 338–39.

20. Nissen, "The Effectiveness and Limits of Labor-Community Coalitions."

21. Brecher and Costello, *Building Bridges*, 333.

22. Margaret Levi, David Olson, and Erich Steinman, "Living Wage Campaigns and Laws," *Working USA* 6, no. 3 (2002–3): 112.

23. Congregation-based community organizing (CBCO) usually consists of between ten and sixty congregations, which through various leadership development strategies seek to gain a place at the local governance table. These networks exist in at least thirty-three states, and each network determines the issues most relevant to their local organizing. Not all CBCO's choose to work on living wage issues.

24. For greater detail on these networks, see Mark Warren and Richard L. Wood, "Faith-Based Community Organizing: The State of the Field" (Jericho, NY: Interfaith Funders, 2001); Wood, *Faith in Action*.

25. Diana Jones, "Organizing through Congregations: Mediating and Moderating Roles of Spirituality"(PhD diss., Vanderbilt University, 2008), 48. Her research focuses most specifically on the PICO network that has a network of fifty federations working in one hundred fifty cities across seventeen states.

26. Helene Slessarev-Jamir, "Exploring the Attraction of Local Congregations to Community Organizing," *Nonprofit and Voluntary Sector Quarterly* 33, no. 4 (2004): 599.

27. This title refers to Acts 2:1–11, where the gift of the Holy Spirit enables people from many different countries and ethnicities to understand the speech of others.

28. Rhys Williams and N. J. Demerath III, "Religion and Political Process in an American City," *American Sociological Review* 56, no. 4 (1991): 426–27.

29. Fred Rose, *Coalitions across the Class Divide: Lessons from the Labor, Peace, and Environmental Movements* (Ithaca, NY: Cornell University Press, 2000), 177–78.

30. Presented at the "Unions 101 Session" at the national Interfaith Worker Justice, June 17, 2007.

31. San Diego Interfaith Committee on Worker Justice, "Living Wage Campaign" (San Diego: Unitarian Universalist Fund for Just Society Proposal, 2003), 8.

32. Clergy describe this model as the last-minute call to have a nominal clergy presence at an event, usually to lead an opening or closing prayer. Clergy regularly complain that they feel "used" by this nonreciprocal relationship.

33. IWJ National Conference, June 2007.

34. This title comes from 2 Corinthians 5:18, which states that believers have been given the "ministry of reconciliation."

35. Silke Roth, *Building Movement Bridges: The Coalition of Labor Union Women*, Contributions in Sociology (Westport, CT: Praeger, 2003), 9.

36. Levi, Olson, and Steinman, "Living Wage Campaigns and Laws," 114.

37. Interfaith Worker Justice, "Why Unions Matter," www.iwj.org/materials/materials_wumtxt.html.

38. Ibid.

39. Robert D. Putnam, *Bowling Alone: The Collapse and Revival of American Community*, (New York: Simon and Schuster, 2001).

40. Smith, *Disruptive Religion*, 17.

41. Ibid.

42. Wood, *Faith in Action*, 134.

43. March 2004 Conference Panel, Vanderbilt University, Nashville, TN.

44. Martin Buber and Ronald Gregor Smith, *I and Thou* (Edinburgh: T&T Clark, 1937).

45. This title refers first to the organizer's quote "fighting over the crumbs," but it also reflects the often controversial Christian biblical passage in Matt. 15:21–28 where a Canaanite women persuades Jesus to heal her daughter despite her lowly social status.

46. Patricia Hill Collins, *Black Feminist Thought: Knowledge, Consciousness, and the Politics of Empowerment*, 2nd ed. (New York: Routledge, 2000).

47. Charlie LeDuff, "At a Slaughterhouse, Some Things Never Die: Who Kills, Who Cuts, Who Bosses Can Depend on Race," *New York Times*, June 16, 2000.

48. Panel presentation, "Red, Yellow, Black and Brown: Building Coalitions to Win Civil Rights for All Workers," IWJ national conference, June 18, 2007.

49. Ibid.

50. IWJ National Conference, June 2007.

51. IWJ 2007 National Conference materials.

52. www.youtube.com/watch?v=KA6M7tUTfRc, posted September 6, 2007.

53. Verba, Schlozman, and Brady, *Voice and Equality*, 18. Hereafter cited in text.

54. See also Snarr, *Social Selves and Political Reforms*.

55. Putnam, *Bowling Alone*.

56. By the time of the public announcement of the Atlanta campaign, the coalition already had the support of ten council members and the mayor Shirley Franklin. This political strength came in part because of the ongoing progressive nature of the Atlanta City Council and also the organizing the coalition did in the mayoral and council elections the previous fall. They sponsored one of the first public forums that

invited all thirty-five candidates running for office (mayoral and council). Twenty candidates showed up and, in front of three hundred to four hundred people, pledged their support of the legislation.

57. Rosetta E. Ross, *Witnessing and Testifying: Black Women, Religion, and Civil Rights* (Minneapolis: Fortress Press, 2003).

58. Mirolla, "Religious Protest and Economic Conflict," 446.

59. Robert N. Bellah, Richard Madsen, William Sullivan, Ann Swidler, and Steven M. Tipton, *Habits of the Heart* (Berkeley: University of California Press, 1985), 72.

60. Verba, Schlozman, and Brady, *Voice and Equality*, 381.

61. Ibid., 381–83.

62. This quote comes from one of the IWJ affiliate's application for a Unitarian Universalist Funding Program grant, which they received.

63. Personal conversation with an IAF organizer, June 2007.

64. Nancy Fraser, "Rethinking the Public Sphere: A Contribution to the Critique of Actually Existing Democracy," in *Habermas and the Public Sphere,* ed. Craig Calhoun, 109–42 (Cambridge, MA: MIT Press, 1992).

65. In large scale projects, such as LA's airport expansion and development of Dreamworks, building trade unions often negotiate their own project labor agreements (PLAs). But as Levi et. al. contend "poor people affected by the projects received no such binding contractual coverage." This conflict meant community groups harbored suspicion of unions intent to cooperate for long-term regional development plans with community guarantees. Levi, Olson, and Steinman, "Living Wage Campaigns and Laws," 118.

66. Kathleen T. Talvacchia, "Learning to Stand with Others through Compassionate Solidarity," *Union Seminary Quarterly Review* 47, no. 3/4 (1993): 221.

67. Pope John Paul II, *Solilicitudo Rei Socialis.*

68. Ibid.

69. Ibid.

70. Douglas A. Hicks, *Inequality and Christian Ethics*, New Studies in Christian Ethics (Cambridge: Cambridge University Press, 2000), 148.

71. Pope John Paul II, "On Human Work: Encyclical *Laborem Exercens,*" sec. 8. Emphasis in original.

72. Ada María Isasi-Díaz, *Mujerista Theology: A Theology for the Twenty-First Century* (Maryknoll, NY: Orbis Books, 1996), 93.

73. Talvacchia, "Learning to Stand with Others through Compassionate Solidarity," 179.

74. Beverly Wildung Harrison and Carol S. Robb, *Making the Connections : Essays in Feminist Social Ethics* (Boston: Beacon Press, 1985), 244.

75. See, for example, Paulo Freire. *Pedagogy of the Oppressed* (New York: Seabury, 1970). As the adult education theorist Tom Heaney explains, conscientization "differs from 'consciousness raising' in that the latter frequently involves 'banking' education—the transmission of pre-selected knowledge. Conscientization means breaking through prevailing mythologies to reach new levels of awareness—in particular, awareness of oppression, being an 'object' in a world where only 'subjects' have power. The process of conscientization involves identifying contradictions in experience through dialogue and becoming a 'subject' with other oppressed subjects—that

is, becoming part of the process of changing the world." Tom Heaney "Issues in Freirean Pedagogy," www.nl.edu/academics/cas/ace/resources/Documents/FreireIssues.cfm#Banking.

76. Sekou Franklin, "Driving toward Poverty: Taxi Drivers in the Athens of the South" (Nashville: Middle Tennessee State University, 2008).

77. Isasi-Díaz, *Mujerista Theology*, 95.

78. Ibid., 93.

79. Marilyn J. Legge, "Wild Geese and Solidarity: Conjunctural Praxis for a Spirit-Filled Ethics," *Union Seminary Quarterly Review* 53, no. 3/4 (1999): 182.

80. The intersectional nature of dominance and oppression means that persons often experience multiple marginalizations simultaneously (race, gender, class, sexuality, and so on) in ways that are not merely the sum of the parts (e.g., race plus class) but rather co-constituted (e.g., a person's race forms their experience of class and vice versa). The complexity of these dynamics can also mean that persons may have more power in one dimension of their identity while being less powerful in others ways (for example, a physically challenged white male). Analyzing the dynamic multidimensional nature of domination is not about determining who is most oppressed. The point is the creation of structures of creativity and accountability that enable greater flourishing; not a zero-sum framework of power swapping.

81. Mary E. Hobgood, "Flag-Waving, Scapegoating, or Solidarity: The Challenge to Whites of the African American Reparations Movement," *Union Seminary Quarterly Review* 56, no. 1/2 (2002): 116.

82. Rauschenbusch, *Christianity and the Social Crisis*, 246.

83. Hobgood, "Flag-Waving, Scapegoating, or Solidarity," 121.

84. Sallie McFague, *Life Abundant: Rethinking Theology and Economy for a Planet in Peril* (Minneapolis: Fortress Press, 2001), 173–74.

85. Harrison and Robb, *Making the Connections*, 245–46.

86. Emilie Maureen Townes, *Womanist Ethics and the Cultural Production of Evil, Black Religion, Womanist Thought, Social Justice* (New York: Palgrave Macmillan, 2006), 157.

87. Ibid., 151, 54–55. .

88. Gerald J. Beyer, "A Theoretical Appreciation of the Ethic of Solidarity in Poland Twenty-Five Years After," *Journal of Religious Ethics* 35, no. 2 (2007): 222.

89. IWJ National Conference, June 2007.

NOTES TO CHAPTER 4

1. Story told by founders of the Atlanta Living Wage coalition in a research seminar at Vanderbilt University in 2005.

2. Nissen, "Living Wage Campaigns from a 'Social Movement' Perspective," 37.

3. "The Self-Sufficiency Standard," University of Washington Center for Women's Welfare, www.selfsufficiencystandard.org/standard.html.

4. Meredith King Ledford, "Equality—State of Opportunity, 2009," The Tides Center, opportunityagenda.org/stateofopportunity/indicators/equality.

5. D. M. Pearce, "The Feminization of Poverty: Women, Work, and Welfare," *Urban and Social Change Review* (1978).

6. U.S. Census Bureau, "Povo3: People in Families with Related Children under 18 by Family Structure, Age, and Sex, Iterated by Income-to-Poverty Ratio and Race: 2008," Current Population Survey (Washington DC, Government Printing Office, 2009).

7. Bray, "Winning Wages."

8. Filion, "Minimum Wage Issue Guide."

9. Sara Lichtenwalter, "Gender Poverty Disparity in U.S. Cities: Evidence Exonerating Female-Headed Families," *Journal of Sociology and Social Welfare* 32, no. 2 (2005): 75–98.

10. Ibid.

11. Leslie McCall, "Increasing Class Disparities among Women and the Politics of Gender Equity," in *The Sex of Class: Women Transforming American Labor*, ed. Dorothy Sue Cobble, 22 (Ithaca, NY: ILR Press, 2007).

12. Heidi I. Hartmann and Stephen J. Rose, "Still a Man's Labor Market: The Long-Term Earnings Gap" (Washington, DC: Institute for Women's Policy Research, 2004), www.iwpr.org/pdf/C366_RIB.pdf.

13. Ibid., 3.

14. Ibid.

15. McCall, "Increasing Class Disparities among Women," 23.

16. U.S. Bureau of Labor Statistics, "Highlights of Women's Earnings in 2008."

17. David A. Cotter, Joan M. Hermsen, and Reeve Vanneman, *Gender Inequality at Work*, The American People. Census 2000 (New York: Russell Sage Foundation, Population Reference Bureau, 2004).

18. Phyllis Palmer, "'The Racial Feminization of Poverty': Women of Color as Portents of the Future for All Women," *Women's Studies Quarterly* 11, no. 3 (1983): 4–6.

19. Valentine M. Moghadam, "The 'Feminization of Poverty' and Women's Human Rights," in *Social and Human Sciences Papers in Women's Studies/Gender Research* (Paris: UNESCO, 2005), 6, www.unesco.org/new/fileadmin/.../HQ/SHS/.../Feminization_of_Poverty.pdf.

20. S. B. Kamerman and A. J. Kahn, *Starting Right: How America Neglects Its Youngest Children and What We Can Do About It.* (New York: Oxford University Press, 1995).

21. Mary Daly and Katherine Rake, *Gender and the Welfare State: Care, Work and Welfare in Europe and the USA.* (Malden, MA: Polity Press, 2003).

22. , Martha E. Gimenez, "The Feminization of Poverty: Myth or Reality?," *Insurgent Sociologist* 14, no. 3 (1987): 7.

23. Gimenez, "Reflections on 'the Feminization of Poverty: Myth or Reality,'" *Critical Sociology* 25, no. 2/3 (1999): 335.

24. Ibid., 336.

25. McCall, "Increasing Class Disparities among Women," 32.

26. IWJ Pre-conference, June 2007. See also Warren and Wood, "Faith-Based Community Organizing."

27. Mark Chaves, Shawna Anderson, and Jason Byassee. "American Congregations at the Beginning of the 21st Century," Report from the National Congregations Study (Durham, NC: Duke University, 2009), 5.

28. Ibid.

29. www.iwpr.org/initiatives/womens-public-vision.

30. www.nywf.org/resources_faith_and_feminism.html.

31. Verba, Schlozman, and Brady, *Voice and Equality*, 18.

32. Ibid.

33. Kay Lehman Schlozman, Nancy Burns, and Sidney Verba, "The Public Consequences of Private Inequality: Family Life and Citizen Participation," *American Political Science Review* 91, no. 2 (1997): 372–89.

34. Caiazza, *Called to Speak*, 9.

35. Ibid., 11.

36. Ibid., 40.

37. Ibid., 45.

38. IWJ National Conference, June 2007.

39. Ibid. The context of the quoted phrase is Matthew 6:28–34.

40. Shared at IWJ Pre-conference, 2007.

41. Nashville female organizer, January 2009.

42. Caiazza, *Called to Speak*, 15.

43. Sue Schurman, "Women Organizing Women" (Washington, DC: Berger-Marks Foundation, 2004), 20, www.bergermarks.org/resources/WOWreport.pdf.

44. Anna Howard Shaw, in *The Dillon Collection—the Shaw Series* (Schlesinger Library, Radcliffe College, n.d.). Quoted in Barbara Andolsen, "Agape in Feminist Ethics," in *Feminist Theological Ethics: A Reader*, ed. Lois K. Daly, 146–59 (Louisville, KY: Westminister John Knox Press, 1994).

45. Valerie Saiving Goldstein, "The Human Situation: A Feminine View," in *Womanspirit Rising*, ed. Carol Christ and Judith Plaskow, 25–42 (New York: Harper and Row, 1980).

46. Niebuhr builds on Anders Nygren's treatise *Agape and Eros,* which saw self-love as a naturally occurring impulse. Nygren argued disinterested love of another (modeled on God's graceful love of sinful persons) best exemplified morality and the immolation of God's love. Anders Nygren, *Agape and Eros* (Philadelphia: Westminster Press, 1932).

47. Andolsen, "Agape in Feminist Ethics," 152.

48. Presbyterian Church (U.S.A.), "The Constitution of the Presbyterian Church (U.S.A.)" (Louisville, KY: Office of the General Assembly, 2004), www.pcusa.org/oga/constitution.htm.

49. Ibid. This is duly noted in the introduction to the PCUSA constitution: "Specific statements in 16th and 17th century confessions and catechisms in *The Book of Confessions* contain condemnations or derogatory characterizations of the Roman Catholic Church. . . . While these statements emerged from substantial doctrinal disputes, they reflect 16th and 17th century polemics. Their condemnations and characterizations of the Catholic Church are not the position of the Presbyterian Church (U.S.A.) and are not applicable to current relationships between the Presbyterian Church (U.S.A.) and the Catholic Church."

50. Suggestions made at IWJ Pre-conference, June 2007.

51. Edward T. Chambers and Michael A. Cowan, *Roots for Radicals: Organizing for Power, Action, and Justice* (New York: Continuum, 2004), 105.

52. Pope John Paul II, "Doctrinal Note: On Some Questions Regarding the Participation of Catholics in Political Life" (Rome: Offices of the Congregation for the Doctrine of the Faith, 2002), www.cacatholic.org/index.php/teaching/.../866-doctrinal-note.html.

53. U.S. Conference of Catholic Bishops, "Faithful Citizenship: A Call to Political Responsibility" (Washington DC: United States Catholic Conference, 2004), www.usccb.org/faithfulcitizenship/bishopStatement.html.

54. Ibid.

55. Frank J. Matera and Daniel J. Harrington, *Galatians*, Sacra Pagina Series (Collegeville, MN: Liturgical Press, 1992), 75.

56. Sheila Briggs, "Galatians," in *The New Oxford Annotated Bible with the Apocryphal/Deuterocanonical Books: New Revised Standard Version*, 3rd ed., ed. Michael David Coogan, 309 (New York: Oxford University Press, 2007).

57. Ibid.

58. Matera and Harrington, *Galatians*, 82–83.

59. Ibid., 83–84. Biblical interpreters who do not focus on the Roman Empire as an essential component in understanding biblical interpretation often limit the scope of "remembering the poor." They often link the phrase with remembering the Jerusalem church (and thus Jewish Christians) that was suffering under a famine. "Remembrance" may have entailed a special monetary collection sent to the Jerusalem church, which would also have attested to the unity of the church.

60. Brigitte Kahl, *Galatians Re-Imagined: Reading with the Eyes of the Vanquished*, Paul in Critical Contexts (Minneapolis: Fortress Press, 2009).

61. Ibid., 276.

62. Thomas Massaro, "Ethics Appropriate for an Empire: A Question Whose Time Has Come," *Political Theology* 10, no. 3 (2009): 501.

63. Ibid., 503.

64. Elsa Tamez, "Neoliberalism and Christian Freedom: A Reflection on the Letter to the Galatians," in *Revolution of Spirit: Ecumenical Theology in Global Context, Essays in Honor of Richard Shaull*, ed. Richard Shaull and Nantawan Boonprasat-Lewis, 107 (Grand Rapids, MI: W. B. Eerdmans, 1998).

65. Kahl, *Galatians Re-Imagined*, 279.

NOTES TO CHAPTER 5

1. From WIN's pamphlet "The Fast for a Living Wage." WIN was operating under the name "Mid-South Interfaith Network for Economic Justice" but subsequently changed their name. There was no change in staffing or organizational structure with the renaming.

2. Michael Lollar, "Living Wage Advocates Rally," *Commercial Appeal* (Memphis, TN), March 13, 2008.

3. David Craig, "Debating Desire: Civil Rights, Ritual Protest, and the Shifting Boundaries of Public Reason," *Journal of the Society of Christian Ethics* 27, no. 1 (2007): 164.

4. Smith, *Disruptive Religion*, 11.

5. Nepstad, *Convictions of the Soul*, 14.

6. Ibid. Nepstad defines collective identity as "the image and definition [of] a group . . . based on its values, beliefs, interests, social location, or practices."

7. Ibid., 163.

8. Smith, *Disruptive Religion*, 11.

9. Nepstad, *Convictions of the Soul*, 149.

10. Doug McAdam defines "risk" as "the anticipated dangers—whether legal, social, physical, financial, and so forth—of engaging in a particular type of activity." Doug McAdam, "Recruitment to High-Risk Activism: The Case of Freedom Summer," *American Journal of Sociology* 92, no. 1 (1986): 67.

11. Ibid.

12. Ibid., 69–70.

13. In the San Diego campaign, carolers were sent to the city council in December to sing "living wage carols."

14. *Bimah* is a raised platform or table where the Torah is read in the synagogue; *Minbar* is where Muslim religious speakers deliver their sermons in mosques.

15. iwj.org/index.cfm/labor-in-the-pulpits. This program is also sponsored by the AFL-CIO and Change to Win.

16. "Living Wage Passes in San Diego," *FaithWorks* (Chicago: Interfaith Worker Justice, October 2005).

17. From IWJ's "Prayer of Blessing the Work of Our Hands" iwj.org/doc/08LipPrayers.pdf. Copyrighted to Diann Neu from Jann Cather Weaver, Roger William Wedell, and Kenneth Lawrence, *Imaging the Word: An Arts and Lectionary Resource*, vol. 1 (Boston: Pilgrim Press, 1994).

18. Pierrette Hondagneu-Sotelo, *God's Heart Has No Borders: How Religious Activists Are Working for Immigrant Rights* (Berkeley: University of California Press, 2008), 114.

19. Ibid., 88.

20. "Living Wage Passes in San Diego," in *FaithWorks* (Chicago: Interfaith Worker Justice, October 2005).

21. Read into the San Diego City Council public record on February 10, 2004.

22. San Diego's mayor was steadfastly opposed to the living wage ordinance and kept it off the council's agenda for several years. Four council members eventually found a rarely used clause in the city charter for a "discharge petition," which bypassed the mayor's control and forced a full council vote—resulting in a 5–4 favorable vote. Conlan, "San Diego Passes Living Wage Law 5–4."

23. Examples taken from San Diego Interfaith Committee for Worker Justice, "Living Wage Campaign" (San Diego: Unitarian Universalist Fund for a Just Society, 2003), 4–5.

24. Conlan, "San Diego Passes Living Wage Law 5–4." See also "Living Wage Passes in San Diego," in *FaithWorks* (Chicago: Interfaith Worker Justice, October 2005). An earlier living wage rally led by members of the ICWJ drew more than four hundred people outside city council. UUFP grant provided to author.

25. Jasper, *Art of Moral Protest*, 184.

26. Hondagneu-Sotelo, *God's Heart Has No Borders*, 21.

27. June Nash, "Religious Rituals of Resistance and Class Consciousness in Bolivia Tin-Mining Communities," in *Disruptive Religion*, ed. Christian Smith, 89 (New York: Routledge, 1996).

28. Conlan, "San Diego Passes Living Wage Law 5–4."

29. Craig, "Debating Desire," 170.

30. Story told by a CLUE LA organizer at a national IWJ conference in June 2007.

31. While I do not see these dimensions as binary opposites, Lincoln and Mamiya provide a helpful distinction between the two in the their study of African American churches. They define priestly functions as "activities concerned with worship and maintaining the spiritual life of members" whereas "prophetic functions refer to involvement in political concerns and activities in the wider community . . . priestly churches are bastions of survival and prophetic churches are networks of liberation." C. Eric Lincoln and Lawrence H. Mamiya, *The Black Church in the African American Experience* (Durham, NC: Duke University Press, 1990), 12.

32. Cal Thomas, "Howard Dean 'Finds' Jesus," *beliefnet* (2004), www.beliefnet. com/News/Politics/2004/01/Howard-Dean-Finds-Jesus.aspx.

33. Alasdair C. MacIntyre and Kelvin Knight, *The Macintyre Reader* (Notre Dame, IN: University of Notre Dame Press, 1998), 83ff.

34. The state action happened so quickly that they had little time to educate members and organize opposition. With only one public hearing that lasted only twenty minutes, the anti-Atlanta state legislature banned living wage ordinances by a two-thirds majority vote. The second most-powerful member of the state legislature's rules committee subsequently called Atlanta's voluntary contractor ordinance "about as voluntary as a baseball bat."

NOTES TO CHAPTER 6

1. The South African title is "Hamba Nathi," www.rockhay.org/worship/music/ hambanathi.htm. The song was also used as an overture in the 2010 original motion picture *Invictus*.

2. With director Jen Kern leaving the ACORN Living Wage Resource Center (to work on passing the Employee Free Choice Act) and then the implosion of ACORN as a whole, the major Web-based clearinghouse for living wage resources is no longer functioning. Kern (now at the National Employment Law Center) and others are still active in living wage conversations, although much energy has shifted to related worker justice issues.

3. Luce, *Fighting for a Living Wage*; Paul Sonn and Stephanie Luce, "New Directions for the Living Wage Movement," in *The Gloves-Off Economy: Workplace Standards at the Bottom of America's Labor Market*, eds. Annette Bernhardt, Heather Boushey, Laura Dresser, Chris Tilly, 269–87 (Ithaca, NY: Cornell University Press, 2008).

4. Sonn and Luce, "New Directions," 276.

5. Ibid.

6. Interfaith Worker Justice, "Immigration through the Lens of Faith" (Chicago: Interfaith Worker Justice, 2010), 1. www.iwj.org/doc/ImmigrationToolkit.pdf.

7. Ibid., 3.

8. Sonn and Luce, "New Directions," 271. Hereafter cited in text.

9. IWJ conference, June 2007.

10. iwj.org/template/page.cfm?id=92, accessed July 20, 2010.

11. IWJ national conference, 2007.

12. Sklar and Sherry, *Just Minimum Wage*, 11.

13. U.S. Census Bureau, "S1703. Selected Characteristics of People at Specified Levels of Poverty in the Past 12 Months."

14. Dockterman and Velasco, "Statistical Portrait of Hispanics in the United States, 2008."

15. Brecher and Costello, *Building Bridges*, 338–39.

16. D. M. Pearce, "The Feminization of Poverty: Women, Work, and Welfare," *Urban and Social Change Review* (1978): 28–36.

17. U.S. Census Bureau, "Pov03: People in Families with Related Children under 18 by Family Structure, Age, and Sex, Iterated by Income-to-Poverty Ratio and Race: 2008," ed. U.S. Census Bureau, Current Population Survey (Washington DC, 2009).

18. Sara Lichtenwalter, "Gender Poverty Disparity in U.S. Cities: Evidence Exonerating Female-Headed Families," *Journal of Sociology and Social Welfare* 32, no. 2 (2005): 75–98.

19. Hartmann and Rose, "Still a Man's Labor Market" (Washington, DC: Institute for Women's Policy Research, 2004), www.iwpr.org/pdf/C366_RIB.pdf.

Bibliography

Allegreto, Sylvia. "Basic Family Budgets: Working Families' Incomes Often Fail to Meet Living Expenses around the U.S." Washington, DC: Economic Policy Institute, 2005. www.epi.org/index.php/phpee/redirect/bp165.

Alpert, Rebecca T. *Voices of the Religious Left: A Contemporary Sourcebook.* Philadelphia: Temple University Press, 2000.

Andolsen, Barbara. "Agape in Feminist Ethics." In *Feminist Theological Ethics: A Reader,* edited by Lois K. Daly, 146–59. Louisville, KY: Westminister John Knox Press, 1994.

Andrews, Irene. "Minimum Wage Comes Back!" *American Labor Legislation Review* 23, no. 2 (1933): 103–5.

Atlanta Living Wage Coalition. "Short-Changed: The High Cost of Working Poverty for Communities and Families." Atlanta: Working Women 9to5, 2003.

Bellah, Robert. "Civil Religion in America." *Daedalus* no. 96 (1967): 1–21.

Bellah, Robert N., Richard Madsen, William Sullivan, Ann Swidler, and Steven M. Tipton. *Habits of the Heart.* Berkeley: University of California Press, 1985.

Bernhardt, Annette D. *The Gloves-Off Economy: Workplace Standards at the Bottom of America's Labor Market.* Labor and Employment Relations Association Series. Champaign, IL: Labor and Employment Relations Association, University of Illinois at Urbana-Champaign, 2008.

Bernstein, Jared. "The Living Wage Movement: What Is It, Why Is It, and What's Known About Its Impact." In *Emerging Labor Market Institutions for the Twenty-First Century,* edited by Richard B. Freeman, Joni Hersch, and Lawrence Mishel, 99–140. Chicago: University of Chicago Press, 2005.

Beyer, Gerald J. "A Theoretical Appreciation of the Ethic of Solidarity in Poland Twenty-Five Years After." *Journal of Religious Ethics* 35, no. 2 (2007): 207–32.

Blow, Charles M. "Rise of the Religious Left." *New York Times,* July 2, 2010.

Bobo, Kim. "Citizen Wealth: Forty-Year Organizing Veteran Wade Rathke Has Plenty of New Ideas." *Religion Dispatches* (2010), www.religiondispatches.org/books/politics/2732/acorn_founder_writes_on_saving_working_families/.

———. "Kim Bobo on Alan Wolfe." *Interfaith Worker Justice Blog,* October 30, 2007, interfaithworkerjustice.blogspot.com/2007/10/kim-bobo-on-alan-wolfe.html..

———. *Wage Theft in America: Why Millions of Working Americans Are Not Getting Paid—And What We Can Do About It.* New York: New Press, 2009.

Boles, Walter E. "Some Aspects of the Fair Labor Standards Act." *Southern Economic Journal* 6, no. 4 (1940).

Bray, Robert, and Max Toth. "Winning Wages: A Media Kit for Successful Living Wages Strategies." San Francisco: Tides Foundation and SPIN Project Independent Media Institute, 2003, www.spinproject.org/article.php?id=95.

Brecher, Jeremy, and Tim Costello. *Building Bridges: The Emerging Grassroots Coalition of Labor and Community*. New York: Monthly Review Press, 1990.

Briggs, Sheila. "Galatians." In *The New Oxford Annotated Bible with the Apocryphal/Deuterocanonical Books: New Revised Standard Version*, 3rd ed., edited by Michael David Coogan, 309–27. New York: Oxford University Press, 2001.

Brubaker, Pamela K. "Sisterhood, Solidarity and Feminist Ethics." *Journal of Feminist Studies in Religion* 9, no. 1/2 (1993): 53–66.

Brueggemann, Walter. "Entitled Neighbors: A Biblical Perspective on Living Wage." *Witness* 85, no. 5 (2002): 18–20.

Buber, Martin, and Ronald Gregor Smith. *I and Thou*. Edinburgh: T&T. Clark, 1937.

Burns, Nancy, Kay Lehman Schlozman, and Sidney Verba. "The Public Consequences of Private Inequality: Family Life and Citizen Participation." *American Political Science Review* 91, no. 2 (1997): 373–89.

Caiazza, Amy. *Called to Speak: Six Strategies That Encourage Women's Political Activism, Lessons from Interfaith Community Organizing*. Washington, DC: Institute for Women's Policy Research, 2006.

Chambers, Edward T., and Michael A. Cowan. *Roots for Radicals: Organizing for Power, Action, and Justice*. New York: Continuum, 2004.

Chaves, Mark, Shawna Anderson, and Jason Byassee. "American Congregations at the Beginning of the 21st Century," Report from the National Congregations Study. Durham, NC: Duke University, 2009.

Citro, Constance F., and Robert T. Michael. "Measuring Poverty a New Approach." Washington, DC: National Academy Press, 1995. www.census.gov/hhes/povmeas/methodology/nas/files/ack.pdf.

Coakley, Sarah. "Why Gift? Gift, Gender, and Trinitarian Relations in Milbank and Tanner." *Scottish Journal of Theology* 61, no. 2 (2008): 224–35.

Collins, Patricia Hill. *Black Feminist Thought: Knowledge, Consciousness, and the Politics of Empowerment*, 2nd ed. New York: Routledge, 2000.

Conferencia General del Episcopado Latinoamericano. "Puebla: Evangelization at Present and in the Future of Latin America." Washington, DC: National Conference of Catholic Bishops, 1979.

Conlan, Mark Gabrish. "San Diego Passes Living Wage Law 5–4." *Zenger's Newsmagazine*, April 13, 2005.

Cotter, David A., Joan M. Hermsen, and Reeve Vanneman. *Gender Inequality at Work*. The American People. Census 2000. New York: Russell Sage Foundation, Population Reference Bureau, 2004.

Craig, David. "Debating Desire: Civil Rights, Ritual Protest, and the Shifting Boundaries of Public Reason." *Journal of the Society of Christian Ethics* 27, no. 1 (2007): 157–82.

Cooperman, Alan and Carlyle Murphy, "Religious Liberals Gain New Visibility: A Different List of Moral Issues." *Washington Post*, May 20, 2006.

Daly, Mary, and Katherine Rake. *Gender and the Welfare State: Care, Work and Welfare in Europe and the USA*. Malden, MA: Polity Press, 2003.

Della Porta, Donatella, and Mario Diani. *Social Movements: An Introduction*. Oxford: Blackwell, 1999.

DeNavas-Walt, Carmen, Bernadette D. Proctor, and Jessica C. Smith. "Income, Poverty, and Health Insurance Coverage in the United States: 2007," edited by U.S. Census Bureau. Washington, DC: U.S. Government Printing Office, 2008.

DiSalvo, Clare. "Working Hard, Falling Short." In *Serving Witness: Religious Leader's Stories of Workers Who Lack a Living Wage*. San Diego: San Diego Interfaith Committee for Worker Justice, 2004, 2.

Dionne, E. J. *Souled Out: Reclaiming Faith and Politics after the Religious Right*. Princeton, NJ: Princeton University Press, 2008.

Dockterman, Daniel, and Gabriel Velasco. "Statistical Portrait of Hispanics in the United States, 2008." Washington, DC: Pew Hispanic Center, 2010. pewhispanic. org/factsheets/factsheet.php?FactsheetID=58.

Dorrien, Gary J. *Social Ethics in the Making: Interpreting an American Tradition*. Malden, MA: Wiley-Blackwell, 2009.

Encyclopedia of Social Theory. Edited by George Ritzer. Thousand Oaks, CA: Sage Publications, 2005.

Farley, Margaret. "New Patterns of Relationship: Beginnings of a Moral Revolution." In *Women: New Dimensions*, edited by Walter Burkhardt, 627–46. New York: Paulist Press, 1976.

Figart, Deborah M. *Living Wage Movements: Global Perspectives*. Advances in Social Economics. London: Routledge, 2004.

Figart, Deborah M., Ellen Mutari, and Marilyn Power. *Living Wages, Equal Wages: Gender and Labor Market Policies in the United States*. Routledge Iaffe Advances in Feminist Economics. London: Routledge, 2002.

Filion, Kai. "Minimum Wage Issue Guide." Washington, DC: Economic Policy Institute, 2009, epi.3cdn.net/9f5a60cec02393cbe4_a4m6b5t1v.pdf.

Fine, Janice. "Community Unionism in Baltimore and Stamford: Beyond the Politics of Particularism." *Working USA* 4, no. 3 (2000–2001): 59–85.

Fischer, Claude S. *Inequality by Design: Cracking the Bell Curve Myth*. Princeton, NJ: Princton University Press, 1996.

Fisher, Gordon M. "The Development of the Orshansky Poverty Thresholds and Their Subsequent History as the Official U.S. Poverty Measure." *Social Security Bulletin* 55, no.4 (1992). www.ssa.gov/history/fisheronpoverty.html.

Franklin, Sekou. "Driving toward Poverty: Taxi Drivers in the Athens of the South." Nashville: Middle Tennessee State University, 2008.

Fraser, Nancy. "Rethinking the Public Sphere: A Contribution to the Critique of Actually Existing Democracy." In *Habermas and the Public Sphere*, edited by Craig Calhoun, 109–42. Cambridge, MA: MIT Press, 1992.

Freire, Paulo. *Pedagogy of the Oppressed*. New York: Seabury, 1970.

Gertner, Jon. "What Is a Living Wage?" *New York Times*, January 15, 2006.

Gimenez, Martha. "The Feminization of Poverty: Myth or Reality?" *Insurgent Sociologist* 14, no. 3 (1987): 5–30.

———. "Reflections on 'the Feminization of Poverty: Myth or Reality.'" *Critical Sociology* 25, no. 2/3 (1999): 333–37.

Goldstein, Valerie Saiving. "The Human Situation: A Feminine View." In *Womanspirit Rising*, edited by Carol Christ and Judith Plaskow, 25–42. New York: Harper and Row, 1980.

Grasska, Denis. "'Living Wage' Gets Push from Religious Community: Workers Will Receive Increases over Three Years." *Southern Cross*, May 12, 2008.

Greene, John, Robert P. Jones, and Daniel Cox. "Faithful, Engaged, and Divergent: A Comparative Potrait of Conservative and Progressive Religious Activists in the 2008 Election and Beyond." Washington, DC: Public Religion Research, Ray C. Bliss Institute of Applied Politics, 2009. www.uakron.edu/bliss/docs/ReligiousActivistReport-Final.pdf.

Hall, Charles F. "The Christian Left: Who Are They and How Are They Different from the Christian Right?" *Review of Religious Research* 39, no. 1 (1997): 27–45.

Harrison, Beverly Wildung, and Carol S. Robb. *Making the Connections: Essays in Feminist Social Ethics*. Boston: Beacon Press, 1985.

Hartmann, Heidi I., and Stephen J. Rose. "Still a Man's Labor Market: The Long-Term Earnings Gap." Washington, DC: Institute for Women's Policy Research, 2004. www.iwpr.org/pdf/C366_RIB.pdf.

Heaney, Tom. "Issues in Freirean Pedagogy." www.nl.edu/academics/cas/ace/resources/Documents/FreireIssues.cfm#Banking.

Heim, David. "The Divided Mind of the Religious Left: Voters and Values." *Christian Century*, August 8, 2006, 26–29.

Hicks, Douglas A. *Inequality and Christian Ethics*. New Studies in Christian Ethics. Cambridge: Cambridge University Press, 2000.

Hinze, Christine Frier. *Radical Sufficiency: The Legacy and Future of the Catholic Living Wage Agenda*. Forthcoming.

———. "Social and Economic Ethics." *Theological Studies* 70, no.1 (2009): 159–76.

———. "What Is Enough? Catholic Social Thought, Consumption, and Material Sufficiency." In *Having: Property and Possession in Religious and Social Living*, edited by William Schweiker and Charles Matthews, 162–88. Grand Rapids, MI: Eerdmans, 2004.

Hobgood, Mary E. "Flag-Waving, Scapegoating, or Solidarity: The Challenge to Whites of the African American Reparations Movement." *Union Seminary Quarterly Review* 56, no. 1/2 (2002): 116–25.

Hondagneu-Sotelo, Pierrette. *God's Heart Has No Borders: How Religious Activists Are Working for Immigrant Rights*. Berkeley: University of California Press, 2008.

Human Nutrition Information Service, Consumer Nutrition Division. "U.S.D.A. Family Food Plans, 1983: Low Cost, Moderate and Liberal," edited by U.S. Department of Agriculture Washington, DC: Government Printing Office, 1983.

Interfaith Worker Justice. "Immigration through the Lens of Faith." Chicago: Interfaith Worker Justice, 2010.

———. "Living Wage Passes in San Diego," in *FaithWorks*. Chicago: Interfaith Worker Justice, October 2005.

——— "Rally Song Book." Chicago: Interfaith Worker Justice, 2005.

———. "Why Unions Matter." www.iwj.org/materials/materials_wumtxt.html.

Isasi-Díaz, Ada María. *Mujerista Theology: A Theology for the Twenty-First Century*. Maryknoll, NY: Orbis Books, 1996.

Jacobs, Jill. "The Living Wage: A Jewish Approach." *Conservative Judaism* 55, no. 3 (2003): 38–51.

Jasper, James M. *The Art of Moral Protest: Culture, Biography, and Creativity in Social Movements*. Chicago: University of Chicago Press, 1997.

"Jen Kern on Peri's Living Wage Research and the Grassroots Movement." www.peri.umass.edu/kern/.

Jenkins, Craig, and Charles Perrow. "Insurgency of the Powerless: Farm Worker Movements." *American Sociological Review* 42 (1977): 249–68.

Johnson, Elizabeth A. *She Who Is: The Mystery of God in Feminist Theological Discourse*. New York: Crossroad, 2002.

Jones, Diana. "Organizing through Congregations: Mediating and Moderarting Roles of Spirituality." PhD diss., Vanderbilt University, 2008.

Jones, Robert P. *Progressive & Religious: How Christian, Jewish, Muslim, and Buddhist Leaders Are Moving Beyond the Culture Wars and Transforming American Life*. Lanham, MD: Rowman and Littlefield Publishers, 2008.

Kahl, Brigitte. *Galatians Re-Imagined: Reading with the Eyes of the Vanquished*. Paul in Critical Contexts. Minneapolis: Fortress Press, 2009.

Kamerman, S. B., and A. J. Kahn. *Starting Right: How America Neglects Its Youngest Children and What We Can Do About It*. New York: Oxford University Press, 1995.

King, Martin Luther, Jr. "Revolution and Redemption." unpublished closing address at the European Baptist Assembly in Amersterdam. August, 16, 1964. King Center Letters Archive.

———. *Where Do We Go from Here: Chaos or Community?* New York: Harper and Row, 1967.

King , Martin Luther, Jr., and James Melvin Washington. *A Testament of Hope: The Essential Writings of Martin Luther King Jr*. 1st ed. San Francisco: Harper and Row, 1986.

Kochhar, Rakesh. "Latino Labor Report 2006: Strong Gains in Employment." Washington, DC: Pew Hispanic Center, 2006. pewhispanic.org/reports/report.php?ReportID=70.

———. "Sharp Decline in Income for Non-Citizen Immigrant Households, 2006–2007." Washington, DC: Pew Hispanic Center, 2008. pewhispanic.org/reports/report.php?ReportID=95.

Lardner, George. "Business Gets Cold Feet on Subminimum Wage." *Washington Post*, March 20, 1981.

Ledford, Meredith King. "Equality—State of Opportunity, 2009." The Tides Center. opportunityagenda.org/stateofopportunity/indicators/equality.

LeDuff, Charlie. "At a Slaughterhouse, Some Things Never Die: Who Kills, Who Cuts, Who Bosses Can Depend On Race." *New York Times*, June 16, 2000, 1.

Legge, Marilyn J. "Wild Geese and Solidarity: Conjunctural Praxis for a Spirit-Filled Ethics." *Union Seminary Quarterly Review* 53, no. 3/4 (1999): 165–85.

Levi, Margaret, David Olson, and Erich Steinman. "Living Wage Campaigns and Laws." *Working USA* 6, no. 3 (2002–3): 111–32.

Levin-Waldman, Oren M. *The Political Economy of the Living Wage: A Study of Four Cities*. Armonk, NY: M. E. Sharpe, 2005.

Levine, Aaron. "The Living Wage and Jewish Law." *Tradition* 41, no. 4 (2008): 8–32.

Levine, Marc. V. "Downtown Redevelopment as an Urban Growth Strategy: A Critical Reappraisal of the Baltimore Renaissance." *Journal of Urban Affairs* 9, no. 2 (1987): 103–23.

Lichtenwalter, Sara. "Gender Poverty Disparity in U.S. Cities: Evidence Exonerating Female-Headed Families." *Journal of Sociology and Social Welfare* 32, no. 2 (2005): 75–98.

Lincoln, C. Eric, and Lawrence H. Mamiya. *The Black Church in the African American Experience*. Durham, NC: Duke University Press, 1990.

"Living Wage Passes in San Diego." In *FaithWorks*. Chicago: Interfaith Worker Justice, 2005.

Lollar, Michael. "Living Wage Advocates Rally." *Commercial Appeal* (Memphis, TN), March 13, 2008.

Long, Michael G. *Against Us, but For Us: Martin Luther King Jr. and the State*. Macon, GA: Mercer University Press, 2002.

Luce, Stephanie. *Fighting for a Living Wage*. Ithaca, NY: Cornell University Press/ILR Press, 2004.

———. "'The Full Fruits of Our Labor': The Rebirth of the Living Wage Movement." *Labor History* 43, no. 4 (2002): 401–09.

MacIntyre, Alasdair C., and Kelvin Knight. *The Macintyre Reader*. Notre Dame, IN: University of Notre Dame Press, 1998.

Martin, Isaac. "Dawn of the Living Wage: The Diffusion of a Redistributive Municipal Policy." *Urban Affairs Review* 36, no. 4 (2001): 470–96.

Massaro, Thomas. "Ethics Appropriate for an Empire: A Question Whose Time Has Come." *Political Theology* 10, no. 3 (2009): 497–512.

Matera, Frank J., and Daniel J. Harrington. *Galatians*. Sacra Pagina Series. Collegeville, MN: Liturgical Press, 1992.

McAdam, Doug. "Recruitment to High-Risk Activism: The Case of Freedom Summer." *American Journal of Sociology* 92, no. 1 (1986): 64–90.

McCall, Leslie. "Increasing Class Disparities among Women and the Politics of Gender Equity." In *The Sex of Class: Women Transforming American Labor*, edited by Dorothy Sue Cobble, 15–34. Ithaca: ILR Press, 2007.

McCarthy, John, and Mayer Zald. "Resource Mobilization and Social Movements: A Partial Theory." *American Journal of Sociology* no. 82 (1977): 1212–41.

McCartin, Joseph A. "Building the Interfaith Worker Justice Movement: Kim Bobo's Story." *Labor: Studies in Working-Class History of the Americas* 6, no. 1 (2009): 87–105.

McDougall, Joy Ann. *Pilgrimage of Love: Moltmann on the Trinity and Christian Life*. Reflection and Theory in the Study of Religion. Oxford: Oxford University Press, 2005.

McFague, Sallie. *Life Abundant: Rethinking Theology and Economy for a Planet in Peril*. Minneapolis, MN: Fortress Press, 2001.

Meeks, M. Douglas. *God the Economist: The Doctrine of God and Political Economy*. Minneapolis, MN: Fortress Press, 1989.

———. "The Economy of Grace: Human Dignity in the Market System." In *God and Human Dignity*, edited by R. Kendall Soulen and Linda Woodhead, 196–214. Grand Rapids, MI: Eerdmans, 2006.

Merrifield, Andy. "The Urbanization of Labor: Living Wage Activism in the American City." *Social Text* 18, no. 1 (2000): 31–54.

Mich, Marvin L. Krier. "The Living Wage Movement and Catholic Social Teaching." *Journal of Catholic Social Thought* 6, no. 1 (2009): 231–52.

Migliore, Daniel L. "The Trinity and Human Liberty." *Theology Today* 36, no. 4 (1980): 488–97.

Milbank, John. *Being Reconciled: Ontology and Pardon*. Radical Orthodoxy Series. London: Routledge, 2003.

Miller, Rev. Elizabeth. "Raise the Minimum Wage." *Morning Call* (Allentown, PA), 2005.

Mirolla, William. "Religious Protest and Economic Conflict: Possibilities and Constraints on Religious Resource Mobilization and Coalitions in Detroit's Newspaper Strike." *Sociology of Religion* 64, no. 4 (2003): 443–61.

Mishel, Lawrence, Jared Bernstein, and Heidi Shierholz. *The State of Working America 2008/2009*. Ithaca, NY: ILR Press, 2009.

Moghadam, Valentine M. "The 'Feminization of Poverty' and Women's Human Rights." In *Social and Human Sciences Papers in Women's Studies/Gender Research*, 1–40. Paris: UNESCO, 2005. www.unesco.org/new/fileadmin/.../HQ/SHS/.../ Feminization_of_Poverty.pdf.

Moltmann, Jürgen. *The Trinity and the Kingdom: The Doctrine of God*. New York: Harper and Row, 1981.

Morris, Aldon D. *The Origins of the Civil Rights Movement: Black Communities Organizing for Change*. New York: Free Press, 1984.

Morris, Aldon D., and Carol McClurg Mueller. *Frontiers in Social Movement Theory*. New Haven, CT: Yale University Press, 1992.

Murphy, Carlyle, and Alan Cooperman. "Religious Liberals Gain New Visibility: A Different List of Moral Issues." *Washington Post*, May 20, 2006.

Murphy, Laura. "An 'Indestructible Right': John Ryan and the Catholic Origins of the U.S. Living Wage Movement, 1906–1938." *Labor: Studies in Working-Class History of the Americas* 6, no. 1 (2009): 57–86.

Nash, June. "Religious Rituals of Resistance and Class Consciousness in Bolivia Tin-Mining Communities." In *Disruptive Religion*, edited by Christian Smith, 87–102. New York: Routledge, 1996.

Neit, Christopher, Greg Ruiters, Dana Wise, and Erica Schoenberger. "The Effects of Living Wages in Baltimore." Washington, DC: Economic Policy Institute, 1999. epi.3cdn.net/63b7cb4cbcf2f33b2d_w9m6bnks7.pdf.

Nepstad, Sharon Erickson. *Convictions of the Soul: Religion, Culture, and Agency in the Central America Solidarity Movement*. Oxford: Oxford University Press, 2004.

Neumark, David. *How Living Wage Laws Affect Low-Wage Workers and Low-Income Families*. San Francisco: Public Policy Institute of California, 2002.

Neumark, David, and William L. Wascher. *Minimum Wages*. Cambridge, MA: MIT Press, 2008.

Niebuhr, H. Richard. *The Responsible Self; an Essay in Christian Moral Philosophy*. New York: Harper and Row, 1963.

Nissen, Bruce. "The Effectiveness and Limits of Labor-Community Coalitions: Evidence from South Florida." *Labor Studies Journal* 29, no. 1 (2004): 67–89.

———. "Living Wage Campaigns from a 'Social Movement' Perspective: The Miami Case." *Labor Studies Journal* 25, no. 3 (2000): 29–50.

Nordlund, Willis J. *The Quest for a Living Wage: The History of the Federal Minimum Wage Program*. Contributions in Labor Studies. Westport, CT: Greenwood Press, 1997.

Nygren, Anders. *Agape and Eros*. Philadelphia: Westminster Press, 1932.

O'Brien, Thomas, and Scott Paeth. *Religious Perspectives on Business Ethics: An Anthology*. Religion and Business Ethics. Lanham, MD: Rowman and Littlefield Publishers, 2007.

O'Keefe, Mark. "Religious Left Makes a Political Push." *Christian Century*, September 21, 2004.

Oberschall, Anthony. *Social Conflict and Social Movements*. Prentice-Hall Series in Sociology. Englewood Cliffs, NJ: Prentice-Hall, 1973.

Olsen, Laura R. "Whither the Religious Left? Religiopolitical Progressivism in Twenty-First-Century America." In *From Pews to Polling Places: Faith and Politics in the American Religious Mosaic*, edited by J. Matthew Wilson, 53–80. Washington, DC: Georgetown University Press, 2007.

Oral history of Frances Perkins, "Reminiscences." *New York Times* Oral History Program, Columbia University Oral History Collection, part 3, no. 182, book 7, 26–27. Glen Rock, NJ: Microfilming Corporation of America, 1976.

Palmer, Phyllis. "'The Racial Feminization of Poverty': Women of Color as Portents of the Future for All Women." *Women's Studies Quarterly* 11, no. 3 (1983): 4–6.

Pasch, Robert E., and Falguni A. Sheth. "The Economics and Ethics of Minimum Wage Legislation." *Review of Social Economy* 57 (1999): 466–87.

Passel, Jeffrey S. "The Size and Characteristics of the Unauthorized Migrant Population in the U.S. Estimates Based on the March 2005 Current Population Survey." Washington, DC: Pew Hispanic Center, 2006. pewhispanic.org/files/reports/61.pdf.

Pastro, Manuel, Jr., and Enrico Marcelli. "Somewhere over the Rainbow? African Americans, Unauthorized Mexican Immigration, and Coalition Building." *Review of Black Political Economy* 31, no. 1 (2003): 125–55.

Pearce, D. M. "The Feminization of Poverty: Women, Work and Welfare." *Urban and Social Change Review* (1978): 28–36.

Peters, Rebecca Todd. *In Search of the Good Life: The Ethics of Globalization*. New York: Continuum, 2004.

Pollin, Robert. *A Measure of Fairness: The Economics of Living Wages and Minimum Wages in the United States*. Ithaca, NY: ILR Press, 2008.

Pollin, Robert, and Jeannette Wicks-Lim. "Economic Analysis of Nashville Living Wage Proposal." Amherst, MA: Political Economy Research Institute (PERI), University of Massachusetts–Amherst, 2009.

Pope Benedict XVI. "*Caritas in Veritate.*" (2009), www.vatican.va/holy_father/benedict_xvi/encyclicals/documents/hf_ben-xvi_enc_20090629_caritas-in-veritate_en.html.

Pope John Paul II. "Doctrinal Note: On Some Questions Regarding the Participation of Catholics in Political Life." Rome: Offices of the Congregation for the Doctrine of the Faith, 2002. www.cacatholic.org/index.php/teaching/.../866-doctrinal-note.html.

————. "On Human Work: Encyclical *Laborem Exercens.*" www.vatican.va/holy_father/ john_paul_ii/encyclicals/documents/hf_jp-ii_enc_14091981_laborem-exercens_ en.htm

————. "*Solilicitudo Rei Socialis.*" (1987), www.vatican.va/edocs/ENG0223/_INDEX. HTM.

Pope Paul VI. "*Octogesima Adveniens.*" (1971), www.vatican.va/holy_father/paul_vi/ apost_letters/documents/hf_p-vi_apl_19710514_octogesima-adveniens_en.html.

Presbyterian Church (U.S.A.). "The Constitution of the Presbyterian Church (U.S.A.)." Louisville, KY: Office of the General Assembly, 2004.

Putnam, Robert D. *Bowling Alone: The Collapse and Revival of American Community.* New York: Simon and Schuster, 2001.

Quigley, William P. *Ending Poverty as We Know It: Guaranteeing a Right to a Job at a Living Wage.* Philadelphia.: Temple University Press, 2003.

————. "The Living Wage Movement." *BLUEPRINT for Social Justice* 54, no. 9 (2001). www.loyno.edu/twomey/blueprint/vol_liv/No-09_May_2001.html

Rauschenbusch, Walter. *Christianity and the Social Crisis.* New York: MacMillan, 1907.

————. *Christianizing the Social Order.* Boston: Pilgrim Press, 1912.

Reynolds, David B. *Taking the High Road: Communities Organize for Economic Change.* Armonk, NY: M. E. Sharpe, 2002.

Rose, Fred. *Coalitions across the Class Divide: Lessons from the Labor, Peace, and Environmental Movements.* Ithaca, NY: Cornell University Press, 2000.

Ross, Rosetta E. *Witnessing and Testifying: Black Women, Religion, and Civil Rights.* Minneapolis, MN: Fortress Press, 2003.

Roth, Silke. *Building Movement Bridges: The Coalition of Labor Union Women.* Contributions in Sociology. Westport, CT: Praeger, 2003.

Ryan, John Augustine. *Economic Justice: Selections from Distributive Justice and a Living Wage.* Library of Theological Ethics. Edited by Harlan Beckley. Louisville, KY: Westminster John Knox Press, 1996.

————. *A Living Wage: Its Ethical and Economic Aspects.* (New York: Macmillan, 1906).

San Diego Interfaith Committee on Worker Justice. "Living Wage Campaign." San Diego: Unitarian Universalist Fund for Just Society Proposal, 2003.

Schlozman, Kay Lehman, Nancy Burns, and Sidney Verba. "The Public Consequences of Private Inequality: Family Life and Citizen Participation," *American Political Science Review* 91, no. 2 (1997): 373–89.

Schurman, Sue. "Women Organizing Women." Washington, DC: Berger-Marks Foundation, 2004. www.bergermarks.org/resources/WOWreport.pdf.

"The Self-Sufficiency Standard." University of Washington Center for Women's Welfare, www.selfsufficiencystandard.org/standard.html.

Sherman, Arloc. *Wasting America's Future: The Children's Defense Fund Report on the Costs of Child Poverty.* Boston: Beacon Press, 1994.

Shierholz, Heidi. "Immigration and Wages: Methodological Advancements Confirm Modest Gains for Native Workers." Washington, DC: Economic Policy Institute, 2010, www.epi.org/publications/entry/bp255/.

————. "New 2008 Poverty, Income Data Reveal Only Tip of the Recession Iceburg." Washington, DC: Economic Policy Institute, 2009. www.epi.org/publications/ entry/income_picture_20090910.

Sklar, Holly, and Rev. Dr. Paul H. Sherry. *A Just Minimum Wage: Good for Workers, Business and Our Future.* Cincinnati: Friendship Press, 2005.

Slessarev-Jamir, Helene. "Exploring the Attraction of Local Congregations to Community Organizing." *Nonprofit and Voluntary Sector Quarterly* 33, no. 4 (2004): 1–24.

Smith, Christian. *Disruptive Religion: The Force of Faith in Social-Movement Activism.* New York: Routledge, 1996.

Snarr, C. Melissa. "Challenging Electoral Hegemonies: The Ethical Potential of (Religiously Attuned) Community Organizing." Paper presented to the American Academy of Religion conference, Chicago, November 1–3, 2008.

———. *Social Selves and Political Reforms: Five Visions in Contemporary Christian Ethics.* New York: T&T Clark, 2007.

———. "Waging Religious Ethics: Living Wages and Framing Public Religious Ethics." *Journal of the Society of Christian Ethics* 29, no. 1 (2009): 69–86.

Snow, David, and Robert D. Benford. "Master Frames and Cycles of Protest." In *Frontiers in Social Movement Theory*, edited by Aldon D. Morris, 133–55. New Haven, CT: Yale University Press, 1992.

Snow, David, Burke Rochford Jr., Steven K. Worden, and Robert Benford. "Frame Alignment Processes, Micromobilization, and Movement Participation." *American Sociological Review* 51 (1986): 464–81.

Sonn, Paul, and Stephanie Luce. "New Directions for the Living Wage Movement." In *The Gloves-Off Economy: Workplace Standards at the Bottom of America's Labor Market*, edited by Annette Bernhardt, Heather Boushey, Laura Dresser and Chris Tilly, 269–87. Ithaca, NY: Cornell University Press, 2008.

Springsteen, Bruce. *We Shall Overcome: The Seeger Sessions*: Sony Records, 2006.

Stabile, Donald. *The Living Wage: Lessons from the History of Economic Thought.* Cheltenham, UK: Edward Elgar, 2008.

Sturm, Douglas. "Martin Luther King Jr. as Democratic Socialist." *Journal of Religious Ethics* 18, no. 2 (1990): 79–105.

Swarts, Heidi J. *Organizing Urban America: Secular and Faith-Based Progressive Movements.* Social Movements, Protest, and Contention. Minneapolis: University of Minnesota Press, 2008.

Swidler, Ann. "Culture in Action: Symbols and Strategies." *American Sociological Review* 51 (1986): 273–86.

Talvacchia, Kathleen T. "Learning to Stand with Others through Compassionate Solidarity." *Union Seminary Quarterly Review* 47, no. 3/4 (1993): 177–94.

Tamez, Elsa. "Neoliberalism and Christian Freedom: A Reflection on the Letter to the Galatians." In *Revolution of Spirit: Ecumenical Theology in Global Context, Essays in Honor of Richard Shaull*, edited by Richard Shaull and Nantawan Boonprasat-Lewis, 105–12. Grand Rapids, MI: W. B. Eerdmans, 1998.

Tanner, Kathryn. *Jesus, Humanity and the Trinity: A Brief Systematic Theology.* Minneapolis, MN: Fortress Press, 2001.

———. "Kingdom Come: The Trinity and Politics." *Princeton Seminary Bulletin*, 28, no. 2 (2007): 129–45.

Taylor, M. P. "Budget Blues." *Dallas Morning News*, March 9, 1993.

Thomas, Cal. "Howard Dean 'Finds' Jesus." *beliefnet* (2004), www.beliefnet.com/News/Politics/2004/01/Howard-Dean-Finds-Jesus.aspx.

Townes, Emilie Maureen. *Womanist Ethics and the Cultural Production of Evil*. Black Religion, Womanist Thought, Social Justice. New York: Palgrave Macmillan, 2006.

UNICEF Innocenti Research Centre. "A League Table of Child Poverty in Rich Nations." In *Innocenti Report Card No.1*. Florence, Italy: Innocenti Research Centre, 2000, www.unicef-irc.org/publications/pdf/repcard1e.pdf.

U.S. Bureau of Labor Statistics. "Characteristics of Minimum Wage Workers: 2008." Washington, DC: Government Printing Office, 2009.

———. "Consumer Expenditure Survey 1998." Washington, DC: Government Printing Office, 1999.

———. "Highlights of Women's Earnings in 2008." Washington, DC: Government Printing Office, 2009.

———. "Record of the Discussion before Congress of the United States on the Fair Labor Standards Act of 1938." U.S. Department of Labor, Washington, DC: Government Printing Office, 1939.

U.S. Census Bureau. "Annual Social and Economic (Asec) Supplement, 2007" Washington, DC: Government Printing Office, 2008.

———. "Povo1: Age and Sex of All People, Family Members and Unrelated Individuals Iterated by Income-to-Poverty Ratio and Race: 2008." Washington, DC: Government Printing Office, 2009.

———. "Povo3: People in Families with Related Children under 18 by Family Structure, Age, and Sex, Iterated by Income-to-Poverty Ratio and Race: 2008." Washington, DC: Government Printing Office, 2009.

———. "S1703. Selected Characteristics of People at Specified Levels of Poverty in the Past 12 Months." Washington, DC: Government Printing Office, 2009.

United Methodist Church (U.S.). *The Book of Discipline of the United Methodist Church, 2004*. Nashville, TN: United Methodist Publishing House, 2004.

United States Conference of Catholic Bishops. *Economic Justice for All: Pastoral Letter on Catholic Social Teaching and the U.S. Economy*. Washington, DC: U.S. Catholic Conference, 1986.

———. "Faithful Citizenship: A Call to Political Responsibility." Washington DC: United States Catholic Conference, 2004. www.usccb.org/faithfulcitizenship/bishopStatement.html.

U.S. Congress. House. Committee on Ways and Means. Subcommittee on Income Security and Family Support. *Measuring Poverty in America : Hearing before the Subcommittee on Income Security and Family Support of the Committee on Ways and Means, U.S. House of Representatives*, 110th Cong., 1st sess., August 1, 2007. Washington, DC: G.P.O.For sale by the Supt. of Docs., U.S. G.P.O., 2008.

Verba, Sidney, Kay Lehman Schlozman, and Henry E. Brady. *Voice and Equality: Civic Voluntarism in American Politics*. Cambridge, MA: Harvard University Press, 1995.

Wallis, Jim. *The Great Awakening: Reviving Faith and Politics in a Post-Religious Right America*. New York: HarperLuxe, 2008.

Waltman, Jerold L. *The Case for the Living Wage*. New York: Algora Publications, 2004.

———. *Minimum Wage Policy in Great Britain and the United States.* New York: Algora Publications, 2008.

Warren, Mark, and Richard L. Wood. "Faith-Based Community Organizing: The State of the Field." Jericho, NY: Interfaith Funders, 2001.

Wartzman, Rick. "Falling Behind: As Officials Lost Faith in the Minimum Wage, Pat Williams Lived It—Historic Shift in Washington Left a Louisiana Worker Struggling to Pay the Bills—a Program that Ike Liked." *Wall Street Journal,* July 19, 2001.

Weisbrot, Mark, and Michelle Sfroza-Roderick. "Baltimore's Living Wage Law: An Analysis of the Fiscal and Economic Costs of Baltimore City Ordinance 442." Washington, DC: Preamble Center, 1996.

Weldon, S. Laurel, and Harry Targ. "From Living Wages to Family Wages." *New Political Science* 26, no. 1 (2004): 71–98.

Williams, Rhys, and N. J. Demerath III. "Religion and Political Process in an American City." *American Sociological Review* 56, no. 4 (1991): 417–31.

Wiseman, Jonathan. "House Passes Increase in Minimum Wage to $7.25." *Washington Post,* January 11, 2007.

Wood, Richard L. *Faith in Action: Religion, Race, and Democratic Organizing in America.* Morality and Society Series. Chicago: University of Chicago Press, 2002.

Index

About the Author

C. MELISSA SNARR is an associate professor of ethics and society at Vanderbilt University Divinity School and the author of *Social Selves and Political Reforms: Five Visions in Contemporary Christian Ethics.*